Dietrich Bonhoeffer—
His Significance for North Americans

Larry Rasmussen
with Renate Bethge

FORTRESS PRESS   MINNEAPOLIS

To friends
in the International Bonhoeffer Society

DIETRICH BONHOEFFER—HIS SIGNIFICANCE FOR NORTH AMERICANS

Cover photos: *Dietrich Bonhoeffer—A Life in Pictures,* ed. Eberhard Bethge, Renate Bethge, and Christian Gremmels (Philadelphia: Fortress Press, 1986), 73-78.

Book design: Publishers' WorkGroup

Library of Congress Cataloging-in-Publication Data

Rasmussen, Larry L.
    Dietrich Bonhoeffer—his significance for North Americans / Larry Rasmussen, with Renate Bethge.
      p. cm.
    Bibliography: p.
    Includes index.
    ISBN 0-8006-2400-9
    1. Bonhoeffer, Dietrich, 1906-1945—Influence. I. Bethge, Renate. II. Title.
BX4827.B57R36 1990
230'.044'092—dc20   89-36037
                                                  CIP

Manufactured in the U.S.A.   AF 1–2400

94   93   92   91   90   1   2   3   4   5   6   7   8   9   10

CONTENTS

Preface   v

Abbreviations   ix

PART ONE: FAMILY

1. Bonhoeffer's Family and
   Its Significance for His Theology   1

PART TWO: SOCIETY

2. Patriotism   31

3. Resistance   43

PART THREE: CHURCH RENEWAL

4. Worship in a World Come of Age   57

5. The Church's Public Vocation   72

PART FOUR: NEW PATHS IN THEOLOGY

6. Method   89

7. Divine Presence and Human Power   111

8. An Ethic of the Cross   144

Afterword   174

Notes   176

Index   196

PREFACE

It was axiomatic for Dietrich Bonhoeffer that Christian life—and reflection upon it—happens most authentically in one's own backyard.
If there are universals, they are best discovered by delving deep into
one's own culture and living out its possibilities and responsibilities.

At the same time, Bonhoeffer learned from those who were at the
edge of his own, most intimate circles. He learned from people notably
different from him. Many of his insights came from experiences abroad.
So it is with us as well.

This volume assumes at least a casual acquaintance with Bonhoeffer
and his writings, and a full acquaintance with life in North America.
The mature work of Bonhoeffer will be examined at some length, but
the purpose for doing so is to give rise to thought about our own
reality on this side of the Atlantic. Christian life on this continent is
the thread of concern in this book. Bonhoeffer is the stimulus for
helping us discern what we are called to be and do. That he is now
of another generation and culture is a marked advantage, not a disadvantage. A different place to stand affords a better gaze.

Only one of the chapters is an exception to the focus on North
American issues. It is the first chapter, written by Renate Schleicher
Bethge, a member of the Bonhoeffer family. Her essay, "Bonhoeffer's
Family and Its Significance for his Theology," serves a double purpose:
it presents Bonhoeffer in the circles most important to him, and shows
how formative, familial influences echo in the themes of his theology
and ethics. This firsthand account thus functions as a personal introduction to Bonhoeffer and as necessary background for the remaining
chapters.

v

The remaining chapters—on society, church, and new paths in theology—move between Bonhoeffer's life and ours. In some cases, a U.S. figure is made to engage in conversation with Bonhoeffer. The Roman Catholic priest Daniel Berrigan, the Protestant theologian Reinhold Niebuhr, and the Jewish rabbi Irving Greenberg—each figures prominently in a chapter. More often, some issue in American life is the focus: Christian patriotism, resistance to the state, the dynamics of church renewal, the form of God's presence. In all cases, Bonhoeffer provides the stimulus for reflection on our own reality.

Two of the chapters are published here for the first time: "The Church's Public Vocation" and "Divine Presence and Human Power." A third, "An Ethic of the Cross," has been previously available only in German. All the essays have been rewritten for this volume. Appreciation is due the following for permission to use materials published by them: "Patriotism Lived: Lessons from Bonhoeffer," *Christianity and Crisis* 45, no. 11 (June 24, 1985): 249–54; "Daniel Berrigan and Dietrich Bonhoeffer: Parallels and Contrasts in Resistance," *Dialog* 11 (1972): 264–72; "Worship in a World-Come-of-Age," in *A Bonhoeffer Legacy: Essays in Understanding*, ed. by A. J. Klassen (Grand Rapids: Wm. B. Eerdmans, 1981), 268–80; "A Question of Method," in *New Studies in Bonhoeffer's Ethics*, ed. William J. Peck (Lewiston and Queenstown: Edwin Mellen, 1987), 103–38; "Ethik des Kreuzes am gegebenen Ort," in *Bonhoeffer und Luther: Zur Sozialgestalt des Luthertums in der Moderne*, ed. Christian Gremmels (Munich: Chr. Kaiser Verlag, 1983), 129–66. The essay by Renate Bethge is translated by Geffrey B. Kelly from "Bonhoeffers Familie und ihre Bedeutung für seine Theologie," which appeared in the series, *Beiträge zum Widerstand 1933–1945*, published under the auspices of the Gedenkstätte Deutscher Widerstand. It also appears in *Widerstand*, ed. by Peter Steinbach (Cologne: Verlag Wissenschaft und Politik, 1987).

I am particularly grateful to the Bethges. Renate Bethge's contribution is most immediately obvious—the lead chapter. But without Eberhard Bethge, Bonhoeffer's friend, editor, and biographer, we would not have had Dietrich Bonhoeffer as the major influence he has become. Gratitude is due also to David Gushee, a Ph.D. candidate in Christian Ethics at Union Theological Seminary, who transcribed the essays from the printed page to computer disks and thus simplified the process of rewriting them; and to Geffrey Kelly, a good friend from the International Bonhoeffer Society who, as noted, translated Renate Bethge's chapter.

We have not altered the language of direct quotations, preferring to leave the historical record as received. But we have made every effort to use non-sexist language in the remainder of the text.

The dedication to good friends in the International Bonhoeffer Society is shared by both Renate Bethge and me. Our work has always been rewarded by their interest, at times generated by it. Most important, however, has been the great pleasure of their company.

LARRY RASMUSSEN
Union Theological Seminary
New York City

ABBREVIATIONS

BOOKS BY DIETRICH BONHOEFFER

AB   *Act and Being*. Translated by Bernard Noble. New York: Harper & Row, 1962. Reprint (same pagination). New York: Octagon Books, 1983.

CC   *Christ the Center*. Revised translation by Edwin H. Robertson. New York: Harper & Row, 1978.

CD   *The Cost of Discipleship*. Translated by R. H. Fuller, revised by Irmgard Booth. New York: Macmillan, 1963. Hardcover reissue (same pagination). Gloucester, Mass.: Peter Smith, 1983.

CS   *The Communion of Saints*. Translated by Ronald G. Smith, et al. New York: Harper & Row, 1963.

E   *Ethics*. Translated by Neville Horton Smith. Rearranged edition. New York: Macmillan, 1965. Hardcover reissue (same pagination). Gloucester, Mass.: Peter Smith, 1983.

Eg   *Ethik*. 6th edition. Edited by Eberhard Bethge. Munich: Chr. Kaiser Verlag, 1963.

FFP   *Fiction from Prison*. Edited by Renate Bethge and Eberhard Bethge with Clifford Green. Translated by Ursula Hoffman. Philadelphia: Fortress Press, 1981.

GS   *Gesammelte Schriften*, 6 volumes. Munich: Chr. Kaiser Verlag, 1958–1974.

LPP   *Letters and Papers from Prison*. Enlarged and edited by Eberhard Bethge, translated by R. H. Fuller, John Bowden, et al. New York: Macmillan, 1972.

NRS   *No Rusty Swords: Letters, Lectures, and Notes, 1939–1945*. Edited by Edwin H. Robertson. Revised edition. Translation revised by John Bowden and Eberhard Bethge. London: Collins, 1970. Original publication by William Collins Sons, London, and Harper & Row, New York, 1965.

SECONDARY LITERATURE

DB   Bethge, Eberhard. *Dietrich Bonhoeffer: Man of Vision, Man of Courage.* Edited by Edwin Robertson, translated by Eric Mosbacher, et al. New York: Harper & Row, 1970. Paperback edition (same pagination), 1977.

DBg   ———— *Dietrich Bonhoeffer. Theologe, Christ, Zeitgnosse.* 5th edition. Munich: Chr. Kaiser Verlag, 1983.

B: EM   ———— *Bonhoeffer: Exile and Martyr.* Edited and with an essay by John W. De Gruchy. New York: Seabury Press, 1975.

1

BONHOEFFER'S FAMILY AND ITS SIGNIFICANCE FOR HIS THEOLOGY

THE FAMILY

Whenever I read or hear anything about Bonhoeffer, I am struck by the close relationship of his thoughts with the attitudes, reactions, thinking, and interests of his family. Indeed, I sometimes recognize sentences that were spoken in a similar way during family conversations. So when in his essay, "After Ten Years," Bonhoeffer writes: "Stupidity is a more dangerous enemy of the good than evil,"[1] the reference is not to intellectual weakness. It is, rather, to those persons who became Nazis out of stupidity. Another example of family thinking is in Bonhoeffer's *Ethics*. There he insists it is not an "absolute good" which is to be realized. Rather, "what is relatively better [is preferred] to what is relatively worse" and "the 'absolute good' may sometimes be the very worst."[2] In an altogether different example, from *Fiction from Prison,* Bonhoeffer is describing family attitudes when Christoph, the main character, says about his parents, "They prefer a good laborer or artisan a hundred times over some conceited person with the title of 'Excellency.' "[3]

But before I go into details, particularly about the period 1933–1945 when I was growing up, I must relate something about the family as a whole, and about how Bonhoeffer was influenced by his family history as he brought forth new ideas and new formulations. I was seven years old when Hitler came to power and nineteen when the war ended. Bonhoeffer was nearly twenty years older than I. My parents' house in Berlin stood next to the house of my grandparents on the Bonhoeffer side of the family.

I remember how concerned all the members of our large family were when Hitler became Reich Chancellor. They had early on perceived a danger in the Nazis. It would not have occurred to anybody to vote for the "National Socialist German Workers Party" (NSDAP). One voted for the "German Peoples Party" or the "German Democratic Party" respectively, or, from 1930 on, the "German State Party." Dietrich's brother Klaus wrote him when Dietrich was in New York in November 1930: "Fond glances are cast in the direction of fascism. I am afraid that, if this radical wave captures the educated classes, it will be all over for this nation of poets and thinkers."[4]

We knew about the brutality of the Nazis, their propaganda filled with lies,[4] and the defamation of the Jews. I for one can still recall the considerable agitation the word "Potempa" stirred up. Later I heard that this was the name of a Silesian village in which S. A. troops had beaten a communist to death before the eyes of his mother in the summer of 1932. Following a judgment against the troops, Hitler and his followers threatened the judge and swore their revenge through a notice published in the newspaper.

Anyone could have known about such things, but many persons were in desperate straits, without work and food, and hoping for a savior. So they believed Hitler's promises, expecting him to abandon the negative side of his program as soon as he came to power. Others did not even notice the negative aspect. Our family was reasonably well off, so it was easier to be alert to the evil around us.

We knew quite early of the existence of concentration camps for those who opposed Hitler, and especially for the Jews. As children we somehow picked up the ditty:

> Dear God, make me stoney deaf,
> So that I can Hitler's words believe;
> Dear God, make me blind,
> So that I in Goebbels an Aryan find;
> Dear God, make me dumb,
> So that I never may in Dachau come!

But we also knew that outside the family we were not to discuss anything that the family said about political affairs.

This became very clear to me during the so-called Röhm putsch. Röhm, an old friend of Hitler, chief of the S. A., and secretly a rival of the "Fuhrer" for party leadership, had become alienated from him over the pace of the revolution. Hitler simply had him and several others, including the former Reich Chancellor, General von Schleicher, together with his wife and other opposition leaders, shot without a trial. To this day it is not known precisely how many victims there were. Recent estimates speak of 150 to 200. At the time, I happened to be visiting my aunt, the youngest sister of my mother and Dietrich, in Lichterfelde, on that June 30th day. When we heard shots from the nearby barracks, my aunt said that with each shot a person who had fallen out of favor with Hitler was being eliminated. I recall the anxious agitation at my grandparents' house as they waited for a courageous word from Minister of Justice Gurtner who, indeed, was no Nazi. I also remember their great disappointment when this word was not forthcoming. The outcome, instead, was merely a declaration after the fact that these measures were properly those of a state emergency.

My grandparents' house was the established meeting place for the family. I remember that people [gathered there] always spoke with deep concern or even outrage, especially when they were at the same time discussing plans that concerned the political situation. Sometimes there was whispering; sometimes a family member would leave to check the door to see if anyone was listening. Often cushions were placed over the telephone because of rumors that the secret police (Gestapo) could listen in even though the receiver was on the hook. Later we children were sent outside to act as lookouts, especially if the family was listening to the BBC news. My grandmother never missed this. If she happened to be with us, she would stand up shortly before ten o'clock, the broadcast time of the BBC news in German, and say, "It's time for devotions!" Such code words quickly became commonplace in the family. They were also spontaneously made up and understood. In this way we could always communicate by telephone and by letter, despite the fact that we had to take into account the possibility of eavesdropping by the Gestapo. If, for example, we wanted to inform someone of a house search, we would say, "By the way, X received a visit yesterday." We still have letters from the 1930s from my grandmother in which she writes about imprisoned acquaintances being "in the hospital" and naturally gives only their first names, even when it was by no means customary to use the first name in speaking about them. We often said some extra things in letters or over the phone for the censor's benefit, especially in the letters that were permitted to be sent to and from prison. For this reason, there are occasional misunderstandings today in reading *Letters and Papers from Prison.* For example, in the letters from Dietrich's mother, she often stressed how she and her husband were old and weak and how urgently in need of the help of their son, then sitting in prison. That this was something written for the benefit of the censor was clear to the family in those days. But, for some people reading these phrases today there emerges the image of an old woman feeling sorry for herself, instead of a woman who was above all actively engaged in the struggle and who never gave up.

The family had a strong sense of togetherness. Besides the parents, four of the Bonhoeffer children lived in Berlin. Dietrich, who always kept his room at his parents' house, was often with them. During the Nazi period this tie was important for him, if only for the sake of political information and discussions available there. The oldest brother, Karl-Friedrich, professor of physical chemistry in Leipzig, and Dietrich's twin sister, Sabine, who lived in Göttingen, also came frequently to Berlin.

I believe that the very size of the family was a factor in explaining why nobody became a Nazi. They were all of the same political persuasion and strengthened one another in it. Indeed, the general attitude of the family did not contain the slightest inclination toward the Nazis. The father, a professor of neurology and psychiatry at the University of Berlin, had a sensitivity and gift for observation that enabled him to see through Hitler and his followers from the very beginning. From the early 1920s in the letters of the brothers and sisters one already sees how negatively the family felt toward the Nazis in political matters. Dietrich's father writes in his memoirs, "From the outset we considered the victory of National Socialism in the year 1933 and Hitler's being named Reich Chancellor as a misfortune. My own aversion for and mistrust of Hitler were founded on his demagogic propaganda speeches, on his telegram of sympathy in the Potempa murder affair, on his habit of driving about the country, riding whip in hand, the choice of his co-workers whose qualities were perhaps better known here in Berlin than elsewhere, and finally, because of rumors that were then being circulated among my professional colleagues about his psychopathic symptoms."[5]

The family held so much importance that it would have been more difficult for an individual member to become a Nazi or even a "fellow traveller" than to take part in the resistance. Moreover, family members were full of various misgivings and therefore on the lookout for every piece of news. Because of our location in Berlin and the men in the family who worked in various ministries there, we were better informed than many others about political events. The main source of information was Hans von Dohnanyi, a lawyer and the husband of Dietrich's sister Christine. He was the first to join and the one most fully involved in the conspiracy. He first worked in the Ministry of Justice under Gurtner and had already begun to document Nazi crimes in 1934, in order to inform the German people in the event of a coup d'état. For a successful overthrow of the government the people would have to have their illusions about Hitler destroyed.

From 1939 on, Dohnanyi worked in the Forcign Office of the Abwehr (part of the *OKW* or Army High Command) under Admiral Canaris, where many strands of the resistance groups soon came together. Together with Colonel Oster, and completely protected by Canaris, Dohnanyi worked there for the overthrow of the regime. He and Oster had already come to know each other as strong opponents of Hitler during the Fritsch crisis. They were assigned to investigate the Fritsch case, Oster for the Wehrmacht (Army) and Dohnanyi for the Ministry of Justice. Both recognized the affair as a plot of Göring against General von Fritsch. From that time on, Oster and Dohnanyi, along with others, forged plans for the coup d'état. These were scuttled time and again because of the irresolution of the generals who were unwilling to act in the face of Hitler's victories. I remember throughout all those years the oft-repeated groans of doubt and disappointment in the generals from members of the family, espccially from Klaus Bonhoeffer and Christine von Dohnanyi.

Dietrich Bonhoeffer was recruited into the political resistance through Hans von Dohnanyi in 1940. He was thereby appointed to the staff of Canaris, and thus exempted from miltary service. Dohnanyi likewise succeeded in freeing some of Bonhoeffer's former students at the Preachers Seminary from the threat of being conscripted. He expected no service from them in return for this favor. On the other hand, he did want to use Dietrich Bonhoeffer's various international contacts for the resistance. Because of Bonhoeffer's employment, he was freed from the obligation imposed earlier by the regime to report regularly to the Gestapo. He actually travelled to Switzerland, to Italy, to Sweden, and to Norway for the resistance in order to find out how the allies would react to the planned coup d'état, that is, what their proposals for a peace treaty would look like in the event of a successful overthrow of the government. Above all, the men of the resistance requested that the allies bring the war activities to a halt in the event of the attempted coup d'état. A positive answer could have been very helpful in making the military more willing to take part in the coup. But no positive answer came. At another level, Bonhoeffer was able to do more of his theologial work.

Klaus Bonhoeffer, also a lawyer and a legal advisor to Lufthansa, likewise worked wholeheartedly for the resistance. Of course, he did not have the advantage of being in a situation like Dohnanyi, whose professional duties included his resistance activity. But he did have, and he sought and found, connections with opposition groups which he, in turn, introduced to one another. Among his personal acquaintances, for example, were his wife's cousins, Ernst von Harnack and Arvid Harnack, also Wilhelm Leuschner, Julius Leber, Johannes Popitz, Joseph Wirmer, Carlo Mierendorff, Jakob Kaiser, Prince Louis Ferdinand, Karl-Ludwig Freiherr von und zu Guttenberg, and, naturally, the brother of his wife, Justus Delbruck, and others. After discussions with these people—occasionally these took place in his own house—Klaus often came rather late in the evening to my parents' or my grandparents' house, sometimes full of hope, sometimes depressed, but always excited and with a sense of accomplishment. Unfortunately, I do not recall the details of what he divulged. He would in any case have been rather cautious when we youngsters were present.

Such prudence was, of course, generally necessary. Indeed, one recorded as little as possible in writing. Much, therefore, can no longer be reconstructed since the Nazis permitted none of the main participants in the resistance to survive. The trials before the people's court, inspired as they were by the hatred of the regime toward its opponents and by the desire to destroy them, and whose conduct is now well known, are considered very limited as sources of reliable testimony for the activity of those in the resistance.

Christine von Dohnanyi, who was likewise an active participant in the work of the resistance—she lived until 1965—was kept thoroughly informed about events in the foreign office of the Abwehr. Unfortunately, she withdrew entirely into herself soon after the war, full of disappointment that the survivors had publicly inflated their own roles at the expense of those who had been killed. The survivors made statements which then had the effect of determining the image of the resistance.

My father, Rüdiger Schleicher, a lawyer completely dedicated to his profession (he refused the position of a bank director because he wanted to be active on behalf of the people) also suffered greatly under that unjust government. He helped the resistance by passing on information from his position in the National Ministry of Air Traffic, whose legal department he headed until 1939. When he became an Honorary Professor at the University of Berlin and head of the Institute for Air Traffic Law there, he collaborated with Dr. Hans John, the brother of Dr. Otto John, Klaus Bonhoeffer's colleague. Hans John was also deeply involved in the resistance. My father made possible his journeys for the conspiracy and covered up for him. The related conspiratorial meetings took place in rooms at his institute and also at our house.

My father, despite his personal attitude, and after much consultation with the family at large, became a member of the Nazi party in May 1933, at the last possible moment before the closure on acceptances. The family was of the opinion that it might be very good for one member of the family to have access to, and direct knowledge of, the Nazi organization. Moreover, with this move, he acquired a certain cover for his resistance activity in the ministry.

The collaboration between my father and Klaus Bonhoeffer, who also worked in the Aviation Ministry, was especially close. Both were imprisoned in the early days of October 1944 and, together with Hans John, condemned to death on February 2, 1945. In the final days of the war they were murdered by the S. S., as were Hans von Dohnanyi and Dietrich Bonhoeffer.

During the first years after Hitler seized power, conversations in the family were mostly centered on the church. Even those for whom the church had previously been unimportant now began to take an interest in it. The church was the only institution that took definite steps to resist Nazi ideology. It formulated public protests and circulated these among the congregations, that is, among the church groups that in 1934 made up the Confessing Church. All other independent or opposing associations and institutions were simply either dissolved or swallowed up by the Nazis. So one no longer viewed the church as looking out only for its own interests; it was now seen as politically important, even more so than it liked. By supporting the Confessing Church, one also hoped to thereby encourage the non-Nazis in the government, the civil authorities, and those in public service. Anyone who was opposed to the Hitler regime could clearly demonstrate this by ostentatious attendance at religious services conducted by pastors of the Confessing Church. In the manuscript of his *Ethics* Dietrich described this experience in 1940 as follows: "The . . . force of order sees in the church an ally, and, whatever other elements of order may remain, will seek a place at her side. Justice, truth, science, art, culture, humanity, liberty, patriotism, all at last, after straying from the path, are once more finding their way back to their fountainhead."[6]

During the early Nazi years, Dietrich and his friend Franz Hildebrandt, a Lutheran pastor of Jewish descent, constantly discussed the political situation with the family and made plans for the Confessing Church. In a special way, my grandmother, Dietrich's mother, was deeply involved in this. She contacted people who had been in the government before Hitler's seizure of power and who still remained there, attempting to smooth the way here and there for people of the Confessing Church. I can still see her telephoning for somebody and without hesitation calling her acquaintances—sometimes rather remote ones—to help in these matters. What is more, she always had several bright ideas at hand. The newspaper *Junge Kirche* ("Young Church") played an important role in her life then. It was always kept close by and discussed. On Sundays she would often travel to Dahlem to attend Niemöller's religious service there. At times she took us children along with her in order to fill up that church, even more, though it was already well attended. The five-mark piece that was pressed into my hand for the collection certainly made the greatest impression on me—since my brother and I together had saved up five marks and had bought a camera with it. My grandmother, of course, was enrolled in the membership lists of the Confessing congregations and therefore had the famous "red card." Susanne Dress, the youngest of the Bonhoeffer children, had received her red card even earlier, namely, on July 23, 1934. The red card, a sign of personal commitment, first came into existence with the Barmen Declaration of May 31, 1934.

Since Dietrich was in London from the end of 1933 until 1935, he constantly kept himself informed about developments in the church through telephone conversations with his mother. Franz Hildebrandt, who had also gone to London at that time, tells the lovely story about how the telephone bill was so astronomically high that both of them went to the central telephone office where the woman in charge there, having scrutinized the bill, realized that such an enormous bill could not be paid, and so without hesitation reduced it by half.

The family was always discussing and making plans for church events, as, for example, in 1936, in connection with the question of whether Dietrich should speak at the Olympic Games or whether his refusal would only let the Nazis present themselves in a more favorable light vis-à-vis foreign countries. He spoke in the context of a lecture series sponsored by the Confessing Church.

Unfortunately, I did not often pay much attention to the conversations of the adults, but I was aware of the highly charged atmosphere that the ever changing moves of the Nazis had rendered commonplace for us. I only recall certain names recurring in the conversations. But I do remember very clearly the arrest of Niemöller, then his acquittal, followed closely by his internment in the concentration camp. That upset everyone terribly. Niemöller's condition was constantly the object of our attention.

In later years the topic of the Confessing Church no longer retained its central place in family discussions. Whether this was because we no longer expected so much from the church, or whether—and this is naturally related to the question—the family became more deeply involved in the political arena, or simply because what was happening politically was so shocking and so ominous that it left no room for other subjects, I do not know.

The "Jewish Question" was certainly the dominant topic of conversation in family circles. Other political matters always seemed intertwined with it. As early as two months after Hitler seized power, the Law for Restructuring the Civil Service was enacted together with other laws. Its third section contained the so-called Aryan Clause which deprived Jews of their right to hold office in government ministries and agencies and in the teaching profession in universities and schools. The infamous Nuremberg Laws followed in 1935. These classified and vilified Jews and their offspring (even in cases where the children were partially Aryan) and imposed severe restrictions on them. We later became obliged to learn these laws and rules in the school course entitled The National Socialist State Structure. Long before Auschwitz, the Jews were subjected to both petty and large-scale harassments. This began with painting on park benches and buildings, "No Jews welcome here," and then turned into the boycott of Jewish shops. It reached a high point with the so-called *Reichs-Kristallnacht* (the nationwide "Crystal Night") in which the show windows of Jewish businesses were smashed, synagogues were set on fire, and Jews were brutalized. And this is to say nothing of individuals who had already been murdered in concentration camps.

On the very first day of the boycott against the Jews, April 1, 1933, my great-grandmother Bonhoeffer made up her mind to counteract this illegal measure. She refused to let herself be restrained from shopping in a Jewish store in Berlin and even broke through the cordon of S. A. guards posted at the entrance. They were taken aback. Later, with purchases in hand, she left the store through the same cordon. Her great-grandson, my nine-year-old brother, tore up signs intended to harass Jews, with the result that S. A. troops appeared at my parents' house to warn them. Such spontaneous, small tokens of resistance had no lasting effect. They were perhaps only undertaken by people who typically were not calculating the consequences or who had not yet arrived at the point of careful calculation.

Prior to this, liberal Christians and liberal Jews in Berlin had lived side-by-side and took each other for granted. Grunewald, where the Bonhoeffers had their home, was also home to many Jews. Nicholas Sombart writes in his *Jugend in Berlin* ("Youth in Berlin") that every third house belonged to Jews. The Bonhoeffers had many close friends who were Jewish. The father had Jewish assistants. Dietrich's twin sister, Sabine, was married to Gerhard Leibholz, who was a man of Jewish descent although he had been raised a Christian. (He later became a high-court judge in the Federal Republic.) The announcement of their intention to marry was treated rather skeptically at first in the family, despite the esteem they had for Leibholz. However, any projected marriage that introduced a partner with a different background, say Catholic, for instance, would have been regarded in the same critically reserved way. Dietrich himself pointed out to my parents, when I intended to marry his friend—though I was only seventeen years old, it is true—that there were certain differences between the families which could create difficulties for me. Giving careful thought to such differences remained an obvious responsibility even for him.

The year 1933 immediately posed the question in the family as to whether and how Jews could continue to live in Germany. Most of our Jewish friends had already left Germany in the first years after Hitler seized power. Dietrich's sister fled with her family in September 1938. I can still clearly recall the many considerations that were brought forward over the years, sometimes with circumspection, sometimes full of emotion, on the issue of whether to emigrate. For a long time we clung to even the smallest indication that the regime could be brought to an end. Every political movement was followed with intense interest. Moreover, the family kept up its contacts with several government people who were opposed to the Nazis in the hope that their intervention could be counted on in an emergency.

However, one never knew whether such people might not suddenly be dismissed and themselves become victims of the regime. The decisive factor in the final decision to emigrate, then, was secret information that passports for Jews would soon be stamped with the notation "Israel," or "Sarah," so that travel abroad by Jews could be immediately checked and stopped.

One of my mother's cousins also emigrated in 1938, since she had married a Jewish lawyer. Their children lived with us during the transition period. Our parents instructed us to answer questions about their possible Jewish extraction by saying that they had Spanish blood.

By the time the deportations began, our Jewish friends and relatives were already outside the country. Of those whom I knew, a family that our household help had befriended fell victim to the deportations and never returned. The woman, together with her two children, had sometimes stayed with us in the house. She would arrive in the morning when it was dark and return home in the evening after it turned dark again. (Because the regime would not have permitted her, as a Jew wearing the "Star of David," in our [Gentile] house.) In addition, the fragile old friend of an acquaintance of my grandparents was taken to Theresienstadt. How she or others were rounded up for deportation, I did not observe. The places where Jews were collected were in other sections of Berlin, and by this time scarcely any Jews lived in our neighborhood anymore. The family, however, knew about the deportations from the beginning and, knowing the Nazis, anticipated the murders and atrocities. When exactly they knew about the mass exterminations, I cannot say. I do remember that the first news of torture and murders in the concentration camps aroused intense anger in the family. Their indignation could hardly have been greater. And yet we came to hear of even more gruesome things. Nonetheless, because of war conditions we were still unable to learn the full extent of the crimes. I myself—and I believe most of the family—felt that the mass exterminations were not some qualitatively new development but were like a dreadful crescendo of what had been organized and carried out from the beginning. It was a huge nightmare that made planning for an assassination attempt on Hitler all the more urgent. But there were continually new hitches and stumbling blocks to the plot and its proper execution.

Despite it all, life went on and people somehow adapted. We children were in the Hitler Youth Movement. I was given an attestation that I had a "weak heart" and after a while I was forgotten, with the result that when I turned fourteen I no longer took part in the organization. My brother with his cello was pressed into the service of the Hitler Youth Amateur Broadcasting Company; instead of doing the customary service he played good music. My very athletic younger sister was even to become a leader of a girls' team, but my parents knew just how to prevent this "on medical grounds" (much, I think, to the displeasure of my sister).

Naturally the schools were also afflicted with Nazi demands. Because of this, there evolved a way to ascertain whether someone really was a Nazi. If the teacher gave the obligatory Hitler salute perfunctorily at the beginning and end of the hour, and went on immediately to the lesson, he was no Nazi; likewise if he spoke of "Hitler" instead of the "Führer." It was not only teachers that we picked out in this way. Another clear indication was the size of the flag that we were required to display on countless occasions. We immediately wrote off those with big flags. My parents had a rather small one; that of my grandparents was so small I was nearly embarrassed by it. I was also proud of them, especially at the thought of malicious Nazis being upset by this. To be sure, in school we simply had to accommodate certain demands of the Nazi administration. Often such demands came from teachers who were by no means Nazis themselves. We were thus required to make a poster on the theme, "Bombs on England," for an art teacher whose sister had been murdered along with her Jewish husband. The family reflected with me about how we might somewhat tolerably design such a poster. We decided on an eagle poised over the British Isles. What was not permitted us children on principal was attending Nazi films, such as "Quex of the Hitler Youth" *(Hitlerjunge Quex)* or "The Jew Süss." [Translator's Note: *Jud Süss* was an extremely anti-Semitic film in which a Jew named Süss is depicted as a vicious criminal type executed for actions destructive of the way of life of an entire village. The film, which was compulsory viewing for all military troops, as well as S. S. and police, is reported to have sparked widespread street demonstrations against the Jews and demands that all Jews be expelled from Germany.] Our parents wrote an excuse note stating that it was too upsetting for us to see such things. So we alone stayed behind while the school, which was closed for the occasion, went off to the movies.

I can, of course, throw light here on only a slender cross section of life during those years. There were many difficulties, but there was also much good to report. We enjoyed music, books, games, and splendid family celebrations of a unique intensity, as if of themselves they compensated for every trouble and provided the balance that was sorely needed. It is astonishing that throughout all those years we never lost hope, even when the five men of the family—the fifth was my husband, who alone survived—sat in prison and both my father and Klaus Bonhoeffer were already sentenced to death.

Likewise, the actions of the family to rescue their men never ceased, even though the chances for success grew slimmer and slimmer. One can hardly imagine all that transpired in the family after the imprisonment of Hans von Dohnanyi and Dietrich on April 5, 1943 (Christine von Dohnanyi was also imprisoned for 5 weeks): seeking advice, decoding messages from books, and direct interventions by my grandfather, who enjoyed a great reputation as a scientist. There were constantly secret discussions held with people who, despite their belonging to the opposition, were well informed about the course of the legal proceedings and developments within the Army and the S. S. These discussions were held by intermediaries who could make discreet contact with persons in key positions without arousing suspicion. My father had also been actively engaged in this task before he was arrested.

My Aunt Dohnanyi had to bear impossible burdens. At her husband's request and in order to render him unfit for interrogation, she sent him food laced with a diphtheria bacillus that made him very ill. Escape plans for Dietrich and for Hans von Dohnanyi were finally set in motion but these came to nothing. My parents and I took the mechanic's uniform in which Dietrich was to have been smuggled out of prison to the guard who had conceived of the plan. But since Klaus and my father had been taken into custody a few days later, Dietrich did not want to further endanger the family by his escape.

Then, on February 2, 1945, my father and Klaus Bonhoeffer were condemned to death. Before then there had been countless discussions and attempts at bribery. Thereafter, we tried further interventions on behalf of Dietrich and Hans and, since they had been transported out of Berlin, we sought to learn their whereabouts.

The end came as a hard blow to us. But we felt that for our family, who had known so much, there had been no other way. We had no other choice. Thus, after the war, my grandfather wrote to one of his former assistants who now lived in America, "I hear you know that we have been through a lot and lost two sons and two sons-in-law through the Gestapo. You can imagine that that has not been without its effect on us. . . . For years we had tension caused by anxiety for those arrested and for those not yet arrested but in danger. But since we were all agreed on the need to act, and my sons were also fully aware of what they had to expect if the plot miscarried and had resolved if necessary to lay down their lives, we are sad, but also proud of their attitude, which has been consistent."[7]

Subsequently, I have sometimes been asked whether I was surprised when I heard that our men were in the resistance. On the contrary, I was somewhat naively surprised, as things became clear to me, that they had not been really active earlier. Did they not from the very beginning speak about the infamous conduct of the government and about the need to overthrow it? However, this political situation, with criminals at the top, had been something completely new to us. At the outset we waited for action to be taken by responsible people in the government who, at that time, were by no means all Nazis. And we hoped that the Nazi regime would perhaps soon collapse because of their mismanagement, as had the other governments from 1918 on. When it turned out that all this was an illusion and we realized for the first time that we ourselves would have to seize the initiative, and that without the military nothing could be done, it was already rather late and everything had become much more difficult.

This failure of readiness to act in such a situation was thus explained by Bonhoeffer in the section on "Civil Courage" in his essay, "After Ten Years":

> In a long history, we Germans have had to learn the need for and the strength of obedience. In the subordination of all personal wishes and ideas to the tasks to which we have been called, we have seen the meaning and the greatness of our lives. . . . This readiness to follow a command from "above" rather than our own private opinions and wishes was a sign of legitimate self-distrust. . . . But in this he [the German] misjudged the world; he did not realize that his submissiveness and self-sacrifice could be exploited for evil ends. When that happened, the exercise of the calling itself be came questionable, and all the moral principles of the German were bound to totter. The fact could not be escaped that the German still lacked something fundamental: he could not see the need for free and responsible action, even in opposition to his task and his calling. . . . Only now are the Germans beginning to discover the meaning of free responsibility.[8]

BONHOEFFER'S THEOLOGY IN THE CONTEXT OF HIS FAMILY

I come now to this question: Which of Bonhoeffer's exciting thoughts, actions, and new formulations can be traced to his family ties? I will mention only a few ideas of his which impressed me because they expressed the general bearing and views of the family or allowed these views to be clearly perceived, even though Bonhoeffer himself articulated them in theological terms.

Naturally such "exciting" things rarely have only one cause. Rather, there are many reasons for their appearance at a given time and place. Here I can and will say something about those aspects that derive from the family. Other sources of Bonhoeffer's sayings have been and continue to be examined by others.

During and just after his years of formal study Bonhoeffer was fully immersed in theology. Here he acquired an intellectual power center from which new dimensions of thought sprang. At the same time he remained close to the world of his family and always maintained an intimate contact with family members. Nevertheless, the two worlds— the theological-ecclesial and the familial-secular—appeared to exist apart from one another for Bonhoeffer.

In the Nazi period this changed. Because of its opposition to Hitler, the church became much more interesting and the family began to make common cause with the Confessing Church. Moreover, Bonhoeffer now linked his theology more and more with what he had assimilated from the family and what he now experienced in and with the family. He reflected on courses of action, values, and estimations of worth in his family tradition, discovered their Christian roots, and consciously and unconsciously incorporated much of this into his theology. He remarked that it was easier to act responsibly and "in correspondence with reality" in this time of crisis on the basis of this tradition than on the basis of the church tradition. This gave him increasing freedom to identify himself with the tradition of his family, in so far as it differed from what was, until then, customary for the church.

I would like now to delineate six points, chosen more or less arbitrarily, where I am struck by Bonhoeffer's conformity to family views that diverge from the viewpoint in vogue in the church during that period. In doing this, I will mention quotations from Bonhoeffer which, on the one hand, shed light on the family and, on the other, are in turn clarified by the family. The six points are:

1. Attitude toward the Enlightenment, Rationality, and Empiricism
2. Emotional Control through Personal Reserve and Guarding One's Feelings
3. "Correspondence with Reality"

4. "Telling the Truth"
5. Persecution for the Sake of Justice
6. Some Theological Catchwords:
    "Costly Grace and Cheap Grace"
    "Who is Christ for Us today"
    "Non-religious Interpretation"
    "Jesus, the Man for Others—the Church for Others"

Attitude Toward the Enlightenment, Rationality, and Empiricism

The time of the Enlightenment and what developed from it, rationalism, empiricism, and liberalism, were regarded with great skepticism by both church and theology. The Enlightenment's rigorous objectivity, on the one hand, and its antidogmatic free thought, on the other, had called into question the credibility of many church views. Hence the church viewed the movements connected with the Enlightenment and the education that promoted them with grave concern, just as it did the one-sided developments spun off by the Enlightenment—one dimensional positivism, for example, or the worldview of social Darwinism. Moreover, the "modern" style of education, based on the model of the natural sciences and striving to inculcate the capacity for critical judgment, was often attacked. Church conservatism and the Nazi antagonism toward science were in agreement in the matter of educating the citizenry, not for critical capability, but for blind obedience. This showed itself in the curtailment of subject matter in both lower and higher education.

So it came about that the church was, indeed, looked on as important for building up character but not as a power that could provide direction to thinking persons conscious of their responsibility for concrete problems and decisions. Bonhoeffer says in a 1931 lecture: "All religion was ultimately pedagogical. It made for a respectable appearance, among other things. But if one outgrew the school, one thereby outgrew the church too."[9] Perhaps here Bonhoeffer was expressing the attitude he found in his home toward his church. However, he was now of the opinion that things need not be such that the church had to reject the growing knowledge God had granted people, a state of affairs in which the church itself had been rejected by many people, especially by those who *wanted* to view reality soberly—such were the intellectuals—or who *had* to view reality that way—such were the workers.

In Bonhoeffer's parents' home the spirit of empiricism, rationality, and liberalism dominated (especially on the part of his father). On his mother's side there emanated a decidedly Christian, though at the same time liberal, attitude. This was joined to a sensitive openness and a prompt readiness for helping out in time of necessity. Here the practical realism of the mother combined with the analytical objectivity of the father.

Bonhoeffer's father rendered his judgment on any given matter only after he had investigated it most thoroughly. He was skeptical toward anything that was not provable. He despised exaggerations, especially the boasting that a person with his bearing and professional experience could not fail but detect. Every arrogance, every measly attempt to deceive oneself or others, was repugnant to him.

Family members were engaged in both the natural sciences and the human sciences. However, the human sciences were approached with a viewpoint drawn from the natural sciences; that is, with the demand for clarity and truthfulness and rejecting of any embellishment (neither Stefan George nor Rilke were held in much esteem). In any event, it was with this same attitude that we, at least on occasion, attended church and listened to and judged sermons. On the whole this was Bonhoeffer's viewpoint as well, and that was probably one of the main differences between him and most of the pastors and theologians of his time. What Bonhoeffer writes in his *Ethics* about the consequences of the French Revolution illustrates this attitude:

> Emancipated reason rose to unsuspected heights. The free exercise of reason created an atmosphere of truthfulness, light and clarity. Prejudices, social conceits, hollow forms and insensitive sentimentality were swept clean by the fresh wind of intellectual clarity. Intellectual honesty in all things, including questions of belief, was the great achievement of emancipated reason and it has ever since been one of the indispensable moral requirements of western man. Contempt for the age of rationalism is a suspicious sign of failure to feel the need for truthfulness. If intellectual honesty is not the last word that is to be said about things, and if intellectual clarity is often achieved at the expense of insight into reality, this can still never again exempt us from the inner obligation to make clean and honest use of reason.[10]

We strove to live with this "honorable and refined use of reason" at home and we also judged the Nazis by these standards. That "intellectual clarity is often achieved at the expense of insight into reality" was, however, quite evident in the Nazi era. Many people used their good sense to find grounds for their pro-Nazi attitude. This is what Bonhoeffer in his essay, "After Ten Years," describes as "stupidity." These people are not exactly stupid but they make themselves dumb. "One feels, in fact when talking to him (the 'dumb' person) that one is dealing, not with the man himself, but with slogans, catchwords, and the like, which have taken hold of him."[11] On the other hand, some people, neither considering themselves smart nor regarded so by others, grasped the reality of the Nazis precisely. (An example of the former is the declaration by the professors of theology at Erlangen, that to some extent there ought to be the equivalent of the Aryan Clause in the church too.) There were continual discussions in the family on this phenomenon. The forsaking of what was the "reasonable" Bonhoeffer refers to in "After Ten Years" and, by implication, in other places as well. From the very beginning Bonhoeffer's parents left no doubt that reason was, indeed, important, but that other things, especially character, were even more important.

Emotional Control Through Personal Reserve and Guarding One's Feelings

Spirit and feeling—as much as possible seasoned with some humor—were looked on as absolute requirements for the family and for those chosen as friends. It was a scathing judgment for one to be considered devoid of spirit, boring, or even "indolent." However, feelings were taken seriously only when they were not manifested too openly but rather when they were expressed indirectly: in what, how, and about which one spoke, in tactfulness and eagerness to be of help, and, also, to be sure, in music and painting. Only from those who did not belong to the family and who were of an exceptionally naive and childlike nature could direct bursts of feeling be accepted with amusement.

We were sensitive to people's feelings as matters of utmost importance and as something that one did not expose to the public. Moreover, we feared cheapening even positive feelings by openly declaring them, something akin to declaring one's affection with words but then not carrying this through with corresponding behavior and making the daily smaller or greater sacrifices that were needed. Rather the family desired—in the measured manner of the father—to talk less, but not to let our actions fall short of our words. So, a "perhaps" in our family was really a "yes." A judgment that something was "nice" might have corresponded to "enchanting" in other families.

We also did not want to intrude upon or to overwhelm anyone with direct outbursts of emotion. That is why his daughter Sabine wrote about her father: "Papa was cautious not to restrict us . . . and did not want to tie us too closely to himself and others."[12] We wanted "to respect the line that has been drawn between us and the other."[13] In *Life Together*, I see many things described or commended that bring back vivid memories of the unspoken principles of our own living together as a family, though naturally now in a different motivational context. Hence one reads in *Life Together*: "Christ stands between me and others."[14]

This perspective is also found in the Christian I-Thou or personalist philosophy and shows how Bonhoeffer was able to unite what he had experienced in his family, what he had thought through in his theology, and what he had tested out in the community of the Preachers Seminary.

In general, therefore, feeling also had to be combined with "reasonable" actions expressed in an almost "matter-of-fact" way. Sentimentality was taboo in the family. However, what psychology recognizes as the ability to empathize (of course, for this to be meaningful it must be tied to practical consequences) played a large role, if not the main role in the family—but without being directly solicited.

To be sure, in prison Bonhoeffer once mentioned that he had perhaps given too little room to personal feelings, that, indeed, he "lived for many, many years quite absorbed in aims and tasks and hopes without any personal longings; and perhaps," he continues, "that has made me old before my time. It has made everything too 'matter-of-fact.' "[15] In prison, he now experiences as enriching the fact that he can allow a personal feeling, that of longing, to completely work its effect upon him. It is a "deficiency" (longing or yearning) that thoroughly fills him emotionally. This experience of personal feelings is in contrast with his previous, active, matter-of-fact period, and in contrast with what was possible for most people, with their general inner "ghostly desolation and impoverishment."[16] He asks: "How many people today allow themselves any strong personal feeling and real yearning?"[17]

The next considerations are connected with the importance of rationality and objectivity in the family.

Correspondence with Reality

Bonhoeffer devotes eight pages to the idea as a subsection of the chapter, "The Structure of the Responsible Life" in *Ethics*. We encounter the idea elsewhere in Bonhoeffer as well. What the thought stands for is a self-evident underlying principle for thinking and acting in the family. "Correspondence with reality" likewise plays a great role in the other aspects and lines of thought we have stressed.

Bonhoeffer sets action in correspondence with reality over against action according to principles or ideologies:

Since we are not concerned with the realization of an unrestricted principle, it is necessary in the given situation to observe, to weigh up, to assess and to decide, always within the limitations of human knowledge in general. . . . One's task is not to turn the world upside-down, but to do what is necessary at the given place and with a due consideration of reality. At the same time one must ask what are the actual possibilities.[18]

The conduct of the responsible person is

not established in advance, once and for all, that is to say, as a matter of principle, but it arises with the given situation. He has no principle at his disposal which possesses absolute validity and which he has to put into effect fanatically, overcoming all the resistance which is offered to it by reality, but he sees in the given situation what is necessary and what is 'right' for him to grasp and to do.[19]

One approached problems in the family in this way, including those problems posed by the Nazis, namely, considerations about resistance. Things were mulled over again and again soberly, with questioning directed to what was realistically possible and always well aware of the changing aspects of the situation. That had the advantage that one knew the reasons for actions when they were taken. It had the disadvantage that one had a more difficult time coming to a decision. There was just "no principle at [one's] disposal which possessed absolute validity."

Rigidly fixed principles were generally rejected in the family. Those who were martinets for principles were derided and avoided as much as possible. The saying in Bonhoeffer's Bible which his mother had inscribed for her son on his Confirmation, also points in this direction: "The letter kills but the Spirit gives life" (2 Cor. 3:6). The saying was characteristic of the mother. She was very free with the letter of the law and with observing rules, but the Spirit, understood as the spirit of loving one's neighbor, was of paramount importance to her.

There was, one must acknowledge, a period in Bonhoeffer's life in which he attempted in a strikingly radical way to be faithful not only to the spirit but also to the letter of the Sermon on the Mount. Although he inveighed theologically against every sort of self-made reduction of Christianity to moral principles, nonetheless, I still have the impression that here something unique was being thought out and lived, which had within itself elements of an ethic based on principles. Perhaps it was for him a special period in which he was testing just how much his ideas on discipleship could bear with respect to the ethos of a renewed church as he first of all looked to the Confessing Church and the paths of action he wanted to urge on it. In the course of the years the extent of the challenge was modified because of the political reality of Nazism's becoming ideologically radicalized in preparation for the war. The chances that the Confessing Church would sustain an attitude of radical discipleship waned. Hence Bonhoeffer, in order to live "in correspondence with reality," quite obviously had to widen his circle beyond the church. He who had been closely connected with pacifism, but who was not a pacifist on principle, would finally become a member of the political resistance ready to use force. The "pacifist" Bonhoeffer was accepted by the family. Bonhoeffer, the man of the resistance, had already been stamped by the family and its attitude toward the Nazis, however.

The unusual step of a Christian participating in the political conspiracy—and a Lutheran theologian at that—gave rise to many questions and reflections which found an explanation of sorts in the idea of "correspondence with reality." This idea was at heart a declaration of why, in these extreme political circumstances, active political resistance, pursuing its most far-reaching consequences, was to be a challenge for those who surveyed this situation. The assassination of the tyrant was a matter of dispute, of course. But in these circumstances it appeared to be the responsible course of action even if not entirely free of guilt.

This debate and its problematic, discussed again and again in the family, is what looms behind the passage in Bonhoeffer's *Ethics* where he writes: "It is not an 'absolute good' that is to be realized; but on the contrary it is part of the self-direction of the responsible agent that he prefers what is relatively better to what is relatively worse and that he perceives that the 'absolute good' may sometimes be the very worst."[20] By this he means that keeping oneself free of guilt—by not doing anything controversial in resistance—effectively continues the abandonment of the victims to their persecutors, and this was "the very worst" thing to do.

For Bonhoeffer, acting in correspondence with reality is based on the incarnation and reconciliation accomplished in Jesus Christ. "Action which is in accordance with Christ is in accordance with reality because it allows the world to be the world; it reckons with the world as the world; and yet it never forgets that in Jesus Christ the world is loved, condemned, and reconciled by God."[21] From Christ "alone there proceeds human action which is not worn away and wasted in conflicts of principle but which springs from the accomplishment of the reconciliation of the world with God, an action which soberly and simply performs what is in accordance with reality."[22] In this connection, he writes further: "All ideological action carries its own justification within itself from the outset in its guiding principle, but responsible action does not lay claim to knowledge of its own ultimate righteousness. . . . The responsible man commits his action into the hands of God and lives by God's grace and favor."[23] Here we detect the writing of a conspirator on behalf of his fellow conspirators. At the same time I note again how Bonhoeffer interprets the family's way of acting from the perspective of Christ. In the family we came to our decisions after thorough deliberations and with a view both to the consequences for those most affected—in this case those being persecuted—and to the wider field of action related to this. The standards, namely the Ten Commandments, functioned as the most important factor, but in an unconscious way, so to speak; one spoke only of the objective situation. If one had to act contrary to such isolated standards, though they were taken seriously in themselves, that would not have prejudiced or interfered with the decision.

"Telling the Truth"

"What is meant by 'telling the truth'?"[24] The answer to this question is closely connected with "correspondence to reality." Hence we read in Bonhoeffer's *Ethics* text: " 'Telling the truth' is also a matter of correct appreciation of real situations and of serious reflection upon them. . . . If my utterance is to be truthful it must in each case be different according to whom I am addressing, who is questioning me, and what I am speaking about. The truthful word is not in itself constant."[25] Bonhoeffer proceeds from the case of a child who, asked by the teacher in front of the class if his father comes home drunk, answers no! despite the fact that his father is a drunkard. Bonhoeffer insists that the child "according to the measure of his knowledge . . . acted correctly."[26] "The question must be asked whether and in what way a person is entitled to demand truthful speech of others."[27] Therefore, it is a question here again of the full "correspondence to reality" of a statement, not of the principle of telling the truth at all costs. In another section Bonhoeffer, to make the point, uses an example from Kant who claims that I would have to reply truthfully to one who had broken into my home seeking to murder my friend, if my friend had taken refuge with me. On this, Bonhoeffer argues that "the refusal to bear guilt for the sake of love of my neighbor sets me in contradiction with my responsibility which is grounded in reality."[28] If one, therefore, speaks the truth without being faithful to his responsibility according to the reality of the situation, one can become guilty of sinning against one's neighbor by the blind following of a principle.

The family, like Bonhoeffer himself, held to this sense of the truth, even before the Nazis arrived. For example, they were quite liberal-minded when it came to writing excuses from school if one of the children acted exhausted, and with confidence they gave cogent reasons for the absence. On occasion the family even permitted lying, such as the denial that a family member was at home if that person did not want to see somebody. Such "lies," though, were not directed against those close to the family. They always originated in a deliberate decision. And one tried to be on one's guard against self-deception.

I have sometimes asked myself what really was the criterion according to which we were guided in this matter, since I have the impression that, with regards to veracity, extra-stringent standards were imposed on us. Many quotations from Bonhoeffer indicate this. Among these references, for example, we could include again the lengthy quotation above in which Bonhoeffer describes the intellectual clarity and honesty that ensued on the French Revolution.[29] Every instance of fibbing to one's family in order to cover up a mistake or to make excuses was punished with disdain by parents or grandparents; and, as we have already indicated, so too was every smallest lie told in order to put oneself in a good light. This disdain, although most often manifest only in short remarks, hurt more than other punishments, and we absolutely avoided exposing ourselves to it. What is more, "lying" through simply being silent, as when one had avoided acknowledging a fault or, without any contrary word, if one had allowed the accomplishments of others to be attributed to oneself, was treated with equal severity. The members of the family themselves naturally acquired this repugnance for such lack of truthfulness early on. But in cases that an outsider would not have been able to understand without uncomfortable explanations, certain "cover-up lies," designed to preserve an urgently needed freedom of movement for oneself, were permitted. The criterion of the "correspondence with reality" is perhaps an answer of sorts, although after several discussions of "What Is Meant by Telling the Truth?", I know that this answer will in no way satisfy everybody.

With respect to the Nazis this practice was absolutely imperative, and the freedom, which one had previously already enjoyed in the family, simplified one's attitude toward them. My father (Bonhoeffer's brother-in-law) was brought up in other family traditions and could hardly bring himself to speak an untruth, something that occasionally made him the butt of friendly teasing in the family. He might be told in a joking way: "You really do come from the last century!" (My father was born in 1895; the others, after 1900.) To become involved in the political action naturally demanded a much greater effort from him.

Although my father recognized this inability to lie under these circumstances as a clear deficiency, he rightly saw himself as acting in accord with church teaching. As with Kant, so also in the church, one had been kept to a narrow, legalistic understanding of truth. Bonhoeffer, therefore, offered something new for many people in the church with his insight into "telling the truth." This, as we are told over and again, can have a very liberating effect. And yet, for many, this can also be rather offensive.

"Blessed Are Those Who Are Persecuted for the Sake of Justice, for the Kingdom of Heaven Is Theirs" (Matt. 5:10)

Matthew 5:10 took on a new reality in the Nazi era. Suddenly there were people "persecuted for the sake of justice." There were some who, in an outspoken way, had stood up for the cause of Christ and were, therefore, made to suffer. But there were also some who would have neither desired nor dared to be regarded as followers of Christ in such a direct way. To them it was a question "only" of the preservation or the restoration of law and justice and, because of this, they were persecuted.

Even in his 1937 book, *The Cost of Discipleship,* where he treats the Beatitudes as a whole, and then also in his *Ethics* where he discusses specific beatitudes, Bonhoeffer expresses his firm conviction that this passage refers to all people who stand up for justice whether they have committed themselves to the cause of Christ or not. He declares that this saying does not refer to the righteousness of God; nor does it refer to persecution for the sake of Jesus Christ. "Rather is it suffering for the sake of a just, true, good, and human cause."[30] Bonhoeffer is disturbed by the "mistaken anxiety" and the "narrowness" of those Christians who keep their distance from suffering "only for the sake of a just cause." And he regards these Christians "as emphatically judged to be in the wrong by this beatitude of Jesus." For Bonhoeffer, Christ and the world belong implicitly together and those who dedicate themselves to justice in the world have the cause of Christ as their cause. Hence Bonhoeffer writes in a letter of January 1935: "There are causes for which an uncompromising stand is worthwhile. And it seems to me that peace, social justice, or, to be precise, Christ himself, are such."[31]

Resistance against the unjust actions of the Nazis was thus judged in every case in a positive light by the family. Without asking about the worldview behind the resistance, we treated with respect and concern those who were persecuted because of it. Nevertheless, the name of Niemöller was held in especially high esteem in the family.

Some Theological Catchwords

In Bonhoeffer, therefore, elements of a Christian-liberal family background converged in a certain tension with the views and principles of the church. New ideas and formulations grew out of this. Some of the now famous key expressions especially reveal their origins in this polarity.

Costly Grace and Cheap Grace. In *The Cost of Discipleship,* Bonhoeffer criticizes the church, which promoted the idea that God's grace be regarded as a reality to be taken for granted. He finds fault with the offer of a "cheap grace . . . without price; grace without cost" through which "the world finds a cheap covering for its sins, no contrition is required, still less any real desire to be delivered from sin."[32] Bonhoeffer speaks instead of a "costly grace." This is grace that has as consequence a life lived in faith and obedience, thus leading to the "discipleship" that concerns the whole person.

Bonhoeffer's anger over the cheap words about God's grace in the church, for which no efforts were required to live according to the demands of being a Christian, correspond to the attitude of his father, who could not tolerate any words that were not backed up by one's entire attitude and by one's deeds.

Who Is Christ for Us Today? In this fundamental question, both Bonhoeffer's reference points are briefly and clearly mentioned by name: first, "Christ," and with him, likewise, the church; and, second, "for us today," and, therefore, also the reality in the world. Bonhoeffer's insistence on both aspects of the question is evident from very early on in the way this reality was reflected in his family.

Non-religious Interpretation. Bonhoeffer's fundamental question is very closely related to his consideration of "non-religious interpretation" or of "non-religious Christianity."[33] He recognizes that religion today functions on the edges of life, "when human knowledge has come to an end, or when human resources fail,"[34] but does not play an important role in the center of life. He wonders whether "religion is only a garment of Christianity" which might impede the work of Christ today, and raises the question what "non-religious Christianity" could possibly be. He asks: "What do a church, a community, a sermon, a liturgy, a Christian life mean in a religionless world? How do we speak of God without religion?"[35] These questions certainly have much to do with the members of Bonhoeffer's family, and also with some people of the resistance who lived as Christians but did not feel at home in a "religious" atmosphere. It was similar even for Bonhoeffer himself. Hence he writes from prison: "While I'm often reluctant to mention God by name to religious people—because that name somehow seems to me here not to ring true, and I feel myself to be slightly dishonest (it's particularly bad when others start to talk in religious jargon; I then dry up almost completely and feel awkward and uncomfortable)—to people with no religion I can on occasion mention him by name quite calmly and as a matter of course."[36]

Jesus, the Man for Others—the Church for Others. An answer to these questions is suggested by this, Bonhoeffer's equally well-known formulation. For Bonhoeffer, "being-for-others" is the central characterization of Christ. Christ suffers with people and for them. In like manner, the Christian ought to participate in his "being-for-others." This is most important since, "it is not the religious act that makes the Christian, but participation in the sufferings of God in the secular life."[37] This is surely not a question of a commitment to one's fellow humans considered by itself, but a commitment that in its motivations and aims is rooted in God's own participation in human life. Because of this, Bonhoeffer, it seems, regards his own family and the others involved in the resistance as those who in a special way are called to Christ's discipleship.

"Being-for-others" had already received heavy emphasis in the upbringing of Bonhoeffer and his brothers and sisters. It was expected of the children that they be aware of anyone needing help, that they not use their position to take advantage of those who were smaller or weaker or absent at the moment, but that they be concerned for their interests as well. The children were severely reprimanded for any offenses in this particular area, whereas other faults might even be overlooked by the mother.

Bonhoeffer contends that the church must likewise be much more a "church for others." "What it means 'to be there' for others"[38] is experienced by the church and by the Christian only through Christ. The life of the church and of the Christian is not thereby exhausted in acting justly for others, but rather consists in "prayer and doing justice." This has also become one of the best known expressions from the period of Bonhoeffer's imprisonment, and calls our attention once again to the two centers of gravity of his life.

THE FAMILY CIRCLE

Finally, let me offer a few of my own impressions and observations. Today some pursue the most remote traces in order to acquire a key to the sources of Bonhoeffer's lines of thought, discovering relationships with Boethius, Teresa of Avila, and others. Something important may be uncovered in the process. But it appears to me that the obvious and basic source, namely, Bonhoeffer's family background, might thereby be easily overlooked. (Naturally there were other families with an entirely similar outlook, though each family had its own slant on things.) With Bonhoeffer it follows that what is most important is generated in the confrontation of what he so evidently lived in his home with what he came upon in church and in theology, brought to a head by the special challenges of his time.

In his coming to grips with the Nazi state Bonhoeffer was able to develop what in his family was in accord with authentic, responsible attitudes in theology and in church proclamation and to do so in such a way that these spheres of interest became creatively interwoven with one another. It is fascinating and rewarding to explore this mutual effect, in the course of which I have obviously proceeded from my own experiences to those of the larger Bonhoeffer family. I frequently discover insights, opinions, and formulations in Bonhoeffer's writings which he has obviously picked up in the family circle and then often developed further. This can be seen, for example, in the critique of the ecclesial-theological world around him, and of his contemporaries, and where he proposes something new to enable the church to seek out different paths and to plan for the future. Without a doubt there was also much controversy in the family, but that must be seen in the context of a stronger togetherness.

The influence of the family's way of life appears to be very far reaching. Even the life of quasi-monastic piety in the Preachers Seminary directed by Dietrich Bonhoeffer at Finkenwalde—something quite unthinkable in the family—stands, nonetheless, in harmony with the demand of his father that one's way of life fully correspond to the convictions one has expressed in words. As I understand it, in order for Bonhoeffer's theology to be credible in the family, he had to live fully immersed in it and in accordance with it. In this, he did not want to pass himself off as someone who only spoke bold words—like many other clergymen at that time—and he certainly did not want to be looked on as one who had contributed nothing of relevance for the period of history in which he lived.

Therefore, he had first of all to take the church and theology very seriously and stand his ground on the basis of his calling as a minister and theologian. How difficult that was for him from time to time, especially during the period before a full personal commitment to his mission had been required—first in the church (and thereby also for the political world) and later for the political world (and thereby also for the church)—is shown in the following quotations. The first is from a letter to Helmut Rössler in which Bonhoeffer asks: "What do you think about the imperishability of Christendom with regard to the general political situation and our own life style?" To which he adds the observation: "This insane, long-standing practice of being thrown back on the invisible God—no one can tolerate this any longer. . . . One really means that something spectacular would have to take place at every moment and yet it is simply a matter of waiting."[39]

The other quotation—less emotional—is not from a letter to a colleague like Rössler, who understands Bonhoeffer's problems as a theologian, but to the eldest brother, Karl-Friedrich. Here his problems are viewed from his family perspective and in an ethical, worldly way of thinking: "But I know that if I were 'more reasonable' I should be honor bound to hang up the whole of my theology. . . . But I now believe that I know at last that I am at least on the right track—for the first time in my life. . . . I believe I know that inwardly I shall be really clear and honest with myself only when I have begun to take seriously the Sermon on the Mount."[40] This letter from 1935, after Bonhoeffer had taken a stand in opposition to the Nazis at several important points, also radiates the conviction that he was "now on the right track." He now sees in a "really clear and honest" way how he can make a relevant impact in the church and theology and, at the same time, in the world. Both were important for him. With his background, he could not live merely in the domain of theology without concrete reference to life; nor could he live in a kind of pious, churchy ghetto. As a theologian he wanted to connect church and world more intimately so that he and people of various backgrounds could and would live with both the church and God.

Near the end of his time in prison, as Bonhoeffer's effectiveness was reduced to the smallest possible sphere, his thoughts were concentrated on what was essential. Hence he writes: "I should like to speak of God . . . at the center . . . in strength . . . in man's life. As to the boundaries, it seems to me better to be silent and leave the insoluble unsolved."[41] He would like to see God in people who are conscious of their strength, who, with God, can achieve something in their freedom, and not solely in those of an anxious, threatened nature. "On the boundaries," indeed, even now on his own "boundaries," Bonhoeffer holds with the reserved, skeptical simplicity of his father in that he accepts the unsolvability of what is "unsolvable," and does not assume an all-knowing piety that could be expected in a person of his profession.

Bonhoeffer was aware of this interconnection with his family and considered it something obvious. In this regard, a word should be said about the sources of Bonhoeffer's thought, lest one be led to make false inferences. The close family ties must be assumed at every level. When there are no letters to attest to this, Bonhoeffer in all likelihood was staying at home. As a consequence, the relationship with his family was especially close. Too, we must keep in mind that, in the case of the letters, the family did not preserve them all. Moreover, the frequent telephone calls, something not so common at that time, were hardly ever logged.

Even during the course of Bonhoeffer's imprisonment there were often, after the bomb alerts, short exchanges of information by telephone through Metz, the prison director. Likewise, after the first few weeks of Bonhoeffer's imprisonment in Tegel, we found many ways to keep informed about one another and to remain in contact. There were, however, no illegal letters between Bonhoeffer and his parents or brothers and sisters, since we had to reckon with the postal censorship.

None of us in the family experienced any impulse on Bonhoeffer's part to distance himself from the family, which some imagine was the case. Another conjecture often put forward, namely, that Bonhoeffer had been a prophetic loner because of the way he had sized up the Nazis, likewise does not correspond to the facts. Rather, he shared actively in the experiences and perceptions of his large family.

Obviously the matters about which I have spoken here have still other, perhaps more important dimensions. Such is the case for Bonhoeffer's specifically theological contribution. But I offer these observations on the family background in the hope that they might shed light on the Bonhoeffer who in the baptismal sermon for his grand-nephew, my son, writes about himself: "He is striving to keep up the spirit—as far as he understands it—that is embodied in his parents' (your great-grandparents') home."[42]

RENATE BETHGE
(*translated by Geffrey Kelly*)

2

PATRIOTISM

In the United States we periodically experience mighty resurgences of patriotism, most recently during the Reagan-Bush administration. Ronald Reagan, who read the cultural script so well, never spurned a chance to be presidentially patriotic. His official opposition, the Democrats gathered in convention in San Francisco and later in Atlanta, wrapped the entire hall in technicolor patriotism and did their best to say they most effectively represented "America." Many businesses, large and small, changed their company colors to red, white, and blue. On its cartons a New York milk company listed the days we should fly the flag, ending with: "Any Day." Manufacturers of U.S. flags said their orders doubled in the 1980s. On many highways Old Glory, waving from each corner of the used-car lots, doubled in size. Schoolchildren collected change to fix up the grand lady on Liberty Island. And at university commencements everywhere, newborn conservatism and patriotism proudly paraded their colors among the young.

This is not emotional tinsel. Feelings are real, and run deep. Ask those who could not be torn from the Los Angeles and Seoul Olympics, or those who unofficially closed out the decade after the fall of Saigon by whiting the canyons of Manhattan with ticker tape, pitching it gently and kindly on a ragged assemblage of almost middle-aged "Nam" vets. "America" apparently had come back and was standing tall. Reagan, though a true believer if ever there was one, was really only massaging the culture, not inventing it.

The religious community joined. At least on the right, religious vitality went hand-in-hand with patriotism. Standard dress became a cross on one lapel, a flag on the other. Family, flag, and faith marched

31

together like the famed "Spirit of '76" trio—battered and patched but steady, musical, and proud. Not for a long time have we experienced such a strong display of religious patriotism.

Reagan consistently set the tone. A typical instance was his nation-wide speech on tax reform, in which he pledged "a future of unlimited promise, an endless horizon lit by the star of freedom guiding America to supremacy." Charles Krauthammer wrote in the *Washington Post*, "You can almost feel your shoes lifting you up and carrying you back to Kansas."[1]

"The star of freedom guiding America to supremacy" certainly captures one strain in the recent fervor. Accompanying it are notions that virtually define the revived patriotism.

"Supremacy" surveys the life of nations as a zero-sum game—our gain is the enemy's loss, the enemy's gain jeopardizes our welfare. Life is fundamentally adversarial. It is essentially competitive. Vigilance and power are the stuff of patriotism.

Yet the spirit of this Social Darwinist patriotism is upbeat: it speaks of "unlimited promise," and "an endless horizon." This is the official optimism of the Opportunity Society. Its standard bent is always to transform the old meaning of the term "frontier," a forbidding and uninviting place, the halting edge of conquest which means making do with what we have, to the true, "American," meaning, "frontier" as the next starting place, an invitation to new conquest and the acquisition of more.

Still, asserted confidence can mask deep fears. In Clarke Chapman's vivid image, we harbor "a suspicion that forward motion—like riding a wobbly bicycle—is at best a postponement of collapse."[2] Indeed, it is the combination of these themes, their playing upon one another, that gives so much American patriotism its warp and woof. Official optimism champions unlimited opportunity for the ambitious and clever in a deeply fearful, zero-sum world of adversarial relationships that threaten our way of life. This demands vigilance, confidence, and, when necessary, brute strength.

But is this true patriotism? If not, what is true patriotism? The exhibits around us certainly offer their interpretations. Yet they must not be approved without qualification; they certainly cannot be the patriotism of any who find themselves rankled by rampant chauvinism and unsettled by jingoism. ("We don't want to fight, but, by jingo, if we do, we've got the ships, we've got the men, we've got the money too.")

We can sharpen the question by adding a qualifier: What is genuinely Christian patriotism?

The answer cannot be simply a definition. Nothing so thick with life, as patriotism is, can be. We instinctively turn to symbols, examples, stories, and real, lived lives. While their meanings do not transfer without remainder from one time and place to another, nonetheless we draw from these in order to fashion our own fragile replies.

What follows is one such life—Dietrich Bonhoeffer's. Perhaps the story surfaces again because of World War II remembrances, D-Day anniversaries, Bitburg, and the Holocaust. Or it may be because of the forty year mark in 1985 of Bonhoeffer's own death in the Flossenburg concentration camp and, in 1984, the rescue of the Barmen Declaration from the archives and the remembrance of the Confessing Church, fifty years later. In any event, the threads run like this.

> To punish sin and to forgiveness you are moved,
> God, I have loved this people.
> That I bore its shame and sacrifices
> And saw its salvation—that is enough.[3]

Bonhoeffer's last extant fragments include this poem, "The Death of Moses." From atop Mt. Nebo Moses gives utterance to his pathos. He can see the promised land, but he cannot enter. And there, on the mountain, he will die.

Yet it is Bonhoeffer rather than Moses who speaks here. The plot on Hitler's life and the overthrow of the state had failed. Now Bonhoeffer must reckon with his own death. "God, I have loved this people" is Bonhoeffer voicing his love—for Germany. The final words are: "Hold me! My staff is sinking; Dear God, prepare my grave."[4]

There is no doubt whatsoever about Bonhoeffer's patriotism. The poetry is only the smallest portion of the proof, however. It is Bonhoeffer's actions that speak most clearly. He could have left Germany permanently in the 1930s. Twice he did leave, once to England and once to the United States. In each case he felt compelled to return, first in 1935 to direct the Confessing Church's seminary at Finkenwalde, then in 1939 to share more profoundly in what he knew would be fateful for his nation and perhaps for his family and himself as well. His stay in the United States lasted no more than six weeks. Explaining his decision to return, he wrote Reinhold Niebuhr to the effect:

> I have come to the conclusion that I have made a mistake in coming to America. I must live through this difficult period of our national history

with the Christian people of Germany. I will have no right to participate in the reconstruction of Christian life in Germany after the war if I do not share the trials of this time with my people.[5]

Testimony near the other end of these ill-boding years ratified the earlier decision. Bonhoeffer had fully identified himself with Germany's fate. He said precisely that in a Christmas letter in 1943.

Now I want to assure you that I haven't for a moment regretted coming back in 1939—nor any of the consequences, either. I knew quite well what I was doing, and I acted with a clear conscience. . . . And I regard my being kept here [in jail] . . . as being involved in Germany's fate, as I was resolved to be. I don't look back on the past and accept the present reproachfully. . . . All we can do is to live in assurance and faith—you out there with the soldiers, and I in my cell.[6]

But this is to start at the end, and that is not where Bonhoeffer's patriotism begins. Moreover, the ugly circumstances and terrible costs of the 1940s do not of themselves really tell us what kind of patriotism this is or what we should make of it. What leads some, like the Bonhoeffer family, to risk death for their country at the moment it is destroying itself and being destroyed, and to do so by playing a conspiratorial role is not obvious. Much less obvious is the reason why it was only along this path that Dietrich learned *faith* (as he himself describes it in the letter of July 21, 1944). The end beckons for the beginning. The story starts elsewhere.

HOME AND HORIZON

It starts with the Bonhoeffer family. History offers no better evidence than the Bonhoeffer household for Charles Dickens's maxim that it is in love of home that love of country has its rise.[7] The most casual reading of Bonhoeffer's letters from prison and earlier correspondence reflects a family life steeped in liberal German culture. With his family as a whole, Bonhoeffer felt himself a guardian of German culture, personally responsible for preserving the best Germany had to offer, for embodying it and passing it on. The entire family opposed Hitler from the very beginning. It did so not only because Hitler meant war but also because Nazism was a thorough barbarization of things German, a vulgarizing and criminalizing of a great cultural legacy. Simply put, the Bonhoeffers resisted Hitler precisely because they were Germans. Dietrich could say with youthful certainty in 1928 (he was 22 at the time): "For what I have I thank this nation, through this nation

I became what I am."[8] But it was the parental home that tendered the national heritage to him, defined it, and nurtured loyalty to it.

If home was the nest of Bonhoeffer's patriotism, it was travels abroad that gave it a distinctive mark. There were many—to Rome during university days, and a trip from there across the Mediterranean with his brother Klaus to Libya; to Spain for seminary internship and again with Klaus to North Africa; to New York for further theological studies and during that year to Mexico and Cuba; to London for two years of pastoral duties and ecumenical work; later to New York again and to Sweden, Denmark, Norway, and Switzerland, on duty either for the ecumenical movement or the resistance movement.

No doubt the family's cosmopolitan disposition and curiosity about all things unknown played itself out here. But there was something else. In Paul Lehmann's words, Bonhoeffer's habit was to focus "on what was most remote from his previous experience,"[9] to understand it on indigenous terms as far as possible, and then to let it adjust his own horizons. Bonhoeffer trekked to what were for him the margins in order to see the center from the edges and, if need be, to relocate his viewpoint. Having no experience at all of African-American culture, he became friends with Frank Fisher and, through him, with Harlem. A total stranger to pacifism, he was instructed by Jean Lasserre—hardly a topic for a German to learn from a Frenchman, with the Versailles Treaty still smoldering in a history of animosities. At home in Berlin he commuted between his parental home in stylish, upper-class Grunewald and an apartment in Wedding, a worker slum, in order to better understand the youth of his confirmation class there.

Even the journeys that did not materialize reveal this distinctive trait of moving to the edges of an experience. Bonhoeffer sought and received an invitation from Gandhi. The church's call to Finkenwalde came before the boat left, so the plan was cancelled. But for a German in the 1930s, the intentions were utterly intriguing and almost unique: to learn resources from the East for the spiritually impoverished West, to practice the arts of disciplined community in an ashram experience, and to study the ways of nonviolence as a practical social force.

Later he would write that the greatest learning of all happened at the edges. Yet not simply the edges, but specifically "from below." An essay written for colleagues in resistance includes a passage that would become a *locus classicus* for liberation theology:

> There remains an experience of incomparable value. We have for once learnt to see the great events of world history from below, from the

perspective of the outcast, the suspects, the maltreated, the powerless, the oppressed, the reviled—in short, from the perspective of those who suffer. The important thing . . . is that we should have come to look with new eyes at matters great and small. . . . We have to learn that personal suffering is a more effective key, a more rewarding principle for exploring the world in thought and action than personal good fortune.[10]

All this crafted Bonhoeffer's patriotism, even when the connections were not always immediately obvious to him. He entered other's lives sufficiently to view his own national and cultural identity from there, and to see Germany as one people amid an array of peoples. Moreover, what he learned abroad was for the sake of Germany. Bonhoeffer was almost deliberate in regarding foreign experiences as training for his responsibilities at home.

CHURCH AND NATION

In the 1930s Bonhoeffer's travels were largely in ecumenical circles. Within them, and because of events at home, the tensions of being Christian and being German drew taut.

His involvement was dual. In Germany it was in the deepening church struggle. The movement of the so-called German Christians *(Deutsche Christen)* trumpeted an acculturated faith in which the *Deutsche Christen* boasted of a profound complementarity between their Christianity and the aggressive German way of life. The neutrals, mostly Lutherans, showed acculturation of a different sort. Theirs was a studied effort to distance matters of the faith from those of the state, leaving politics to the latter and the unencumbered preaching of the Word to the former, each viewed as a necessary complement of the other. The Confessing Church, not without struggle, resisted both the Aryanizing of the church and the totalitarian claim of the Führer.[11] Through most of these years, Bonhoeffer periodically worked on a tract of the times, which was eventually published as *The Cost of Discipleship*. ("We Lutherans have gathered like eagles 'round the carcass of cheap grace and there have drunk the poison that has killed the life of following Christ.")[12]

Bonhoeffer's other arena of passionate involvement was the *oikoumenē* (ecumenical movement). Later, when Bonhoeffer's active participation in the ecumenical movement necessarily came to an end, he wrote that it had become "foundational for my whole thought and life."[13]

It had become that, but the tie to his patriotism was not at all clear. If anything, Bonhoeffer had subordinated his national citizenship to membership in the transnational church. Not only Bonhoeffer's priority, but his very identity was first church, then Germany. Loyalty to the nation was drastically relativized. All the nation's claims were qualified by membership in the Body of Christ as a concrete, international reality. He made his position clear at the 1934 Fanø meeting of Life and Work and the World Alliance for Promoting International Friendship, in which he served as a youth secretary. His sermon address on "The Church and Peoples of the World" said it clearly:

> This Church of Christ lives at one and the same time in all peoples, yet beyond all boundaries, whether national, political, social, or racial. And [those] who make up this Church are bound together . . . more inseparably than men are bound by all ties of common history, of blood, of class, and language. All these ties, which are part of our world, are valid ties, not indifferent; but in the presence of Christ, they are not ultimate bonds.[14]

The meeting had been called to discuss whether the international church was empowered to take sides in international disputes, the lengths to which it might go in such cases, and the means which might be considered. Due in part to Bonhoeffer's influence, the focal issue became peace. His words still carry an eerie relevance:

> How does peace come about? Through a system of political treaties? Through the investment of international capital in different countries? Through the big banks, through money? Or through universal peaceful rearmament in order to guarantee peace? Through none of these, for the single reason that in all of them peace is confused with safety. There is no way to peace along the way to safety. For peace must be dared. It is the great venture.[15]

Moreover, Bonhoeffer continued, Christians dare not take up arms against one another. For in doing so, they take dead aim at Jesus Christ himself.[16]

Evidently the ecumenical basis for his "whole thought and life" lasted to the end. On the final day of his life, Bonhoeffer sent a message to a dear friend in England, George Bell, Bishop of Chichester, via a fellow prisoner, the Englishman Payne Best: "Tell him that for me this is the end but also the beginning—with him I believe in the principle of our universal Christian brotherhood which rises above all national interests, and that our victory is certain. . . ."[17]

What then of the tension of being both Christian and German, and of Bonhoeffer's patriotism, stretched between these poles?

The German ethos in both church and society made ecumenical participation uncomfortable and sometimes dangerous. Most Germans were extremely hostile toward it. The *oikoumenē* was home to "decadent internationally minded democrats," to recall the common epithet for suspected enemies of national pride.[18] When Bonhoeffer took seminarians to Sweden in 1936, Bishop Heckel of the Church Office for External Affairs responded. The Reich Foreign Ministry would take care of the foreign policy concerns, he wrote, but

> I feel impelled . . . to draw the attention of the Provincial Church Committee to the fact that the incident has brought Lic. Bonhoeffer very much into the public eye. Since he may incur the reproach of being a pacifist and an enemy of the state, it might well be advisable for the Provincial Church Committee clearly to distance itself from him and take steps to ensure that he no longer train German theologians.[19]

(As a consequence of this journey, the Reich Ministry of Education terminated Bonhoeffer as a lecturer at Berlin University.)

In such an atmosphere, it is understandable why the Confessing Church was reticent about ecumenical representation. This was true as much for positions it favored as for those it opposed. As Bonhoeffer wrote to Danish Bishop Ammundson in connection with possible actions desired by the Confessing Church: "It's possible that our side may be terribly cautious for fear of seeming to be unpatriotic."[20] The reticence was not simply tactical, however. Segments of the Confessing Church reflected German society on two of Germany's most uncompromising themes—sincere nationalism and ardent anti-communism. The internationalism of ecumenical meetings challenged and tempered both. For the Confessing Church it was all quite uncomfortable.

Still, what was Bonhoeffer's own posture? He assumed what was for him a characteristic stance. On the one hand, he pressed for stronger anti-Nazi stands than even the ecumenical movement was willing to take. At the very same time he used the international forum to be heard as a German on questions vital to his country. He spoke of the wrongs of Versailles, for example. He let non-Germans know which policies of other European nations and the United States made Nazism itself more appealing to Germans. And he was delighted when non-Germans, like George Bell, Bishop of Chichester, showed understanding and empathy for his homeland. It was, all in all, an easily misunderstood stance. Representing and interpreting Germany out of deep love for it, he called upon the church to take forceful anti-Nazi actions which were interpreted at home as anti-German. All this transpired in a transnational church where he now lodged his own citizenship.

Or did he? Ecumenical connections offered him an easy way to escape the draft in 1939. ("I am thinking of leaving Germany sometime," he wrote Bell. "The main reason is the compulsory military service. . . . It seems to me conscientiously impossible to join in a war under the present circumstances. . . .")[21] Abroad he could then devote himself to theology, his first love. But after initially accepting the offer, he knew almost immediately that it was wrong. He boarded the boat again, this time eastbound. Paul Lehmann tried to persuade him to stay in the United States, but could not. Conscientious objection to serving in Hitler's army, uncompromising as it was for Bonhoeffer, was apparently not as strong as conscientious participation in Germany's fate.

Had Bonhoeffer's priorities shifted? From church/Germany to Germany/church? From ecumenism to patriotism? In fact, it was his ecumenical patriotism quietly showing its true colors. For by this time the truth deep in Bonhoeffer's bones faced itself—"a debt had accumulated for every German, which had to be paid off" is Bethge's way of naming it.[22] While Bonhoeffer never forsook the citizenship that "rises above all national interests," patriotism now meant for him a full identification with Germany's destiny and a shouldering of responsibility for its crimes. The privilege of ecumenical refuge had to be set aside for the sake of being an authentically Christian German. Bonhoeffer understood exactly what de Mores, a Brazilian poet, later penned: "You can't be universal anywhere except in your own backyard."

TRAITOR OR PATRIOT?

Now we enter a world of mottled greys. The scene is the little town of Memel, June 17, 1940. Bethge recalls:

> While we were enjoying the sun, there suddenly boomed out from the cafe's loudspeaker the fanfare signal for a special announcement: the message was that France had surrendered. The people round about at the tables could hardly contain themselves: they jumped up, and some even climbed on chairs. With outstretched arms they sang *Deutschland, Deutschland, über alles* and the "Horst Wessel Song." We had stood up, too. Bonhoeffer raised his arm in the regulation Hitler salute, while I stood there dazed. "Raise your arm! Are you crazy?" he whispered to me, and later: "We shall have to run risks for very different things now, but not for that salute!"[23]

Bonhoeffer's double life had begun. The pastor and professor became the conspirator. The seminary director took on the grotesque "vocation" of an agent in Hitler's own army intelligence unit, where the resistance movement itself was headquartered. The citizen of high bourgeois standing, schooled in civil responsibility, labored to topple his government. Eventually it would land him in jail and take him to the gallows. In 1941 and 1942, while employed as a courier in the Army Intelligence Unit (*Abwehr*), he used his ecumenical contacts to inform the Allies of the resistance movement's plans to overthrow Hitler and to ask that the Allies not prosecute the war further once the coup d'état was under way. He also helped smuggle Jews into Switzerland with falsified papers provided by the *Abwehr*. But when Bonhoeffer and his brother-in-law, Hans von Dohnanyi, were arrested and sent to Tegel Military Prison in 1943, the reason was not the discovery of actions treasonous to the national security. Rather, the Gestapo, in its running battle with the *Abwehr* over control of intelligence operations, uncovered sufficient bureaucratic irregularities and suspicious connections to serve as a pretext for disabling the *Abwehr*. It was considerably later, in the aftermath of the failed plot of July 20, 1944, that the work of *Abwehr* resistance was itself uncovered. Bonhoeffer was then transferred to the Gestapo prison and from there to concentration camps for the final weeks of his life.

If there is any laughter here, it is the laughter of hell. Bonhoeffer, by disposition reflective, in taste and temperament aristocratic and nonviolent, now had to learn the Nazi arts that so repelled him. From prison, and again in poetry, he confessed the agony of clandestine resistance.

> We too had learned to lie before long,
> and adapted ourselves to public wrong
> and when the defenceless were felled by force,
> we took it all as a matter of course.

> And that [which] within our hearts still flamed
> remained unspoken and unnamed;
> we checked the blood's insurgent flow
> and trampled out the inward glow.[24]

This only begins to chart the moral and emotional turbulence of the times. They were surreal in ways that are still hard to grasp. For most, the days of the Third Reich began in utter exhilaration. The vast majority welcomed the early 1930s as deliverance from the malaise of the Weimar Republic and the runaway inflation and unemployment of the Depression. There was a mighty surge of national pride, prestige, power, and prosperity. Even those who later became anti-Nazi Christian heroes drank this heady brew—Martin Niemoller rejoiced that Germany was back and standing tall after the national humiliation of the previous war and the shameful terms of defeat. With almost everyone else, he was feeling good about being German. Bonhoeffer wrote to Erwin Sutz: "Naive visionaries like Niemoller continue to think they're the true National Socialists."[25] Gradually, however, the folly and evil of militant racist nationalism displayed its wares. Consequently, "the slow sure doom [fell] pitiless and dark" on Germany and Europe, to adopt Bertrand Russell's words. The horrors of the Holocaust and the awesome waste of war descended on the world.

To continue to be what it already was, Bonhoeffer's Christian patriotism had to change course. It had been the courageous, morally clean, uncompromising public witness so powerfully presented in *The Cost of Discipleship*. Now the sharp, unequivocal moral profile was submerged, and in its place appeared, like some figure in a dark alley, the terrible patriotism of conspiracy. Earlier Bonhoeffer had followed a truly "countercultural" Jesus, rendered visible in bright evangelical witness. Now Bonhoeffer walked with the Jesus of sorrows, the one for others who does not speak, but in dreadful silence takes upon himself their guilt. The same identification with Jesus that had led Bonhoeffer to say a bold *Nein!* to the patriotism of flags, party rallies, and the Berlin Olympics, now led him to say yes to another, very different kind of love for country. His resistance expressed his understanding of Jesus Christ, as did his patriotism, and both were enacted with utter seriousness. To be a Christian, he wrote, is to stand by God in God's own hour of grieving;[26] and God was grieving in Germany, because of Germany. Bonhoeffer had to be there, precisely as a German. And like Jesus in Gethsemane, he had to drink the earthly cup to the dregs.

So what is Christian patriotism for us in North America and specifically the United States? It was a theological axiom for Bonhoeffer that "backyards" are not identical and that the ecumenical church in each locale has the task of discerning "who Christ really is, for us, today."[27] The task of local discernment is ours. Bonhoeffer cannot simply be "applied." Indeed, it is precisely because Bonhoeffer was martyr and patriot in his own backyard that he has become an authentic ecumenical teacher. To assist our own quest, however, we can summarize his patriotism. It is rich substance for our reflection.

• He was a grateful heir and genuine guardian of his country's cultural wealth, a conserver of the best of its past.

• Through experiences with others unlike him, at home and abroad, he entered into their lives sufficiently to view his own nation from what were, for the nation and himself, external and marginal points of view. From there he saw Germany afresh, as one nation amid a world of nations and peoples.

• He worked vigorously in the international church and in the resisting church in Germany. He represented his country's legitimate aspirations and strengths in transnational church circles, and he offered the perspectives and gifts of non-German Christians to his home church. His patriotism was always qualified and instructed by the cosmopolitanism of the Body of Christ.

• He identified with those Germans, some of them Christian, many not, who risked all in an attempt to save their country from utter destruction, from even more crimes against humanity and further unrelieved guilt. In this solidarity Bonhoeffer died, as an ecumenical Christian, for Germany.

Whatever else true Christian patriotism is, it is a profound "acceptance." Not in the sense of uncritical affirmation, with or without the chauvinism of "supremacy"; but "acceptance" in its genuine sense: "to take on," "to receive willingly." What is taken on are the culture's gifts, in order to cherish them and pass them on, and a deep responsibility for the culture's crimes and victims, in order to atone for them and to help prevent their recurrence. Community, solidarity, responsibility, and sacrifice—these are the values of Christian patriotism.

> God, I have loved this people.
> That I bore its shame and sacrifices
> and saw its salvation—that is enough.

3

RESISTANCE

A volume on Bonhoeffer for North Americans should mention some Americans by name and give them due attention. Accordingly, there are separate chapters on Daniel Berrigan, a Roman Catholic priest; Reinhold Niebuhr, Protestant theologian; and Irving Greenberg, a Jewish rabbi. Daniel Berrigan is the subject of this chapter. He is often mentioned in the same breath with Bonhoeffer because of common associations with protest and resistance, and because both are widely read. It is common for admirers as well as the simply curious to compare Bonhoeffer and Berrigan. Christians engaged in political resistance invariably do so.

There are striking parallels—and contrasts—in their lives as resistance figures. In part this is because Bonhoeffer's life and thought have influenced Berrigan, by Berrigan's own testimony. In particular, Berrigan is familiar with the context and course of Bonhoeffer's resistance.[1] When Berrigan went underground in 1970 to elude the FBI, he took along Bethge's manuscript biography of Bonhoeffer and "meditated on the volume, and set down preliminary notes, a work of some two weeks."[2]

But the similarities derive from more than Berrigan's reading of Bonhoeffer and being influenced page-by-page. Rather, the similarities themselves disclose the reasons for the discernible influence of Bonhoeffer upon Berrigan, especially if Robert Coles is correct that Berrigan's interest in Bonhoeffer is not best understood as a search for clues for the course of his own life (Berrigan's), but rather as a sympathetic and empathetic response rooted in correlative thoughts, experiences, and events.[3] Several of these shared characteristics follow.

PARALLELS

1. A strong *theologia crucis* (theology of the cross) is evident in the writings of both. They share a conviction of the power of suffering love and a vision that what marks Christians is that they stand by God while God suffers in the midst of people's very "worldly" lives. For both, siding with the defenseless, the poor, the weak, the prosecuted, and the persecuted is understood as part of a *theologia crucis* and is viewed as a theological and ethical test case.[4]. The impulse to resistance is intensified by this shared picture of Jesus—the radical and human Jesus of the passion.[5] There are surely major differences in the theologies of these men. Yet the centrality of the cross is a powerful common strain, without which any understanding of their resistance remains obfuscated.

2. There are striking similarities in their understanding of and stance toward the church. Bonhoeffer and Berrigan bear a love/hate relationship toward the church because of the following: the common experience of a civil religion confused with Christianity—and this in a decadent social order; deep disappointment in the national church, that is, their respective denominations, for its failure to act decisively and uncompromisingly on the great moral issues facing society, then disappointment in the lack of unanimity and effectiveness among dissenting ranks in the church; and the experience of discovering non-Christians to be doing what Christians ought to be doing, while Christians have failed to do so. Berrigan and Bonhoeffer both have a passion for church renewal, and both prefer the *ecclesiolae in ecclesia*, the small gatherings of close and disciplined communities directed toward outward service. Just as Jesus is "the man for others" (Bonhoeffer's phrase), so the church is to be "the church for others."

3. Both exhibit a common religious style, a dialectic of "arcane discipline" and "religionless Christianity." The movement is between meditation and prayer in reflective solitude, or with small groups of clearly committed Christians, on the one hand, and making common cause with non-Christians in the public arena, on the other.

4. There is an intense sense of national and ecclesiastical guilt and a patriotic response that drive both Bonhoeffer and Berrigan to political action. A corollary of their patriotism is that neither seriously considers emigrating from the nation. Or, if either does, he regards it as a temptation or a mistake. In short, "geography"—home turf as the place of responsibility—counts for both. The first citation below is a familiar one from Bonhoeffer. The second is from Berrigan.

Now I want to assure you that I have not for a moment regretted coming
back in 1939—nor any of the consequences, either. I knew quite well
what I was doing, and I acted with a clear conscience. I have no wish
to cross out of my life anything that has happened since, either to me
personally . . . or as regards events in general. And I regard my being
kept here [in prison] . . . as being involved in the part that I had resolved
to play in Germany's fate.[6]

I could not remain at peace at the center, so the issue continues to be
spatial—an issue of one's geography, one's place, one's decision to stand
here, not there, and for this rather than that.[7]

5. Both share intimate knowledge of the horrors that impel them
to action. Bonhoeffer had knowledge of German war crimes, Berrigan
accused the United States of crimes in Southeast Asia and Latin America,
both of which he visited amidst the strife. For Berrigan, as for Bonhoeffer, travels abroad yielded perspectives that heightened opposition
to home government policies and to the home society's way of life.

6. Both felt the attraction of Gandhi and the way of non-violence.
Both held a commitment to pacifism and a strong sympathy for conscientious objectors.[8] Berrigan continues to do so. Bonhoeffer appears
to differ from Berrigan on the matter of violence, as we shall see. Yet
it is surely important that Bonhoeffer, too, wrestled with the issue of
violence, that for an important time in his life he regarded himself a
pacifist, that he sought and succeeded in obtaining an invitation from
Gandhi to learn the arts of meditation, community, and nonviolence,
and that he sought and succeeded in evading conscription into the
army.

7. The range of moral, intellectual, and esthetic sensibilities is striking
for these two Christians. The sketchy accounts of Berrigan's response
to prison experiences are much like Bonhoeffer's. Fellow prisoners
testify to a certain "sovereignty" each carried in his bearing. Both
demonstrate an ability to concentrate on intellectual projects of their
choosing and even continue much of their pre-prison life-style, including the cultivation of their sensitive esthetic tastes. Although Bonhoeffer, unlike Berrigan, was a novice, he, too, wrote poetry and tried
his hand at a novel and a play. Both seem capable of multiple perspectives and of criticizing points of view with which they are most
in sympathy.

8. Both Bonhoeffer and Berrigan come to the conclusion, reluctantly,
that some drastic action of resistance must be taken. "The times are
inexpressibly evil," Berrigan says. Bonhoeffer claimed the same for his.

Both feel "compelled" to do what "must" be done, and exercise "free responsibility" (Bonhoeffer's phrase). The following, which refers to the Berrigans and others who poured blood on government files in Catonsville, Maryland, is equally true of Bonhoeffer:

> The defendants might have just as readily led the lives they had selected and for which they had been trained—nurse, teacher, priest, missionary, even the life of the struggling artist—if it were not for the times we live in.[9]

In this regard, a deep conviction about the virtual unredeemability of the present national order is clearly a major factor in the choice of each to undertake drastic action.

These are strong and significant similarities. They help explain Bonhoeffer's impact upon Berrigan. There are significant differences between these men, however. The following remarks trace these. Foremost among the differences are those that arise when Christians become both dissenters and serious resisters.

The following statements by Noam Chomsky and David O'Brien are abbreviated, but they accurately plot Daniel Berrigan's course of resistance, together with that of his brother Philip.

> The Berrigans have argued, with care and patience, that such circumstances [circumstances under which civil disobedience, even sabotage, is legitimate] now exist: specifically, that non-violent resistance to the Indo-China war is a legitimate response to criminal acts of the American executive, and that a legitimate component of such non-violent resistance is the destruction of property that has no right to exist in that its immediate function is to implement these criminal acts. They have suggested that such a response is not only legitimate in principle, but also that it may be efficacious in restricting, perhaps terminating the criminal violence of the American way. They have not been content merely to present the argument, or—as many others have—to construct the case from which the conclusion follows, without explicitly drawing it. Rather, they have pursued the logic of the argument to its conclusion and have acted accordingly, destroying property that (they argue) has no right to exist. They have also denied that the state has the right to prosecute those who act to restrain its criminal violence; and, again, they have acted accordingly, refusing to yield themselves voluntarily to state authorities.[10]

> At first they had expected and welcomed the prospect of jail. . . . But later they concluded that "the courts have become more and more the instruments of the warmakers," that the entire judicial system lacked moral and legal justification. They therefore decided to evade arrest and were jailed only after pursuit by federal authorities.[11]

Keeping this in mind for Berrigan, Bonhoeffer's criteria for measuring the appropriate time for and kinds of resistance can be listed. Attention focuses on active resistance and the employment of violence. Bonhoeffer's criteria for sanctioning extreme active resistance and the *ultima ratio* use of violence (last resort use) were the following.[12]

1. There must be clear evidence of gross misrule that threatens possibly irreparable harm to the citizenry.

Rule by elites is not of itself misrule for Bonhoeffer. He was totally opposed to totalitarian rule, insisted upon the rule of law, believed in a distribution of powers, and promoted the guarantee of certain rights. But he was not in principle opposed to all forms of strong government and he was not an unqualified democrat. He probably was closest to a studied, morally responsible Prussian conservatism. For Daniel Berrigan, by way of contrast, elitist rule as such is misrule.

2. For Bonhoeffer the scale of political responsibility must be respected. Men and women in the lower ranks of the hierarchy or outside it can take on heavy political responsibility only after it has been abdicated by those placed higher, or after these have been restrained. This is a version of "estates theory" in Bonhoeffer. Here Bonhoeffer is clearly not the democrat Berrigan is. There are statements in Bonhoeffer's *Ethics* on the Christian's political responsibility which Berrigan simply would not accept.

> Is there a political responsibility on the part of individual Christians? Certainly the individual Christian cannot be made responsible for the action of government, and he must not make himself responsible for it; but because of his faith and his charity he is responsible for his own calling and for the sphere of his own personal life, however large or however small it may be. If this responsibility is fulfilled in faith, it is effectual for the whole of the *polis*. According to Holy Scripture, there is no right to revolution; but there is a responsibility of every individual for preserving the purity of his office and mission in the *polis*.[13]

3. Hard coercion must be the last of the last resorts. All nonviolent and legal means must first be exhausted or known in advance to be clearly unavailing before one considers violent and illegal means. Here Bonhoeffer's contrast with Berrigan appears significant. It is true that both men respect such scales and begin with a commitment to legal and nonviolent means of effecting change. But Berrigan appears to stop with illegal and nonviolent means (toward persons) while Bonhoeffer allows the use of violence toward persons, including the possibility of assassination. Granted, it is the most extraordinary exception

for Bonhoeffer, and nearly unthinkable. But it is real, nonetheless—he approved of tyrannicide in the case of Hitler.

Just how extensive the parting of minds is here is not easily determined. In Bonhoeffer's case, the rationale is highly abbreviated. But it is clear. The policies of the Third Reich meant a forfeiture of its legitimacy as the state. The situation then is a condition called the "necessity of state," that is, the necessity of the restoration of the rule of law by extraordinary means. The means used to reestablish a genuine state may, in fact, include those employed by the Nazis themselves: deception, force, and violence. But the ends and dispositions are anti-Nazi. Contrasting ends include the return of justice via law, against the continued rule of barbarity via laws and orders arbitrarily formulated and enforced. Contrasting dispositions are reflected in Bonhoeffer's statement that the one who uses exceptional violence will acknowledge the guilt he or she incurs in its use, and will seek forgiveness. When violence is the last of the last resorts, when the extraordinary exception is never allowed to become standard policy, and when the ends and dispositions are themselves just, then the extremes of active resistance might be turned to in order to topple an order that cannot be healed from within. This is Bonhoeffer's stance.

In Berrigan's case, the parallels follow to a certain extent. Many of his statements echo Bonhoeffer's conviction that the state's policies can mean a forfeiture of its legitimacy as the state. Further, Berrigan says that a temporary and exceptional recourse to violence by such as the Weathermen (a body of politically radical students of the late 1960s) is far different from a use of violence as standard operating policy in keeping with a reigning ideology (by such as the Ku Klux Klan, for example). Berrigan's thought here approaches Bonhoeffer's statement, "Baldwin was right when he said that there was only one greater evil than violence and that this was violence as a principle, a law and a standard."[14]

Berrigan also notes that, given the moral ambiguity of resistance, one may need to risk joining those who take recourse to sporadic, exceptional violence. But such solidarity is not approval of the violence, nor does it compel one to undertake it for oneself. Further, Berrigan would, as he told the Weathermen, disassociate himself fully from them if and when their violence became policy and belonged intrinsically to the ideology held in their ranks.[15]

Berrigan has articulated his own scale for assessing revolutionaries. In this instance the subjects are Fidel Castro, Che Guevara, and Ho Chi Minh.

Each is deserving of praise . . . in proportion as he assiduously placed limits on violence, and made the creation of human structures his main life task. Conversely, the task is tarnished in proportion as it invokes violence as exemplary, as inevitable.[16]

Revolutionaries are heroic and praiseworthy, in proportion as they surpass the methods of the enemy, and teach the people to do the same.[17]

Bonhoeffer would subscribe to this assessment, provided he could sanction revolution at all. Yet, the extent of his agreement with Bonhoeffer notwithstanding, Berrigan makes clear that he cannot follow Bonhoeffer on the matter of exceptional use of extreme violence, that is, killing violence. In his review of Bonhoeffer's biography, Berrigan writes:

He joined in a conspiracy to assassinate Hitler, in order to bring down the Third Reich, and open the way for negotiations with the Allies. Now presupposing, as I firmly believe, that the Vietnam war is comparable in its genocidal character to Hitler's war and his near extinction of the German Jews, one asks himself whether Phil and I would at this stage, or any immediate future state (or indeed at any point in the past four years), venture in any such direction. We would not, by any means.[18]

The disagreement may revolve around the relation of ends and means. Berrigan follows Gandhi in saying that means are invariably a rehearsal of ends, or are ends-in-process, and thus cannot be out of character with the ends sought. Bonhoeffer responds, in effect, "Yes, normally, but not always." The disagreement may rest elsewhere, in the conviction of limits upon the kind of action which a Christian, *as* Christian, may undertake in active resistance. It appears in any case that Berrigan's refusal to follow Bonhoeffer's highly qualified sanction of the use of violence is not only argued on pragmatic grounds[19] but is grounded in a commitment to nonviolence on a more transcendent plane and as an uncompromised way of life.

4. Only the minimum force and violence that is required to abolish the abuses of misrule can be used. Berrigan would underwrite this criterion of Bonhoeffer's. His brother Philip says explicitly that the Christian may approve and support a violent revolution when political and social injustice have reached intolerable limits and hope of redress is absent. But the *Christian* must never personally partake of this admittedly necessary violence. So Bonhoeffer's criterion stands, though qualified by the Berrigans in a way with which Bonhoeffer disagrees. The minimum *violence* that is necessary for overthrow may be morally allowed for non-Christian co-resisters. But it cannot be the action of

Christians, according to the Berrigans.[20] Bonhoeffer, after what seems an analogous position in *The Cost of Discipleship*, came to regard such a distinction as parasitic and irresponsible.

Whatever the reasons in the end, their positions contrast in an interesting way. Bonhoeffer appears much less willing than the Berrigans to support revolution. He is far more cautious about overthrow.[21] But he is more willing than they to participate in its violence if and when the extremely rare moment of justified revolt does occur.

5. There must be reasonable assurance that extreme action will be successful. The individual, acting alone, acting even from compassionate motives and a genuine willingness to sacrifice his or her life, cannot justifiably undertake actions that involve the lives of thousands unless that action is coordinated with a group capable of assessing the situation and quickly occupying the organs of government. This is Bonhoeffer's conviction. He grew ever more convinced of the importance of calculating consequences and ever less enamored with the voice of impassioned conscience as sufficient authorization of action. From *The Cost of Discipleship* to *Letters and Papers from Prison* he moves further away from the bold, public, prophetic, consequences-be-damned witness, and closer to the actions of the careful planner and the realist politician. The policymaker and politician is, to be sure, no less the practitioner of courageous and highly precarious moves than the prophetic figure.[22] Both must take risks.

A difference between Bonhoeffer and Berrigan emerges here, but it is so closely tied to other matters in need of explication that comment can be deferred.[23]

In the review of Bonhoeffer's biography, Berrigan writes:

> The serious question for us if we are to continue faithful to the impulse that led us to Catonsville is not the question of our own welfare but the moral trajectory of our act—that it fly undeflected, to the heart of the matter, which is the infamy of the widening war, the grief torture dislocation death rape murder terrorism inflicted by our government upon the innocent.[24]

Bonhoeffer wrote in his account of the lessons learned in resistance:

> The ultimate question for a responsible man to ask is not how he is to extricate himself heroically from the affair, but how the coming generation is to live.[25]

Is there a difference here? Bonhoeffer certainly agrees that there comes a point when the Christian must act under moral compulsion.

And Berrigan certainly hopes the political consequences of following the moral trajectory will be the desired ones. So perhaps perceived differences dissolve with these qualifications. Yet it is quite likely that contrasting views about the purpose and justification of resistance lie behind these two statements. The difference may explain the apparent divergence between Bonhoeffer and Berrigan on the question of violence.

The dissimilarity of the two, larger even than differing views of violence per se, can best be seen in light of several representative quotations from Berrigan.

> The symbolism of Catonsville may become a permanent method and symbol. Of what? Of moral process.[26]

> The revolutionary quest, according to the hypothesis of guru John [of the Cross], is nothing more than the quest for moral change.[27]

> I *have* to be caught. . . . The whole point of all these weeks underground is to stand witness all over—here and there, and God willing, everywhere possible.[28]

> Something is happening to me and something is (I believe) happening to the others with whom I am staying and spending my time; and maybe the "something" has to do with the development of consciousness—that could be one way of putting it. It seems fairly certain, as far as one can be certain in very obscure times, that like it or not my brother and I are involved in a struggle for a certain kind of moral awareness.[29]

> How useful were the acts of the martyrs? How many martyrs ever had any practical programs for reforming society? Since politics weren't working anyway, one had to find an act beyond politics: a religious act, a liturgical act, an act of witness. If only a small number of men could offer this kind of witness, it would purify the world.[30]

> The New Left suffers from American pragmatism. . . . It fights violence with the tools of violence. I fight it with Gandhian and Christian dimensions of non-violence. They measure effectiveness by pragmatic results, I see it as immeasurable, as the impact of symbolic action.[31]

When contrasted with Bonhoeffer's purposes and justification of resistance against the state, these quotations reveal dissimilarities on at least two fronts. (They may be parts of one complex, however.)

First, there is a contrasting ethic. In the case of the Berrigans, we face an ethic of witness and parabolic action that is an apocalyptic ethic held by those with no present intents of attaining ruling power. In the case of Bonhoeffer and his coconspirators, the ethic is one of consequences held by those committed to attaining precisely such power.

Second, there exists on Berrigan's part a concern for moral purity, or at least certitude, which Bonhoeffer rejects.

Sketching Bonhoeffer's position will make it clear why these dissimilarities are significant. At the time of *The Cost of Discipleship* Bonhoeffer did make it a test of Christian character that any political resistance be open, public, candid, and unambiguous in its statement. It should be morally beyond reproof, and an unequivocal witness to life on another plane. The disciple's resistance is an expression of moral rectitude and single-minded obedience to a commanding Christ.

After Bonhoeffer enters the conspiracy, something subtle happens to this. Bonhoeffer does talk (in *Ethics*) of the Christian's obligation to obey divine *law*. But he immediately sets out a discussion of the "deed of free responsibility." This is his rationale for what in the eyes of the state is seditious action. It includes a notion of freedom, granted by Christ, to violate not only civil law, but divine law as well. Justification is thrown into the hands of God alone. It is "justification" by grace—and mercy—alone.

There may be severe problems in Bonhoeffer's thoughts at this juncture. But that is not the point. The matter is rather to indicate Bonhoeffer's acceptance in the 1940s of working from within the Nazi war machine, and cultivating Nazi arts for the purpose of jamming that machine. This is for him a moral boundary situation that he accepts. He recognizes it as a severe ethical maelstrom he cannot avoid.

Bonhoeffer does not calculate his actions on the basis of their true course on some moral trajectory. (This is Berrigan's procedure.) Nor does he keep in view a purpose of action such as witness to a better order, the pricking of consciences, keeping alive a civil morality in a barbaric ethos, or embodying the moral configurations of the "new man." These are worthy enough, to be sure, but they are not precisely Bonhoeffer's undertaking in the 1940s. Earlier, in *The Cost of Discipleship,* following Christ entails prophetic witness and moral certainty; but in *Ethics* and *Letters and Papers from Prison* discipleship involves morally disorienting tasks which, if one can hold out in the ethically chaotic and turbulent boundary situation, might bring about at least the possibility to work for a better future.

In the course of the resistance, Bonhoeffer became self-critical of the pacifism he held at the time of *The Cost of Discipleship.* As mentioned, he came to regard it as irresponsible and parasitic. If morally sound people intent on just ends were working to overthrow Hitler, and only violence would attain the goal, then the Christian must join them and not simply approve their course and share the benefits. Resistance as dramatic public witness might, on one level, appear to be a morally upright course. Clean hands, a courageous spirit, and innocence maintained are not to be scorned. But Bonhoeffer saw this as less responsible toward the coming generation than resistance as clandestine realpolitik. Paul Schneider chose what was precisely Bonhoeffer's stance in the 1930s, and Philip Berrigan tellingly chooses Schneider over Bonhoeffer as his moral model.[32] (Paul Schneider was tortured to death in Buchenwald for openly disobeying bans on his protest activities.)

If this assessment is correct, Philip's choice arises from a combination of moral rectitude and resistance as prophetic witness. If Daniel Berrigan joins his brother here, as clearly seems to be the case, they part company with Bonhoeffer. Bonhoeffer respected such a morally uncompromising stance to the end, just as he respected Paul Schneider's martyrdom in the same way a just-war adherent might respect a vocational pacifist. But Bonhoeffer found it a less responsible route than the conspiratorial one, even with the unclean hands and intrinsic moral ambiguity of the conspiracy.

Roger Shinn's question is surely appropriate for comparison and evaluation of the Berrigan/Bonhoeffer contrast.

> What human crises require us to shift from a pragmatic ethic concerned with tactics for change and expectations of some improvement of the present situation, to a more nearly apocalyptic ethic that puts aside orderly calculations and simply raises a flag of protest and affirmation, regardless of the cost?[33]

We will not pursue this question here but only add that it can be reversed. What human crises require us to shift from an ethic of witness which puts aside orderly calculations and simply raises a flag of protest and affirmation, whatever the cost, to a more calculating one concerned with tactics for change and expectations of an improved situation?

ETHICS AND CONSCIOUSNESS

The human crises surrounding one's actions are vital to understanding them. Even more vital are the *perceptions* of those crises. A person's ethic conforms closely to the configurations of personal perception and consciousness. We will be taken deeper into the cases of Bonhoeffer and Berrigan by asking about the character of their moral consciousness.

John Raines believes the Berrigans are driven by a new consciousness. It is rooted in a recognition on their part that such assumptions
as the continued existence of humankind, the resources of the planet,
and "the future of the future" can no longer be presupposed. With
such apocalyptic elements central to their sense of reality, radical
action becomes realistic action; and the older "realistic" action is
hopelessly "utopian" in the pejorative sense of that word.[34]

A felt wave of threatening doom is not the only element in Berrigan's
apocalyptic consciousness. Whatever the foreboding, and whatever
the sense of a crisis of massive proportions and multiple dimensions,
Berrigan also sees the present as a time of the emergence of "new
men" (his phrase). This is intimately tied to "moral process" and to
the kind of ethic implicit and explicit in the following quotations.

> How are we to live our lives today? We are in the dark preliminary stages
> of a new humanity together.[35]

> Am I suffering delusions, or can others see with me the stunning op-
> portunity that opens like a grace before us?[36]

> We are called to grow new organs . . . new ways of perceiving, of living
> in the world.[37]

> The biology of the spirit is really exploding in this country . . . trying to
> break through to another stage of human development.[38]

In the fashion of Teilhard de Chardin, Berrigan sees a new beginning
in the midst of the end. He exults in the real possibility that what is
occurring is a quantum jump in human evolution. Its manifestations
may well be "the Movement" of the 1960s and its successors.

The contrast with Bonhoeffer is considerable. To take things in order:
Remarkably absent in Bonhoeffer's picture of things, despite his times,
is a sense of apocalypse. His ethic of resistance is not an apocalyptic
one.[39] Bonhoeffer does recognize a new era (he calls it "the world
come of age"), and he does sense that the times are full of historic
change. But, despite similarities, this is not the precise parallel of
Berrigan's development of consciousness through heightened moral
awareness, consummating in "new men."

This point needs elaboration. Berrigan's interpretation of the bor-
derline case *(Grenzfall)* is a telling one when compared with Bonhoeffer's. Berrigan regards risk-taking in the boundary situation as the
means by which breakthroughs of consciousness occur.[40] Such breakthroughs are part of the "dark preliminary stages of new humanity."
In Berrigan's view, resistance then becomes "the stage of life itself"

which will surely extend beyond "our lifetime."[41] Resistance belongs, part and parcel, to the early stages of the next step of that slow evolution which, in this Teilhardian vision, centers now in the growth of a planetary consciousness. Resistance thus becomes the way or style of living appropriate to "new men" in times both foreboding and hopeful. Resistance actions are the standard fare of an eschatology in the process of being realized. While they are indeed concrete protestations against particular policies, their larger meanings reside in their symbolic significance as moral trajectories in the "history of goodness."[42]

Bonhoeffer certainly does regard his present and the future as a new era, one that forces the Christian to rethink the most basic tenets of the faith and to find new ways of being the church. But this is not Berrigan's emerging new humanity,[43] nor is it Berrigan's reading of the times. Furthermore, the *Grenzfall* for Bonhoeffer is far less a breakthrough of consciousness in Berrigan's Teilhardian sense, despite its epistemological richness. It is simply holding out in a situation experienced as one of extreme moral and ethical ambiguity and turmoil. To be sure, Bonhoeffer did regard "the view from below" as more revealing of the truth about life than places of privilege, and resistance placed him next to the victim and the victim's important perception of things. But this is not part of a cosmic optimism spurred by resistance as an ongoing way of life.

In short, on the matter of consciousness Bonhoeffer and Berrigan are at a certain distance from one another, whatever the intriguing similarities.[44] This distance makes the purpose and understanding of resistance in the case of one different from that of the other. Berrigan's resistance belongs to an ethic of parabolic action embodying the moral configurations of "new men" ahead of their times. Despite Bonhoeffer's attraction to world-come-of-age citizens, his resistance ethic is much more focused upon strictly political consequences over a shorter haul, and is not seen as a central element in a life-style of emerging prototypical human beings. Yet subtleties matter, and we will argue in a later chapter that Bonhoeffer's thinking about Christian responsibility in a new era is deeply indebted to his experience with fellow resisters. This is an important experience he and Berrigan share, despite subtly different perceptions of it.

The enduring differences are nicely captured in Berrigan's writing some sixteen years after he took the biography of Bonhoeffer along during his time underground, just beyond the reach of the FBI. In his own biography, *To Dwell in Peace*, Berrigan maintains his commitment to unexceptional nonviolence. But he, now an older man, shifts somewhat in his expectation of results.[45] He writes that "it was one thing to follow Christ; it was quite another to live in the world that the world, however reluctantly, might turn its adamant face in a new direction. The world was like a mountain. . . ."[46] Berrigan says he "whispered into ears of stone his riddle—Turn, turn, turn"[47] but the world did not turn. He concluded that he should "concentrate . . . on simpler and closer matters. What did a truly human life look like, in such times as we were enduring?"[48] Berrigan thus moves from concentration on epochal consequences to the witness of the disciple's life, a life not unlike the disciples' Lord and his cross with its "pristine rigor and crude innocence."[49] In a word, Berrigan in the late 1980s ends as the friend of the Bonhoeffer of *The Cost of Discipleship*. He continues his disagreement with *Ethics* and the conspiracy, although he is now sobered by the world's intransigence.

Times for resistance wax and wane. They can and often do emerge rather unexpectedly and before we have given the religious and moral dimensions sufficient thought. North Americans have seen the occasions come and go in virtually every decade for several centuries, a condition of history that we can fully expect will not disappear.

Both Bonhoeffer and Berrigan carry the precious currency of freedom and courage for resistance in uncommon measure, and they cause many to invoke their witness whenever the conversation turns to responsible Christian resistance. They are, to be sure, of different generations, and they cannot make our future assessments and decisions for us. Nor are they of one mind, despite deep affinities. But assuming that occasions for resistance will persist, these two offer a range of intriguing similarities and dissimilarities that extend far beyond personality quirks. They present a set of crucial, subtle, and vital issues and perspectives, and a liberal fund for reflection.

4

WORSHIP IN A
WORLD COME OF AGE

Worship in a world come of age is a topic given very little attention
thus far in Bonhoeffer studies and in the spate of literature on liturgical
renewal. Perhaps this is just one of those oversights that occurs even
in four decades of close scrutiny. But should we not be rather amazed
at the omission, for the question of worship was very much on Bonhoeffer's mind? In the very first of those pathfinding theological letters
from prison, after he raises the leading question ("what is bothering
me incessantly is the question what Christianity really is, or indeed
who Christ really is, for us today"), he goes on to say that "today" is
a religionless time: "People as they are now simply cannot be religious
any more."[1] That uncovers many questions for Bonhoeffer, among them
the meaning of worship in such a time. "The questions to be answered
would surely be: What do a church, a community, a sermon, a liturgy,
a Christian life mean in a religionless world?"[2] Further along, Bonhoeffer again asks: "What is the place of worship and prayer in a
religionless situation? Does the secret discipline . . . take on a new
importance here?"[3]

Even more indicative of this topic's importance is the place Bonhoeffer gives it in his future plans. When he came upon the momentous
insight of the world's coming of age, he set aside what he had only
recently named as his major life task, writing his *Ethics*, and set out
on a new work. Unfortunately, only the outline survives. The manuscript itself was a victim of his enthusiasm. He took it as one of his
few chosen possessions to the Gestapo prison. There it was lost to the
chaos of the last year of the war. But in the surviving outline, "cultus"
is listed as one of the main sections in the critical chapter, "The Real

57

Meaning of Christian Faith." Considerable frustration accompanies the notes, for Bonhoeffer scribbled simply: "Cultus. (Details to follow later, in particular on cultus and 'religion')."[4] Yet the point is that when Bonhoeffer stakes out his own future theological project, cultus in a religionless time has a place that is far from peripheral. Thus it is a surprise that the treatment of worship is virtually absent from the crowded shelves of Bonhoeffer studies.

The surprise is underscored if we note the pattern of Bonhoeffer's life, and not only the priorities for his writings. What is striking in those letters and papers from the jail cell is the intense piety: Paul Gerhardt's hymns, a memorized stanza of *"Frölich soll mein Herz springen"* commended to a friend, daily use of the Herrnhuter *Losungen*, prayers, a sermon or two, poetry, and so on. Yet even these constitute second-order examples. The telling point is that in prison, while he lamented "religion" and applauded the world's coming of age, Bonhoeffer practiced regular prayer and meditation (surely part of what he meant by "secret" or "hidden" discipline (*Arkandisziplin*). He in fact lived by the church year, often dating his mail by the ecclesiastical calendar. His last action in community was to conduct a worship service among fellow prisoners on the way to the last concentration camp, and his last action in solitude was to pray quietly, on his knees and naked, before the steps of the gallows. Cultus counted for Bonhoeffer in his life and thought, in his last days, and for the future he envisioned. It is a surprise, then, that worship in a world come of age has been given so little attention by so many scholars.

Or is it? In that first letter about religionless Christianity, just after the questions about "the place of worship and prayer in a religionless situation," Bonhoeffer continues: "I must break off for today, so that the letter can go straight away. I'll write to you again about it in two days' time. . . ."[5] The succeeding discussions are equally abbreviated, and the typical outcome is the same postponement we noted in the book outline: "details to follow later. . . ." Thus we come away nearly empty-handed, with apparently little more than a clear indication of the topic's importance to Bonhoeffer. It is hardly a complete surprise that there has been little follow-through. Bonhoeffer himself supplied little.

Again, if we look to Bonhoeffer's life and not just his unfinished thoughts, we are faced with that common situation in which, while actions certainly do speak louder than words, they often do not tell us what we most need to know. Bonhoeffer did indeed worship in the world come of age, and that says much. But what shall we make of that for his own answers to his own questions about cultus in a religionless time? Perhaps he, like many of us, is anachronistic, talking and sometimes acting radically, but when the pressure is most intense, responds in the familiar; speaking freely and excitedly about the new setting of a religionless world but, under stress and facing death, answers in a manner marked by the most traditional cultic forms. Thus Bonhoeffer's actions, which speak so movingly, still do not supply for us what we most need to know. Perhaps.

There is a final reason our topic did not become Bonhoeffer's in the space of those pages he left behind. He held some convictions about prior questions and attendant ones. And until the former are answered, the latter cannot be. Bonhoeffer was serious when he wrote, "What is bothering me incessantly is what Christianity really is, or indeed who Christ really is, for us today."[6] Or, in another place, "The question is: Christ and the world that has come of age."[7] When these first-order questions are answered, then perhaps the clues will emerge for church renewal, meaningful worship forms, and the actions of a Christian style appropriate to a drastically altered setting. The order of topics in Bonhoeffer's outline is not arbitrary: (1) A Stocktaking of Christianity; (2) The Real Meaning of Christian Faith; (3) Conclusions (for the Church).[8]

Answering the basic questions will take a long while. In the baptismal sermon from prison, Bonhoeffer includes this:

Today you will be baptized a Christian. All those great ancient words of the Christian proclamation will be spoken over you, and the command of Jesus Christ to baptize will be carried out on you, without your knowing anything about it. But we are once again being driven right back to the beginnings of our understanding. Reconciliation and redemption, regeneration and the Holy Spirit, love of our enemies, cross and resurrection, life in Christ and Christian discipleship—all these things are so difficult and so remote that we hardly venture any more to speak of them. In the traditional words and acts we suspect that there may be something quite new and revolutionary, though we cannot as yet grasp or express it. That is our own fault. Our church, which has been fighting in these years only for its self-preservation, as though that were an end in itself, is incapable of taking the word of reconciliation to the world. Our earlier words are therefore bound to lose their force and cease, and our being Christians today will be limited to two things: prayer and action. . . . We are not yet out of the melting time [trans. corrected] and any attempt to help the church prematurely to a new expansion of its organization will merely delay its conversion and purification. It is not for us to prophesy the day (though the day will come) when men will once more be called so to utter the word of God that the world will be changed and renewed by it. It will be a new language, perhaps quite nonreligious, but liberating and redeeming—as was Jesus' language. . . . Till then the Christian cause will be a silent and hidden affair, but there will be those who pray and do right and wait for God's own time. May you be one of them.[9]

If "the Christian cause" is "a silent and hidden affair" for the foreseeable future, waiting "for God's own time" and awaiting the conversion of the church, and if Christians are being driven by the world's coming of age "right back to the beginnings of [their] understanding," then it is surely little surprise that the matter of worship in a religionless time must join the long labor and endure the hard pangs of the church's rebirth. That will take a while, for clearly the answers to these priority questions of what Christianity actually is and who Christ really is for us today are not armchair discourses. We cannot simply think through to the answers. They must be lived into, and emerge as the outcome of daring Christian practice. This is, Bonhoeffer knew, a generational endeavor.

Perhaps it is no surprise, then, that worship in a world come of age has been given so little attention. Bonhoeffer's own utterances dictate a necessary restraint. But if the topic is to be pursued at all, at least the place to begin is clear. We must discern the meanings of "world come of age" and "religion."

RELIGION AND WORLD COME OF AGE

In a rich discussion of Bonhoeffer's later writings, Roger A. Johnson sorts the thoughts about religion and world come of age by clustering them around three interacting themes. (1) Sometimes Bonhoeffer's discussion comprises what is virtually a psychological typology of religious personality and mature, or world come of age, personality. These are distinct types with contrasting psychological traits. (2) Other remarks sketch a movement of Western history that locates us now in a "religionless situation," or is leading toward a "time of no religion at all." Here the contention is that a particular historical development is occurring on a grand scale. It began about the thirteenth century and is reaching a certain culmination in the present or the near future. (3) Finally, many of Bonhoeffer's ruminations constitute a theological critique of religion and a theological search for a response to the world come of age.[10]

Discussing the first two of these three (religion and world come of age as personality types and as a historical movement) can best be done with the rubric of "consciousness." The term is itself in need of definition, all the more so because it is not Bonhoeffer's way of unveiling his own categories. By "consciousness" is meant that configuration of values, knowledge, feelings, judgments, and opinions that makes up the picture of reality or the "sense" of reality which an individual or group holds. Consciousness sets our angle of vision and thereby largely determines the way we see life, think about it, and live it out. It selects, sorts, and interprets our experience.

Several notations must be made. The first is that consciousness is historically mutable. Pictures or understandings of reality vary greatly from time to time and place to place, from one age to another, one society to another, even from one person or group to another, and sometimes within the course of the life of the same person or group. Discontinuity as well as continuity characterize consciousness. Its content changes.

The second notation is that a widely shared consciousness—a collective consciousness—may undergo massive change. Then a new way of seeing life, thinking about it, and living it out comes about for a people or a nation, for a whole society or some group within a society. A revolution of consciousness occurs and, however long it is in coming, a new sense of reality dawns for large numbers of people.

The third item is that consciousness is a basic shaper and interpreter of human needs. Of course, there are some basic physiological determinants of our needs, and we all have "needs of first necessity"—food, clothing, and shelter. These influence all varieties of consciousness. But beyond these and other elemental stipulations, what we regard *as* our needs is very much a function of our perception of things, that is, our consciousness.

What does this simplified profile of consciousness mean for Bonhoeffer's discussion of worship in a world come of age? Almost everything. For him, "religion" belongs to a longstanding, now changing, and for many, a passing consciousness. "World come of age" belongs to an ascending consciousness. He surmises that we are living in something approaching an axial period and that many people are moving from a "religious" consciousness to a "world-come-of-age" consciousness. These are fundamentally different ways of seeing life, thinking about it, and living it out. Both the psychological dynamics of the people and the *Zeitgeist* of a whole period are undergoing a massive mutation. When Bonhoeffer says, "We are moving toward a completely religionless time; people as they are now simply cannot be religious any more,"[11] his reference is to the eventual outcome of major changes in a previously shared consciousness.

The implications are startling, even for Bonhoeffer. He is rejecting a religious apriori supposedly constitutional to human nature. There is no inborn God-shaped blank that must be filled if a person is to lead a life of meaning, purpose, and integrity. More accurately stated, if some set of religious needs *does* exist which only God or at least "religion" can meet, such needs are integral to, and relative to, that person's consciousness. A need for God and for religion is not a "given" of being human. Humankind *qua* humankind is not *homo religiosus*, although some men and women are, depending upon their sense of reality.

Bonhoeffer is not saying that people no longer have a felt need for God and religion. He is saying that such needs are those of people possessed of a particular consciousness. It is one with a very long history; it is also currently on the wane. He is saying further that the consciousness of some others has already altered in such a way that they get on well without religion, indeed they fare better than religious people. These are people of world-come-of-age consciousness. In part that means that their way of seeing life is such that God and religion are not indispensable to a satisfactory vision of life, to a humane morality, and to living lives of integrity.

There is more. Bonhoeffer observes that Western Christianity in all aspects—doctrine, liturgy, ethics—has cast its content in the material and forms of "religion." Western Christian edifices rest on religious footings. Thus if ours is indeed a religion*less* time, "the foundation is taken away from the whole of what has up to now been our 'Christianity'."[12] In other words, Christians in the West have been—and are—people of a religious consciousness who now find themselves in a world in which that consciousness is in the process of slow expiration.[13]

It is clear why Bonhoeffer calls for a religionless Christianity for a world come of age. It is also clear why he thinks it will be a long time before that is forthcoming, before religious Christians become world-come-of-age Christians. And it is clear why he asks what shape that worship, which has been encased in religious rubrics for so long, will take, and what meaning and place it will have in a time of "no religion at all."

What criteria would measure "religionless" worship in a world come of age? How would it be characterized? Answering such questions requires an exact description of "religion" and "world come of age." Since forty years of Bonhoeffer scholarship have attended to this with a happy outcome,[14] we need not include more than a sketch here. In this sketch the reader should be attuned to the way in which the elements of religious consciousness and world-come-of-age consciousness contrast with one another on point after point.

For the person of religious consciousness, God is a working hypothesis for explaining whatever is unexplainable, or seems so. Contrasting with this is a characteristic of the world come of age, the growth of human autonomy through the increase of human knowledge and powers. Humankind in a world come of age, using its autonomous reason, can and does interpret natural and social processes and can and does face and answer life's questions without the tutelage of a divinity, that is, from premises that need not and do not posit God. Where God or the gods were once employed to account for almost everything, now other explanations suffice; or they suffice at least as well as religious ones. God is not necessary to those understandings which enable us to come to terms with our world and its matrix of obligations. The ensemble of explanations in sphere after sphere is assembled without God's necessary participation.

All this may be so commonplace in some quarters as to be a dull statement of fact. But the implications for "God" and "religion" in a world come of age are nonetheless momentous. When God is a working hypothesis for explaining the unexplainable, God becomes associated with or situated in the unknown rather than in the known. As the known increases, God is farther and farther removed from the center of life and pressed ever outward toward the boundaries, boundaries that are themselves pushed back as human knowledge and powers increase. Ironically, in religious consciousness God is marginalized!

What happens to religion itself? It becomes a separated sector of life, a diminishing sector of the unknown and unexplainable, rather than the central dimension in the overriding sense of reality. It becomes a certain genuinely alienated—and alienating—division in life.

The God of religious consciousness is also the deus ex machina. In the plays of antiquity, whenever the normal course of human events simply could not muster some action essential to the plot, a god or goddess intervened and did his or her job. The business of life and the plot could then move on to the next dramatic episode. Bonhoeffer contends that people of religious consciousness turn to God and religion only (but always) when their human resources fail to secure "solutions" to problems that exhaust them or that they regard (or choose to regard) as insoluble or interminable. God and religion "rescue" us from dangers we encounter but cannot face or control. Or they function, in some grand theodicy, sooner or later to right all those wrongs we are too tired to right as our passion for justice wanes but our complacency does not.

The contrast with characteristics of world-come-of-age consciousness is stark. The growth of human autonomy through the increase of human powers and accountability means that human destiny falls into human hands in ever greater measure. And people possessed of world-come-of-age consciousness, whose answers are arrived at without recourse to God and religion in the first place, regard themselves irrevocably accountable for their answers to life's questions, together with the consequences of the answers chosen and acted on. When there is failure, as there most certainly will be, there is no ready recourse to God and religion. The buck is not deposited with "God," "circumstances," "fate," or any other religious or quasi-religious account.

It should be noted in passing that by "world come of age" Bonhoeffer does not mean moral maturity. He means psychological maturity and moral accountability, or responsibility. When he speaks of the "adulthood" of the world, a synonym of world come of age, he does not mean that humankind has achieved a degree of moral accomplishment never before attained. He means that humanity is responsible for the uses of increased knowledge and powers, whether they are exercised in a morally mature manner or not. And he means world-come-of-age people accept that responsibility without trying to deny or deflect it. There is no returning to an adolescent dependence on a father—even a Heavenly Father—on whom final responsibility falls. For world-come-of-age people, humankind's future or lack of future rests in human hands.

When God is the deus ex machina, the consequences for religion can be readily be seen. God is not experienced by people in their achievement and strength; God is experienced in people's weakness and resignation. Religion is for people in their trouble, rather than for people at their best. At their best, people are "nonreligious." Since God is on the margins and depended upon only (but always) when human powers peter out, then people are at their most religious when they are most exhausted, defeated, and self-denigrating. They are most religious when they are most turned in upon themselves and preoc-cupied with their troubles. But on their own, and in their "world-come-of-age" moments, people are self-confident, responsible, and strong, exercising powers in full consciousness of a common destiny of all with all. In short, for religious consciousness, humanity is "less" when it is most with God, and "more" when most god-less.

One last matter must be extracted from Bonhoeffer's discussion. There are two poles in religious consciousness. At the one pole is a God who is located beyond the world, rather than in the midst of it. At the other is an interior realm within the individual which serves as the place of contact with this God beyond. Religion then, as Bon-hoeffer says, is a matter of "individual inwardness." For individual inwardness, God is removed from the world except for a speaking place in the recesses of the soul, and religion is removed from critical engagement in the public arena. Religion again becomes a separate sphere, now located in an inner sanctuary to which one withdraws in order to encounter God. Thus Bonhoeffer jotted in the outline for the new book, "Pietism as a last attempt to maintain evangelical Christianity as a religion. . . ."[15]

We have presented Bonhoeffer's sketch of religion and the God of religious consciousness in admittedly skeletal form. He laments such religion and he applauds the world's coming of age. Thus he laments religious Christianity and religious worship, and calls for religionless Christianity and the "nonreligious interpretation of biblical concepts."

Bonhoeffer is aware that a certain irony and tragedy wait in the wings. The church will fight the world's coming of age and do all in its power to save a place for God and religion. The clergy will, in Bonhoeffer's language, use all their "clerical tricks" to retain religion as a sector of life. They will do this by marketing certain questions and problems—death and guilt, for example—"to which [supposedly] only 'God' can give an answer."[16] The irony is that world-come-of-age people are, in their godlessness, actually closer to confronting the God of the Bible who calls people to become fully responsible for their world, than are religious Christians and the church in their alliance with the "God" of religion. The tragedy is that the church will be the strongest opponent of the rediscovery of Christianity in its nonreligious biblical roots and will be the ablest opponent of its own conversion. (Conversion here means a deeply altered consciousness.) Bonhoeffer's language is anything but timid.

The attack by Christian apologetics on the adulthood of the world I consider to be in the first place pointless, in the second place ignoble, and in the third place unchristian. Pointless, because it seems to me like an attempt to put a grown-up man back into adolescence, i.e. to make him dependent, and thrusting him into problems that are, in fact, no longer problems to him. Ignoble, because it amounts to an attempt to exploit man's weakness for purposes that are alien to him and to which he has not freely assented. Unchristian, because it confuses Christ with one particular stage in man's religiousness, i.e., with a human law.[17]

But what does all this mean for worship? First, to satisfy Bonhoeffer, worship in a world come of age must strive to be nonreligious worship for religionless Christians. If it does not become this, if it remains religious worship in a world come of age, it will participate in that ignoble, pointless, and unchristian "Christian" apologetic that tries to soften up a place for God and religion in world-come-of-age people. In Bonhoeffer's language, worship will try to communicate to such people that they are dependent on things on which, in fact, they are no longer dependent, thrust them into problems that are no longer problems to them, and play on their weaknesses in such a way as to smuggle God into some last secret and vulnerable place in their lives. Or, if world-come-of-age people choose to ignore the church alto-gether, religious worship may well continue, but it will be part of the baggage of people in quiet retreat from the world, people who tragically believe themselves to be preserving Christianity in the very act of fortressing themselves against forces which offer opportunity to re-discover and recover it. Worship may continue to be "meaningful" for them, to be sure, but precisely because it is irrelevant to the world that surrounds them. Worship, then, is meaningful because it protects against the promising vulnerability that world-come-of-age conscious-ness includes. (*Etsi deus non daretur!* "as though [the] God [of religion] did not exist.")

Second, a brief, quite different point: religion for Bonhoeffer does not refer to the liturgical elements as such—sermon, sacrament, Scrip-ture, doctrine, prayer, meditation, confession. Any and all of these may be interpreted and employed in either a religious or a nonreligious manner.

Concluding the discussion to this point, we can contrast religious worship and nonreligious worship, using familiar phrases from the prison letters. Nonreligious worship would, using the liturgical ele-ments, help us "find God in what we do know," not "in what we do not know," which would be religious worship. Nonreligious worship would help us, through the liturgical elements, to realize God's presence in those problems that are solved, not simply in "unsolved problems" (which would be religious worship). Nonreligious worship would help us speak of God "at the center of life," not "on the boundary" (which would be religious worship). It would help us discern "the beyond in the midst of life," not point away to some other life in some beyond (which would be religious worship).

Nonreligious worship would thrust us "unreservedly [into] life's duties, problems, successes and failures, experiences and perplexities" in such a way as to take seriously "not our own suffering, but the sufferings of God in the secular life." By contrast, religious worship would aid and abet our efforts "to try and make something of ourselves, whether it be a saint, a converted sinner, or a churchman . . . a righteous man or an unrighteous one, a sick man or a healthy one." Nonreligious worship would help us, through the liturgical elements, experience God in the meeting with the neighbor and being for him or her in that meeting. By contrast, religious worship would experience God in a private encounter of the single self and God in some inner sanctuary of the individual.

Surely more could be said. It would include Bonhoeffer's theological critique of religion and his efforts at nonreligious interpretation of biblical concepts for religionless Christianity (for example, Jesus as "the man for others"). Further discussion would soon find its limits, however, for the reason cited earlier: Bonhoeffer's conviction that Western Christianity is so soaked in religious consciousness that the answers to those prior questions of what Christianity really is, indeed, who Christ is for us in a religionless time, will be answers a long time in process. We cannot be clear about the gestalt of religionless Christianity, including the gestalt of religionless worship, until we are well into the struggle that might yield foundational answers.

THE DYNAMICS OF RENEWAL

We would be remiss to draw the curtain here, however. Bonhoeffer leaves a last trace about how the movement toward religionless Christianity and worship might proceed. Two quotations cited earlier serve as texts:

> What is the place of worship and prayer in a religionless situation? Does the secret discipline . . . take on a new importance here?[18]

Our being Christians today will be limited to two things: prayer and doing justice among men. All Christian thinking, speaking, and organizing must be born anew out of this prayer and action.[19]

If we set these few lines within Bonhoeffer's own practice, they become suggestive for the rhythm of Christian living in a world come of age. In fact, they reflect a lively dialectic Bonhoeffer lived out in the church struggle of the 1930s and the resistance movement of the late 1930s and early 1940s.

What are the poles of the dialectic? Naming the first is easy, because Bonhoeffer does so, taking the early Christian community's name: the hidden, or arcane, discipline. Naming the second is not as easy because Bonhoeffer does not provide the term. It concerns "doing justice among men" or, viewed in its theological dimension, with participation "in the sufferings of God in the secular life." For lack of a better term, we shall here call it "costly worldly solidarity."

Arcane Discipline

Bonhoeffer says "back to the conventicles" more than once. The goal is focused, inner concentration for discipleship. Bonhoeffer sees the church of the future as a kind of low-profile order in the world as the world come of age. In this order, arcane discipline is the focused inner concentration. Bonhoeffer's continuing fascination with Gandhi was partly due to the fact that Gandhi offered the disciplines for a discipleship community. Also, Bonhoeffer's visits to Anglican monastic communities were in preparation for his own community of arcane discipline, the seminary at Finkenwalde. His look to the future in the "Outline for a Book" is on the same track.

Arcane discipline means that worship in a world come of age is not for everyone. It is for small groups of committed Christians who comprise an intense community on the basis of their intense loyalty to Christ. Their expression of the meaning of that loyalty is communicated with one another in worship, but not to and with all. Worship as arcane discipline is not for the streets, the posters, or the mass media. It is certainly not Hollywood Bowl and drive-in Easter sunrise services, nor Sunday East Room exercises in American civil religion in the White House, nor Astrodome rallies of religiosity. It is not bumper-sticker and slick paper Christianity. If Bonhoeffer were to have his way, the church would begin by giving up its property for the sake of the needy, would be devout in its practice of disciplines, and demanding in its stipulations for participation. It would be a poor and apparently powerless church that would dispense costly grace, rather than a rich and privileged church that offers cheap grace.

Arcane discipline means a concentrated nurturing of the varied elements of the Judeo-Christian heritage. At the time when the secular theologies were in their heyday, worship and tradition were often neglected, occasionally forthrightly downgraded. At a critical point those theologies missed Bonhoeffer almost entirely, even when they were partly inspired by him. They overlooked a focus in the dialectic: his genuinely pious observing of the liturgical traditions. Bonhoeffer did not want less to do with the ancient symbols and archaic confessions of the church. Nor did he want less to do with the lives of all those bizarre saints, with the details of that hoary tradition, with all the "—gesimas" of the liturgical year. What he wanted was to know what we still really believed of all that. And he wanted to be clear that the materials involved, including the biblical materials, were in need of nonreligious interpretation. They still carry their treasures for life in our own time, but they must not be retained in such a way as to make "religion" a necessary condition for salvation, as they have in the past.[20]

The concentrated nurture includes worship, both in solitude and with others. Bonhoeffer's own daily meditation and prayer in prison is an example of the former. The personal confession of one brother of Finkenwalde to another and the common celebration together in communion is an example of the latter. Thus one ongoing element in the rhythmic process of answering the first-order questions is the hidden discipline of intense nurture and disciplined worship of small groups of strongly committed Christians who make up the church as a kind of low-profile Christian order in the world come of age.

Costly Worldly Solidarity

This element—costly world solidarity—refers to the engagement that arcane discipline nurtured. It means groups of Christians operating rather incognito in the world, making common cause with the non-Christian and the nonreligious, all without ecclesiastical and theological pretense and qualification. Bonhoeffer's resistance activity is itself paradigmatic here. This second pole is doing justice in secular ways in public arenas. It is justice as *mitleiden* (suffering with those who suffer). The informing vision is that of the theology of the cross, and the mission is understood as part of the *missio Jesu* itself. It is costly solidarity as participation in the sufferings of God in the secular life.

The dialectical movement is critical. Arcane discipline left to itself would easily revive the worst of the sectarian style. The Christian in-group would soon become a pious and self-righteous ghetto. Its "otherness" would become fetid particularism. Costly worldly solidarity by itself would result in Christianity as a soon burnt-out case. The rich paths in spirituality of arcane discipline would soon lose themselves in the worthy—but eventually shallow—crusades of a one-dimensional secularism. Arcane discipline by itself would soon become just another form of spiritual tribalism, and worldly solidarity by itself another round of exhausting partisan involvement.

But in dialectic, arcane discipline provides the sustenance for suffering with non-Christians for the common good. And costly discipleship provides the mode of public engagement for that hidden nurture. Even more, costly worldly solidarity provides the very means and materials necessary for discovering religionless Christianity in a world come of age. (The church learns from the world.) The "otherness" of arcane discipline brings to expression the transcendent elements of worldly solidarity (being-for-others as the "realization of reality," Bonhoeffer's theme in *Ethics*). And the solidarity with others breaks again and again the easy propensity of Christian particularism to close in upon itself.

An edited look at an earlier excerpt must suffice as a summary:

> Our being Christian today will be limited to two things: prayer [shorthand here for arcane discipline] and doing justice among men [shorthand for costly worldly solidarity]. All Christian speaking, thinking and organizing must be born anew out of this prayer and action.[21]

In the end we do not know for certain the gestalt of nonreligious worship in a world come of age. That awaits our conversion from religious consciousness to world-come-of-age consciousness, the renewal of our minds in a new era. Yet by taking our cues from Bonhoeffer, we inherit a rich fund of resources and are shown how to proceed.

These thoughts of the mid-1940s remain lively and appropriate. For in virtually all of North America, from Mexico to Canada, there is a great ferment in church and society. There is much innovation and revision in worship itself and new interest in the public arena. There is an explosion of various forms of "base Christian communities" and local ecumenism. Yet all this happens amidst evidence of the vitality of "old-time religion" in Bonhoeffer's sense. (He badly misjudged its demise.) It also happens amidst evidence that "world-come-of-age" consciousness exists and is struggling to find its way in a new human epoch. In short, both Christian faith and moral responsibility for a world of heightened human power are being recast in our time. Bonhoeffer had a profound sense for this. His dynamic for renewal and his analysis of consciousness is most timely!

5

THE CHURCH'S
PUBLIC VOCATION

A sense of history comes easily. I write in the apartment that was Reinhold Niebuhr's and look across the quadrangle to the room where in 1939 Bonhoeffer made his fateful decision to return to Germany. He had only just come, in large part through Niebuhr's assistance.

A sense of orientation to the subject of this chapter comes easily as well. From the start Niebuhr practiced theology as a public vocation and did so with an effectiveness unsurpassed by any other twentieth-century theologian in the United States, with the exception of Martin Luther King Jr. Bonhoeffer was less self-consciously a theologian of public life and came to it via the hard and harsh path of the Church Struggle and the Resistance, though the foundational sense of public responsibility and the most immediate and long-standing impulses were familial. In any case, and quite unlike Niebuhr, Bonhoeffer had to exercise his public vocation more behind closed doors than in the public square. Nonetheless, both these men orient their readers to public engagement as the theologian's proper activity.

But this is to speak of the public vocation of a theologian, not of the church's as such. Here Bonhoeffer offers much, perhaps more than Niebuhr, for Bonhoeffer thought in ecclesial terms. From *Communio Sanctorum* through "Outline for a Book" in *Letters and Papers from Prison,* the church is identified as that piece of the world with the public vocation of showing the concrete social form of Christ existing as community. Niebuhr, while the practitioner par excellence of the theologian's public vocation, did not fully develop a doctrine of the church as a community with a public vocation, even though he was an activist in the church at local, national, and international levels.[1]

From Niebuhr is gathered an unrelenting insistence upon public theology in North America, from Bonhoeffer the equally forceful insistence that it be *ecclesial* in character.

The approach to this chapter was to be Bonhoeffer's Lutheran-based theology of the cross; and so it is, with one major emendation. What I did not know, until rereading a portion of the Niebuhr corpus, was how deeply Niebuhr himself draws from this tradition, both for his theological ethics and his theology of history. Strong echoes of the *theologia crucis* can be heard from both men.

Niebuhr's presence affects this presentation in yet another way. Few have been abler interpreters of, and better "worriers" about, "America." This chapter was stimulated by some patriotic worry and is indebted to Niebuhr for a view of the behavior of the United States as a powerful nation-state. From Bonhoeffer is drawn a similar patriotic worry about the nation's way in the world,[2] as well as special concern for the church's public responsibility both nationally and ecumenically.

Space does not permit the details of my patriotic worry. Yet this chapter makes little sense apart from that concern and some sense of the reasons for it. The following paragraphs must suffice, not as analysis and argument, but as orientation.

• "Public" here refers to the realization that we humans are "a company of strangers" (Parker Palmer) who will, for the most part, remain strangers to one another. But we are strangers who occupy a common space, share common resources, are increasingly tied to one another in a common fate, and must learn to live together on common ground. Either we carry or fashion deep identity as "public" persons, or we bracket from our vision and action that which is most obvious and important to being human in the late twentieth century.

• Yet, as has been noted at least since de Tocqueville's *Democracy in America*, published more than 150 years ago, our U.S. sense of "public" is extremely thin as a matter of identity, just as our sense of the common good and the public welfare is thin in our moral traditions. The public sector itself is seen as existing for the sake of enhancing the private. And the private sector is regarded as the place where the good life happens. Perhaps only in the United States can one use an oxymoron like "private citizen" and not intend or get a laugh.

• If a sense of public is fragile within the nation, it is even more so ecumenically—and that at a time when nationalist patriotism is often very chauvinistic, even militaristic. (The large murals in the entrance of the most popular visitor attraction in the United States, the Air and

Space Museum in Washington, D.C., orient the entire solar system from the position of the United States. The one item to be identified on the farther planets is a United States flag.)

There is little sense of the global good here, except as a magnification of what we regard as good for us. That comes as little surprise within a Niebuhrian analysis. Yet it is hardly reason to ratify the present international projection of the United States, which is something akin to this. We continue to fascinate others with the lure of individual freedom and the pull of material prosperity. Simultaneously, however, we appear as an imperial schemer, a blundering, half-blind leviathan, an arrogant ally, an unpredictable foe, a fount of decadent, materialistic values, of paganism with a Judeo-Christian patina. Though there is a somewhat different tone in the Bush-Quayle Administration, the Reagan-Bush Administration seemed almost dedicated to pushing each of these terms to new heights.

• There is a growing recognition that "public life" and the "common good" are slender notions in our collective morality, and that there is a paucity of coherent moral traditions in and for public life in the United States. Few citizens dispute the contention that a "naked public square" exists (Richard Neuhaus). Instead, most argue about what moral configuration and policy configuration should fill it.

• Of the configurations, the leading candidate of late seems to be "Judeo-Christian values," "the Judeo-Christian tradition," or, even more nebulous, "traditional values." It is hard to avoid the conclusion that the majority of advocates rushing to repair the torn moral fiber and fill the empty moral spaces with "Judeo-Christian" values and traditions are actually engaged in a legitimation of "America" as a righteous empire in a world read largely in Manichean terms. The actual social substance of these values and traditions has almost nothing to do with Jewish, with Christian, or even with simply righteous people. It has everything to do with "America," which, it turns out, means only the United States. The quest is for the preservation of a powerful place in the world at high levels of affluence, and effective warding off of threats to that—all this by a nation that comprises a tiny percentage of the world's population (6%).

The sure clue that this discussion is about American and not Judeo-Christian traditions is buried in the fact that Jewish and Christian values are not really asked about, nor—the clincher—is their substance used for serious *critical moral analysis* of the national culture and of domestic and international policies. Rather, what substance is publicly presented is done in such a way as to buttress "America" in a bewildering and sometimes fearful world.

Said differently, both neoconservative and neoliberal uses of "Judeo-Christian" candidates for populating "the naked public square" are uses of religion as a custodian of the dominant culture. And a closer look into the square itself shows that values are, in fact, already present—chiefly "private sector" values. It is these that reign and welcome direct and indirect religious legitimation.

• With some exceptions, the condition of the churches does not inspire optimism. While there is much moral restlessness, there is even more enculturation. While parallels with Bonhoeffer's context would be misleading if not altogether wrong, the double dialectic he pressed for should be ours as well. We should strike the sharp differences of "Christ" and "culture" in the United States and involve ourselves in two movements simultaneously: (a) the church's own conversion (*discovering* Jewish and Christian faith "for us today") and (b) "world-come-of-age" efforts to fashion a public good appropriate for this age, including a new "Germany" ("America") as one nation among many nations.[3] We should emphasize "the narrow pass of Christianity" (Eberhard Bethge's phrase) at the same time as we vigorously engage in a public vocation.

Against this backdrop, with some resources drawn from Bonhoeffer and Niebuhr, we now turn to our theme, the church's public vocation.

ESCHATOLOGY AND ETHICS

The discussion now diverges somewhat from Bonhoeffer. The starting point here is neither precisely his nor Niebuhr's. It is eschatology, even apocalyptic eschatology.

There are good reasons why neither Bonhoeffer nor Niebuhr was attracted to apocalyptic eschatology, as well as good reasons why it is theologically and morally attractive here. Exploring the omission in Bonhoeffer and Niebuhr is not the task, however. Suffice it to note that while Niebuhr's social ethic is fundamentally structured by prophetic eschatology and the cross, apocalyptic eschatology in particular is eschewed, at least as an informing tradition of the church's public vocation. And suffice it to note as well that Bonhoeffer was apparently almost immunized against whatever "elective affinities" (Max Weber) might have been drawn between the "apocalyptic" character of his time and place and apocalyptic themes in Scripture.

We contend here that the public vocation of the *ecclesia crucis* (church of the cross) is sharpened by apocalyptic eschatology, and that the themes of the New Testament's theology of the cross and apocalyptic eschatology converge, although the Lutheran heritage both Niebuhr and Bonhoeffer drew upon obscured this badly. Niebuhr substitutes an *ideal* for apocalyptic eschatology (the ideal of individual agapeic love) and thereby loses the eschatological community's identity and vocation. Bonhoeffer suffers a theological education that, after Albert Schweitzer's work on eschatology, found apocalyptic eschatology an embarrassment for ethics. Bonhoeffer also suffered an education in which Lutheran core doctrine, such as justification by grace, had long since lost sight of its biblical roots in apocalyptic eschatology.

Because Christian social ethics in much of North America lacks a positive tradition of apocalyptic eschatology as its ecclesial framework (African American churches are an important exception), and because Bonhoeffer omits it as well, some basic exposition is necessary. Then it will be possible to discuss the implications of this eschatology for public vocation.

Apocalyptic literature arises among people whose experience of life is persistently, agonizingly "from below." Very often this is the experience of direct oppression; invariably it is one of suffering. The writings of suffering peoples—or, more frequently, the songs, the oral traditions, and other yearnings of hope—are "apocalyptic" because the explosive double theme is the theme of apocalypse: the destruction of evil forces and the "up-rising" of new creation amidst the old. The language of the Magnificat or of Luke 4 is typical: the mighty are cast from their thrones, the poor have good news preached to them, the prisoners are set free, the lame and the blind are healed. The tale is about the promised end of evil itself, the victory of justice, the spread of peace, and the abiding presence of sufficient abundance. God is portrayed as implacably set against all evil and is seen as the power of the new age in deadly struggle with the old. Apocalyptic literature is always about great moral struggle, with life itself at stake.

Jesus' own eschatology appears to be an apocalyptic variant of the Jewish restoration eschatology widespread in the Israel of his time. The common themes of restoration eschatology were the gathering of Israel, a new or renewed temple, repentance, judgment, and the admission of the Gentiles into the way of the covenant. The apocalyptic variant included time-hastening hopes for national liberation (freedom from Roman rule) and the formation of an avant-garde community of

Israel which would also be a proleptic community of the new creation itself, a faithful social embodiment of what God intended for all creation.

For apocalyptic eschatology the time is messianic, announced and enacted in an initial way by God's agent, the eschatological prophet. The signs of the times, indeed the seismic tremors of the reign of God *(basileia tou theou)*, are seen and felt in healings, exorcisms, and meals of celebration which include the impoverished, disenfranchised, and outcast. There is also the announcement of impending reversals of fortune (such as the Lukan Beatitudes). In this ending of the present age, the proleptic community struggles to structure itself by the coming order of God, and show the beginnings of new Israel and new creation.

It is relatively easy to see this as the provenance of Jesus and his community, as that is glimpsed in, with, and under the Gospel writings and the authentic Pauline letters. Here Ernst Käsemann and others are persuasive—the milieu of Paul's themes of "justification by faith," "the righteousness of God," "new age," "new humanity," "new creation" and "new world" is apocalyptic eschatology, though not exclusively that (Jewish mysticism is equally vital). "Justification" is Paul's borrowed language (from the Roman legal system) to say what in the mouth of Jesus is the coming reign of God (or "the kingdom of heaven," in Matthew's coinage). And Nils Dahl contends that *basileia* (kingdom) and justification by grace already have social reality in the transformation of relationships between Jew and Greek, male and female, bond and free, and richer and poorer. The same contention is considerably expanded and deepened in the work of Elisabeth Schüssler Fiorenza. (That patriarchy and other cultural forces often blunted and frequently reversed this transformation does not refute the point. It does render credible Jesus' and Paul's description of the powers of "this present age" as forces capable of contesting God's power and sovereignty.)

What, then, is justification? It is eschatological reality already present. In Gerhard Forde's words:

> Justification is the creative act of God which ends all previous schemes and begins something new . . . [Justification] is a way to communicate God's radical creative act in a new reality, a new age, a new creation, a new humanity.[4]

The theological legacy in Bonhoeffer's Germany, however, was drained of an eschatological dynamic intrinsically bound to a dynamic ecclesial consciousness. Justification did not communicate the presence of new-community power which relativizes all other authorities and pioneers new social realities. Instead, justification became something like consolation: when we fail in our schemes to do as we ought, we say in resignation, "Clearly we're sinners; but thank God we're justified!" Then justification is rescue in the face of recurring failure, rather than the onset of something radically new. It is a word preached to pick us up when we are down. In the end it functions as bourgeois therapy. This is what justification came to mean, rather than the power of a community of the cross whose only authority and power is the justifying and "apocalyptic" God.

Because of this history, Bonhoeffer does not readily associate his Lutheran legacy with the apocalyptic eschatology of Paul. Nevertheless, there are remarks in *Ethics* that link the two:

> The point of departure of Christian ethics is not the reality of one's own self, or the reality of the world; nor is it the reality of standards and values. It is the reality of God and [God] is reveal[ed] in Jesus Christ.[5]

> What is of ultimate importance now is no longer that I should become good, or that the condition of the world should be made better by my action, but that the reality of God should show itself everywhere to be the ultimate reality. Where there is faith in God as the ultimate reality, all concern with ethics will have as its starting point that God shows [God's self] to be good, even if this involves the risk that I myself and the world are not good but thoroughly bad.[6]

Before turning in earnest to further resources in Bonhoeffer (and Niebuhr), we must ask about the dynamics of apocalyptic eschatology for public life. Eschatology fundamentally structures social ethics in two ways: (1) a posture of radical critique of the going order or "age" and (2) efforts to fashion new community in accord with the anticipated reign of God. We take each in turn.

Unrelenting Criticism

A striking mark of Jesus, expressing apocalyptic eschatology, is that he lives as though God reigns and no one else has any power over him. So does the Jesus community (on its better days)! This public posture relativizes all other authorities, whether of polity or culture, and breaks the hold of controlling ideologies. This in turn makes possible "world-switching" (Robin Scroggs)—opening up new, alternative social possibilities via a transformed perspective (cf. Romans 12).

The dynamics can be described with the help of the sociology of ideology. "World," or "this present age," refers to the two processes of the "social construction of reality" (Berger and Luckmann): (1) the objectification of society through its institutions, roles, and traditions, and (2) the legitimation of society by "giving normative dignity to its practical imperatives."[7] "World" thus means the going arrangements and their ratification "in the heavens"—to allude in particular to religion's role.

In the legitimation process, ideology works in such a way as to supply one simple, crucial conviction: the present world's arrangements are necessary. This conviction stabilizes the social order among strong and weak alike, rich and poor together. The people say, in effect: "Things might not be all they should be. But we can't make a living, raise the kids, attend the college of our choice, and protect what we have, other than by way of what is." When the people have said that, the ideology of controlling power has become the power of controlling ideology, and the league of kindred spirits holding dominant power has successfully shared its own illusions about the necessity of things. The ideological cocoon is never wholly spun, or without flaw, to be sure. But for all practical purposes, it is complete. It is complete whenever strong and weak, powerful and powerless, dominant and subordinate groups alike share the same definitions of power and its patterns. When they perceive reality similarly, albeit from different social strata and experience, then ideology has had its way.

The ideological cocoon only unravels under the force of tumultuous events that drastically alter the social arrangements, or if some group harbors the dangerous eschatological "memory" of some alternative vision, or when both occur simultaneously. It happens where a "contrast-society"[8] musters public presence and gets some attention during a period of social crisis.

What does a "contrast-society" of apocalyptic persuasion effect? Living as though God reigns and no one else has power over the community means that moral legitimation is peeled from present cultural patterns and social forms. "In the power of the Spirit" the prevailing family patterns, economic arrangements, community polity, and, not least, the standard ordering of ideas itself—ideology—are all moved rather abruptly from necessity to possibility. They may still be provisionally valid, but only that. No particular arrangements are indispensable, nor any forbidden. The forms for governance, material provision, family and community life are as open-ended as the imaginations and the resources of those struggling to live as the community of the new age. In parts of the New Testament the way of God, as glimpsed in Jesus, means exactly this kind of radical freedom.

"Glimpsed in Jesus . . ."—Jesus' ministry itself shows this relativizing of the world. The parables play out another world where the power relations and social givens of the current age and its habits of mind and heart are momentarily suspended. More than that, those patterns are examined, sometimes subverted, even shattered. The miracles, or "signs and wonders," are moments of demonstrated eschatological power as the new age touches human life and transforms it. So Jesus demystifies the world as a given, renders it a "problem," conscienticizes his hearers (this empowers some and threatens others), and embarks upon the gathering of an alternative, restored society.

The unrelenting criticism and openness to alternative possibilities mean empowering moments in some quarters. Paulo Friere writes:

> In order for the oppressed to be able to wage the struggle for liberation, they must perceive the reality of oppression not as a closed world from which there is no exit, but as a limiting situation they can transform.[9]

Apocalyptic eschatology, when it is a community public presence, breaks open the present order to different possibilities by presenting "no-exit necessities" as limiting situations that can be transformed. Moreover it pictures the suffering ones themselves, those willing prisoners of ardent eschatological hope, as agents with God in dramatic social transformation. Those who have for too long seen life "from below" now become intoxicated with a new reality against which, they are convinced, even the gates of hell will not prevail. Indeed, they live as though God reigned and no one else has lasting power over them.

Pioneering Creativity

"An eschatological orientation requires eschatological communities."[10] Demystification is not all that is glimpsed in Jesus. It is coupled with attempts to forge a community in keeping with the character of God's way for Israel and all creation. In Jesus' case that means efforts to strike the barriers between groups at enmity with one another, or benignly neglecting one another. It means altering the relationships between those at odds with one another across hostilities of religion, nation, race, sex, culture, and taxes! This is more than simply a "constrast-society." Its character is one of pioneering creativity in which the borders are rather fluid between the eschatological community and the wider world of which it is part. While constantly trying to discern the way of God's *basileia* as present power and reality, the community does so with a posture of social experimentation and innovation. Forms of governance and family style, material provision and distribution, liturgical, pedagogical, and moral expression all require review, and may well embark on new paths.

If a public ethic of unrelenting critique and social creativity sounds relatively trouble-free, that is not the presumption of apocalyptic eschatology. The picture there is one of new age powers doing deadly battle with old age powers. This hope, as this grace, is costly. The "lordship" of Jesus, to use early theological vocabulary, is contested until the very end of the age, embattled all the way. The outcome itself is certain only as a matter of the confident hope of the resurrection. The public life of the church is, in a word, the way of the cross as a community ethic. It will not cease to be cruciform until evil's powerful reign is itself ended.

We close this section with a comment about Schweitzer and Bultmann, both of whom uncovered the apocalyptic eschatology of Jesus but dismissed it as irrelevant for the social ethics of a church with "time" on its hands. Schweitzer and Bultmann both assumed that relevance for ethics turned on a matter of chronology. "As every schoolboy knows,"[11] Bultmann wrote, the world did not come to an end. Thus any inclusion of an eschatological component for ethics had to happen in some other way than direct warrant for a transforming social drama. For Niebuhr—to indulge in an aside—the solution was to cast eschatology in the form of the judging ideal (*agape*) that probes and purges all our efforts to live in accord with it, and as a revelation of God's character as finally gracious and merciful toward us in our failures— and successes! This stance helped make Niebuhr the unmasker of ideology he was, almost without peer. It also supplied a spirituality of grace and forgiveness which refreshed him for further moral struggle.

What is suggested here is that Schweitzer and Bultmann misunderstood "world." Chronology is not decisive in the dynamics of new age and old. Rather, with Dominic Crossan, apocalyptic eschatology is better understood as the ongoing dynamics of living by the powerful presence of a suffering God set implacably against evil and struggling against it in this and every age.[12] God is the shatterer of the "world" as a comprisal of the present forms of harm, just as God is simultaneously the community-creating God. This community-creating God engenders faith first of all among the marginalized and the victimized, but welcomes people of all strata and persuasion. Apocalyptic eschatology, then, is "permanent eschatology" with a preferential option for the suffering. But what must be underscored is that its dynamics of radical critique and pioneering creativity are the dynamics of the public vocation of the church as an eschatological community. With that emphasis registered, we return to Bonhoeffer's writings.

21 August 1944

Dear Eberhard,

It's your birthday in a week's time. Once again I've taken up the readings and meditated on them. The key to everything is the "in him." All that we may rightly expect from God, and ask him for, is to be found in Jesus Christ. The God of Jesus Christ has nothing to do with what God, as we imagine him, could do and ought to do. If we are to learn what God promises, and what he fulfills, we must persevere in quiet meditation on the life, sayings, deeds, sufferings, and death of Jesus. It is certain that we may always live close to God and in the light of his presence, and that such living is an entirely new life for us; that nothing is impossible for us, because all things are possible with God; that no earthly power can touch us without his will; and that danger and distress can only drive us closer to him. It is certain that our joy is hidden in suffering, and our life in death; it is certain that in all this we are in a community that sustains us. In Jesus God has said Yes and Amen to it all, and that Yes and Amen is the firm ground on which we stand.[13]

This letter carries themes familiar to apocalyptic eschatology: an entirely new life for us . . . nothing is impossible . . . no earthly power can touch us . . . danger and distress drive us closer to God . . . we are in a community that sustains us. . . .

But the letter is also a classic statement of the *theologia crucis in nuce:* The key to everything is "in him." All that we may rightly expect from God is to be found in Jesus Christ. The God of Jesus Christ has nothing to do with what God, as we imagine God, could do and ought to do. If we are to learn what God promises, and what God fulfills, we must persevere in quiet meditation on the life, sayings, deeds, sufferings, and death of Jesus.

With the addition of Niebuhr's voice, these two sets of themes—eschatology and the theology of the cross—lead us into further discussion of the public vocation of an eschatological community as a community of the cross.

A Public Stance that Takes Life in Stride

Living the theology of the cross is hardly living the Golden Mean! Aristotle would never have been found a worthy candidate for crucifixion. Yet there is in the *theologica crucis* a view toward life which tends to avoid overly emotional extremes, while at the same time emboldening the community for courageous, even radical, action. Apocalyptic eschatology and the theology of the cross share what Pinchas Lapide, an Orthodox Jew, finds as the strong traits of the rabbi from Nazareth: utter realism about human nature, which includes realism about the presence and power of evil; and utter seriousness about the presence and power of God. This means facing the wretchedness of the world while yet insisting that history is meaningful, even in moments of the eclipse or absence of God. "Our joy is hidden in suffering, and our life in death" is Bonhoeffer's way of stating it. "Beyond tragedy" is the way Niebuhr describes this outlook.[14]

But what is the public stance this represents? What outlook does it cultivate for public life? How does it differ from the dominant cultural ethos of the United States and other sectors in North America?

The sharpest difference is that the community of the cross (*ecclesia crucis*), living by the "permanent eschatology" of the apocalyptic variant, is nontriumphalist. It is nontriumphalist in a nation with a virile "theology of glory" (see chapter 4). Such a nation cannot be honest and realistic about evil. Instead it must either project it upon others, or deny it, as it must deny death. An "official optimism" (Jürgen Moltmann, Douglas John Hall) must reign, an optimism which works in quasi-religious fashion to bolster public confidence and infuse threatening events with a meaning that keeps faith with this optimism.

One example will represent many. What follows is most of the text of President Reagan's address to the nation the evening after the explosive dismemberment of the space shuttle *Challenger* and the fiery and watery death of its crew.

> Nancy and I are pained to the core by the tragedy of the shuttle *Challenger*. We know we share this pain with all the people of our country. This is truly a national loss. . . . We've never had a tragedy like this. And perhaps we've forgotten the courage it took for the crew of the shuttle. But they, the *Challenger* crew, were aware of the dangers and overcame them and did their jobs brilliantly. We mourn seven heroes. . . . To the families of the seven, we cannot bear as you do the full impact of this tragedy. But we feel the loss and we're thinking about you so very much.

Your loved ones were daring and brave, and they had that special grace, that special spirit that says: "Give me a challenge, and I'll meet it with joy." They had a hunger to explore the universe and discover its truths. They wished to serve, and they did. They served all of us. They, the members of the *Challenger* crew, were pioneers. And I want to say something to the schoolchildren of America who were watching the live coverage of the shuttle's takeoff. I know it's hard to understand, but sometimes painful things like this happen. It's all part of the process of exploration and discovery. It's all part of taking a chance and expanding man's horizons. The future doesn't belong to the fainthearted. It belongs to the brave. The *Challenger* crew was pulling us into the future, and we'll continue to follow them. . . . Nothing ends here. Our hopes and our journeys continue. . . . The crew of the space shuttle *Challenger* honored us with the manner in which they lived their lives. We will never forget them or the last time we saw them, this morning, as they prepared for their journey and waved good-bye and slipped the surly bonds of Earth to touch the face of God. Thank you.

When the crushing reality was brokenheartedness, the President spoke of "faintheartedness." He had to insist, against all deep knowledge, that "nothing ends here." In keeping with triumphalist optimism, the final scene must be a happy one; it must be covered with quasi-religious fulfillment ("they . . . waved good-bye and slipped the surly bonds of Earth to touch the face of God").

There is no truth-telling here, except the illusory truth of a theology of glory. Yet short of an alternative perspective that can face death, evil, tragedy, and yet affirm meaningful historical existence, this is the only truth that consoles. For this reason its illusions must be maintained.

If the illusions are not maintained, there is a long slide into despair and cynicism, a cosmic pessimism, or even nihilism. That is not only dangerous for the individual, but also a sickness unto death for society and culture. The effect is to "write off the world prematurely" (Bonhoeffer) by losing self in "otherworldly" indulgences—or to retreat into the kind of hedonism that will play loose with mega-death weapons at the same time as it aspires to live the present moment as intensely as possible. The contrast with the way of the community of the cross is stark, for the insistence there is to care passionately for the earth, and, in good Jewish fashion, even hold God accountable for it and demand that the suffering God show divine saving presence. At the very same time the community holds to the goodness of creation, despite the corruptions of existence, and rejoices in the "powers of good"[15] while combating the corruptions. "Our joy hidden in suffering; and life in death."

During the Reagan years U.S. society vacillated between wild, illusory optimism and a void of meaninglessness just below the surface, meaninglessness that led many to hedonism and a few to suicide. An apocalyptic community of the cross is utterly serious about the evil, but takes life in remarkable stride. There is a "serenity" at the heart of things, to use Niebuhr's word, even amidst convulsive events. There is also, to stay with Niebuhr's theology of the cross, the avoidance of utopianism and of pessimism and cynicism as life-orientations.

Salvation as Engagement
Rather than Resolution

These terms are Douglas John Hall's in "The Cross and Contemporary Culture."[16] He uses them to describe Niebuhr's rejection of both perfectionist ethics (hoped-for perfection in history is one kind of resolution in the quest for salvation) and ethical passivity (salvation as either other-worldliness or as a matter of interiority only is another kind of resolution). Instead, Niebuhr's ethic locates salvation in engagement—in the participation of suffering love in history against powerful evil forces but without assurances that goodness will be the victor on the scale and the terms we set.

Bonhoeffer, too, found salvation as engagement rather than resolution. Jesus did not come to "solve our problems," he says, and indeed "has nothing to do with what God, as we imagine [God], could and ought to do." "Salvation" comes by "living unreservedly in life's duties, problems, successes and failures, experiences and perplexities," "throw[ing] ourselves completely into the arms of God, taking seriously, not our own sufferings, but those of God in the world. . . ."[17] To be a Christian is to stand by God in God's hour of grieving (for the life of the world).

Commentary on contemporary culture need not continue at this point. We can see the profile of the church's public life clearly enough. An eschatological community of the cross moves, like Jesus, to those places in society where the mortal flaws of human community are most obvious. There it takes up its ministry, as participation in God's suffering with and for others. Almost by definition those are the abandoned places of the forgotten, powerless, exiled, or poor. By definition, then, the community of the cross looks for salvation where the wider public normally does not look. It is not surprised, however, to find that the ranks of the compassionate draw from all sorts and conditions of human beings and that "Christ" is the Christian's symbol for a salvatory presence borne by a strange assortment of vulnerable beings who may or may not name the power in that way. It is indeed a transcendent power, a divine power and presence, but it is wholly hidden, as it was in Yehoshua ben Josef, Miriam's son, one Jesus from Nazareth from the far region of Galilee.

THE PUBLIC ROLES

We close by simply listing the public roles of an eschatological community of the cross. Together they comprise the church's public vocation. The vocabulary will be neither Bonhoeffer's nor Niebuhr's but they have been important resources for what follows. We should add that neither Bonhoeffer nor Niebuhr looked to the church alone as a public agent. Both pursued the public vocation of the church through alliances with many who were not members, and thought the church relatively impotent apart from these alliances. Both Bonhoeffer and Niebuhr resisted with all their might any sense of a church living only to itself.[18] This, of course, does not diminish the public vocation of the church. It only makes clear that the church/world boundaries are fluid and open and that alliances are always necessary.

• A community of radical critique. No slice of the world, including the church, wants every layer of its life seen in cross-section. But an eschatological perspective is a perspective *sub species aeternitatis* (from the vantage point of eternity). Thus a vital public task of the church as an eschatological community is to communicate a purging judgment, both in the public square and in the sanctuary. Whether the slogan is the young Marx's, "the relentless criticism of everything that exists," or the young Luther's, "crux probat omnia" (the cross probes all things), the outcome is the same. The piercing light cast by the reign of God demands that what is illumined be named and truth be spoken to power.

• An anticipatory community of inclusive membership and social exploration. If the conviction of the theology of the cross is that as the human Jesus is, so God is,[19] then the Way of Jesus exemplifies the Way of God. Jesus' ethic, as a way of life, death, and hope, stands in the long Jewish tradition of an imitation-of-God ethic. As an eschatological ethic, it means mirroring, in this present time, what God anticipates for the wider world, indeed all creation. Such a restored society is one where all belong, sharing the same loaf and drinking from the same cup, acknowledging a fundamental equality as members of the same social body. Such inclusiveness happens only by persisting struggle to remove human barriers through "dehostilizing love."[20] That inevitably means ongoing social experimentation and exploration because new barriers always arise in society and in the church. Gains in the direction of inclusiveness are never exempt from corruption. *Ecclesia reforma, semper reformanda* is a necessary principle, applicable to both the church and the wider world. To view the Christian ethic as inherently an ethic of social experimentation is to encourage the ongoing practice of this vital principle.

• A community of relentless honesty about good and evil, and of salvation as participation in the sufferings of God in the life of the world. The twenty-first thesis of Luther in the "Heidelberg Disputations" (1518) contends that the theology of glory "has to call evil good and good evil, but the theology of the cross calls the thing what it really is." This immodest claim for the theology of the cross cannot be sustained in such pure form. Here even Luther underestimated the human propensity to ideological self-deception, which is never greater than when it is "religious." Yet the unremitting realism of an eschatological theology of the cross does counter the common drives to (1) make one's own worse case sound the better and (2) inflict upon ourselves a blindness to the good present in others, including the enemy.

Too, the church's preferential option for the suffering, with its view from the precarious edges, sharpens insight even more. "Personal suffering is a more effective key . . . for exploring the world in thought and action than personal good fortune."[21]

Yet the purpose of entering the suffering, and not denying its presence when and where it exists, is to join God's struggles to end it. In the perspective of a cruciform eschatology, salvatory action is the power of God calling people together in covenant intimacy for the creation of a new order. Jesus' crucifixion is for the purpose of ending all other crucifixions. The church's ministry is here, as participation in the public sufferings of God in the life of the world in order to help realize this new order. This is the "realization" in this world of the reality already fashioned by God in Jesus Christ.

The public vocation of the eschatological community is, then, three-fold: radical critique of society and self, pioneering community creativity, and ministry centered in the flawed places of human life as that is manifest in suffering of all kinds. There is celebration of every evidence and instance of the routine goodness of creation. Even deeper joy issues from the vigorous hope that God's power is sufficient to end evil. A sustaining joy, and an ability to take life in stride, issues from participation in "a community that sustains us"[22] in God's "Yes and Amen to it all."[23]

6

METHOD

Questions of method in Christian ethics are always important, but infrequently asked. How ought Christians to approach a moral issue? How are decisions made, on what grounds and by what procedures? Might it be of value to North American Christians to ask about Bonhoeffer's method in ethics?

On the face of it, the answer might be negative, since Dietrich Bonhoeffer never completed his work in ethics. As we know from the gratifying detail supplied by Clifford Green[1] and Eberhard Bethge,[2] the posthumously published *Ethics* is comprised of different and incomplete approaches to the volume Bonhoeffer planned.

Each of these approaches contains penetrating themes for Bonhoeffer's method. "Proving the will of God," "conformation," "the ultimate and the penultimate," "the command of God"—these are different entry points for writing an ethic. Any one of them would be worthy of study. This chapter chooses two of them—"conformation" and "command"—for comparison. The reasons are simple. Bonhoeffer is most explicit about ethical method in these sections, and they carry the longest history in his writings. Our time is best invested here.

Hanfried Müller contends that these two—"Ethik als Gestalt" (ethics as formation) and "Ethik als Gebot"[3] (ethics as command)—constitute two clearly different methods in Bonhoeffer's ethics. That remains to be demonstrated. That they are separate treatments of method by Bonhoeffer is clear. Yet they may be but different approaches to what in the end is a single method. Comparing these treatments, in order to arrive at a statement of Bonhoeffer's methods, or method, is the task at hand.

There is a major impediment—the fragmentary character of Bonhoeffer's *Ethics*. It is immediately obvious to any reader, since a number of chapters break off at clearly unfinished points. Moreover, we now know that no chapter was ever completed to Bonhoeffer's satisfaction. Only one was even reworked. Some finish with outlines of what is to come, once the author can return to his work. He was never able to do that, however. And beyond the incomplete chapters Bonhoeffer did draft, much of the remaining material is in smaller segments still— pages of notes of varying length, on papers of varying size and sort, all awaiting the chance to get on with *Ethics*.

The fragmentary character applies in a larger sense. The book as a whole is assembled from four clearly different beginnings. These were undertaken off and on through the years 1939–1943, between assignments for the Army Intelligence Service and the resistance cell located there. To these beginnings Eberhard Bethge has added five other pieces. While they are pertinent to any discussion of Christian ethics, they were not written explicitly for the volume Bonhoeffer conceived as his major work.[4]

Considering the difficulties of deciphering the almost illegible manuscripts, and considering the problems of putting the various parts in order and dating the larger divisions, it is little wonder Bethge has referred to the *Ethics* as "an absolute fragment."[5] The foreword to the sixth German edition, like Green's careful reconstruction, reads like an essay in *Redactionsgeschichte*.

Ethics is fragmentary in yet another way. It was Bonhoeffer's judgment that not only the manuscripts, but also his ideas were unfinished.[6] In short, the reader intent upon uncovering Bonhoeffer's method in ethics is greeted with both literary and intellectual fragmentation.

This is not all loss. Few of us have polished methods of Christian moral judgment. To watch a thoughtful Christian deliberate about method over a season or two of his or her life, usually entertaining more than one approach, can itself be instructive. It certainly reflects our actual experience more than does a finely honed, settled, and unchanging scheme. In any event, there are two beginnings by Bonhoeffer which are explicit about method and which let us see his thought in process. The first is "Ethics as Formation," written in the fall of 1940. The second is entitled "The 'Ethical' and the 'Christian' as a Theme," written the winter of 1942–43. The motif in the latter is ethics as command. To these we turn.

ETHICS AS FORMATION

In the Christology lectures of 1933 Bonhoeffer spoke of Christ as the center of humanity, nature, and history. "The one who is present in Word, sacrament and community is in the centre of human existence, history and nature. It is part of the structure of his person that he stands at the centre."[7]

The full elucidation of this was foreshortened by the semester's end. But we have sufficient indication of the line to ethics as formation. "The character of the statement about his centrality is not psychological, but ontological-theological."[8]

Christ as the center of humanity, history, and nature means "Christology is *logology*."[9] "Christology is *the* science, because it is concerned with the Logos."[10]

The point is that Bonhoeffer understands reality christologically. This is most clearly drawn out in *Ethics*, where Christ's taking up the world into himself establishes an ontological coherence of God's reality with the reality of the world.

> Whoever sees Jesus Christ does indeed see God and the world in one. He can no longer see God without the world or the world without God.[11]

> In Jesus Christ the reality of God entered into the reality of this world. The place where the answer is given, both to the question concerning the reality of God and to the question concerning the reality of the world, is designated solely and alone by the name Jesus Christ. God and the world are comprised in this name. In Him all things consist (Col. 1:17). Henceforward one can speak neither of God nor the world without speaking of Jesus Christ. All concepts of reality which do not take account of Him are abstractions.[12]

The ontological coherence of God's reality and the world's in Christ leads Bonhoeffer to discuss moral action in two ways. In the end, they are the same—"conformation to Christ" (*Gleichgestaltung*)[13] and action "in accordance with reality" or "with due regard to reality" (*Wirklichkeitsgemässheit*).[14] After discussing the relation of Jesus Christ to reality, he makes the point straightforwardly. "Our conclusion from this must be that action which is in accordance with Christ is action which is in accordance with reality."[15] Ethics as formation rests in the ontological coherence in Christ of God's reality and the world's.

If the student judges ethics as formation to be the heart of Bonhoeffer's entire ethic, then Heinrich Ott's thesis can be affirmed as the key to Bonhoeffer's method.

> Bonhoeffer's ethic as a whole is the attempt to make these thoughts about conformation to Christ into *the* principle of the Christian ethic from this standpoint.[16]

Accepting this judgment for the moment, we could construct Bonhoeffer's procedure along these lines. The Christian answers the question, "What am I to do?" by first answering the question, "How is Christ taking form in the world?" or, as it is put in *Letters and Papers from Prison*, "Who is Christ for us today?"[17] Alternatively, it could be stated in the following way. The first question is, "What is the real?"; the second is, "What action on my part would be in accordance with reality?"[18] In this scheme moral action is action that is in conformity to Christ (in accord with reality); immoral action is action that deviates from Christ's form (from reality). Moral discernment means sensing the presence in our world of "the cosmic reality given in Christ."

> In Christ we are offered the possibility of partaking in the reality of God and in the reality of the world, but not in the one without the other. The reality of God discloses itself only by setting me entirely in the reality of the world, and when I encounter the reality of the world it is always already sustained, accepted and reconciled in the reality of God. This is the inner meaning of the revelation of God in the man Jesus Christ. Christian ethics enquires about the realization in our world of this divine and cosmic reality which is given in Christ.[19]

Ethics as Formation— Relational and Contextual

Reality is one. But reality has a history. Christ is the same yesterday, today, and forever. Yet the ways Christ gains gestalt vary through time. "Who is Christ for us today?" Christian ethics must be contextual ethics. Ethics is "a matter of history" and "a child of the earth."[20] "The 'ethical' as a theme is tied to a definite time and a definite place."[21]

The historical character of reality and the polyphonic character of Christ's gestalt results in a relational, contextual ethic. It is contextual for the reason given—who Christ is for us today may not be who Christ was for us or others yesterday. "What can and must be said is not what is good once and for all, but the way in which Christ takes form among us here and now."[22] It is relational because it is Christ gaining gestalt. Here "the direction of action is shaped by the sense of excitement or gratitude which arises from a live, dynamic, and compelling encounter with the source of moral guidance."[23] Indeed, Bonhoeffer uses not only relational but intensely personalist language in his discourse on ethics. Yet that corresponds to the very nature of reality. "Reality is first and last not lifeless; but it is the real man, the incarnate God."[24] "Reality consists ultimately in the personal."[25] Christian ethics can only be relational when the actions emerge from a "live, dynamic and compelling encounter" with "the real man, the incarnate God," "the source of moral guidance."

> Whenever [the Scriptures] speak of forming they are concerned only with the one form which has overcome the world, the form of Jesus Christ. Formation can come only from this form. But here again it is not a question of applying directly to the world the teachings of Christ or what are referred to as Christian principles, so that the world might be formed in accordance with these. On the contrary, formation comes only by being drawn into the form of Jesus Christ. It comes only as formation in His likeness, as *conformation* with the unique form of Him who was made man, was crucified, and rose again.[26]

An important, logical question for any relational, contextual ethic is whether it bends toward atomism and relativism. Is the "here and now" so separated from the "there and then" and the present situation so unique that each ethical decision is a case unto itself? In an atomistic contextual ethic, each case must be approached methodologically as sui generis. If not, damage is done to the very integrity of the ethical. Bonhoeffer's 1929 Barcelona lecture presents such an ethic.

> From all this it now follows that the content of ethical problems can never be discussed in a Christian light; the possibility of erecting generally valid principles simply does not exist, because each moment, lived in God's sight, can bring an unexpected decision. Thus only one thing can be repeated again and again, also in our time: in ethical decisions man must consider his action *sub specie aeternitatis* and then, no matter how it proceeds, it will proceed rightly. . . . The decision which is really required must be made freely in the concrete situation.[27]

At least for matters of ethical method, the significance of this passage is that it was written before Bonhoeffer took up the *Gestalt Christi* in his ethics. After he does so, the ethic loses its atomism while carrying its contextualism. It even develops a kind of christocentric natural law. "Natural life is formed life"[28] bearing universal rights, duties, and relationships.[29] Natural life is formed life because Christ himself entered into the natural life, and it is through the incarnation of Christ that the natural life becomes the penultimate which is directed towards the ultimate. Through the incarnation of Christ we have the right to call others to the natural life and to live the natural life ourselves, Bonhoeffer writes.[30]

With the christological treatment of the natural, the penultimate, and the mandates, considerable moral content becomes part of Bonhoeffer's contextual ethic. Christ has taken form in the world; reality has a discernible structure; and because Christ is the same yesterday, today, and tomorrow, there is coherence and continuity in his gaining gestalt. Methodologically, Bonhoeffer's remains a relational contextual ethic. But the atomistic character recedes as Bonhoeffer draws out the full force of the Incarnation and expands the arena and content of conformation. As the elaboration of universal laws, rights, duties, and relationships occurs, the method of deciding, still done contextually, takes the form of something approaching casuistic reasoning.

These points—and some others—can be made by surveying the Bonhoeffer corpus.

The Path of Ethics as Formation

The Communion of Saints (1927) is not a book on ethics. Its key term, however, is a critical notion for Bonhoeffer's ethics: "Christus als Gemeinde existierend"—"Christ existing as community."[31] The intimacy of Christology and sociology is worked out as the social character of revelation. The Incarnate God, existing "in, with, and under" social relations, is the only one we know. For us no other God exists than the incarnate, present one. Bethge's sentence, summarizing Bonhoeffer's discussion, is succinct: "All we know, and this is breath-taking, is that the incarnated concreteness is *the* attribute as far as we can think."[32]

In *Act and Being* we again meet the concrete *Gestalt Christi.* As in *The Communion of Saints,* Christ's form is in the ecclesial community.

> God is not free *of* man but *for* man. Christ is the Word of his freedom. God *is there,* which is to say: not in eternal non-objectivity but (looking ahead for the moment) 'haveable,' graspable in his Word within the Church.[33]

More explicit discussion of the meaning of the *Gestalt Christi* for ethics emerges as conditions worsen in Germany and Bonhoeffer becomes involved in the first stirrings of the church struggle. In the 1932 seminar, "Gibt es eine christliche Ethik?" ("Does a specific Christian ethic exist?"), student manuscript notes share the following:

> The possibility of judging whether our action is good lies alone in Christ, the present and future One. All other "secure" possibilities, which appear to give continuity to the action, are to be rejected: (1) the orders of creation; (2) conscience; (3) a Christian principle of love; (4) the situation itself; (5) laying claim to the forgiveness of sins; (6) the Law, even in the form of the Sermon on the Mount.[34]

Another passage reads:

> Action is based in the coming Christ; therein consists its continuity. We stride into the future and our action must be determined through the Christ coming to us, from this Thou.[35]

It is questionable whether the student notes are entirely faithful in stressing the coming Christ even more than the present Christ. In any event, Bonhoeffer's concentration is upon the latter in the Christology lectures given that winter and in a major theological address delivered during the time the seminar was conducted.[36] Yet the salient item is Bonhoeffer's rejection of any basis for Christian moral judgment outside Christ.

Ethics as formation in Christ is even more clearly present in *The Cost of Discipleship*.

> To be conformed to the image of Christ is not an ideal to be striven after. It is not as though we had to imitate him as well as we could. We cannot transform ourselves into his image; it is rather the form of Christ which seeks to be formed in us (Gal. 4:19), and to be manifested in us. . . . We must be assimilated to the form of Christ in its entirety, the form of Christ incarnate, crucified and glorified. Christ took upon himself this human form of ours. He became Man even as we are men. . . . He has become like a man, so that men should be like him. And in the Incarnation the whole human race recovers the dignity of the image of God. . . . Through fellowship and communion with the incarnate Lord, we recover our true humanity.[37]

This is language striking in its similarity to the section, "Ethics as Formation," written in the fall of 1940.[38] But a difference does exist, and it is of momentous importance for ethics as formation. The difference is the expanded arena of conformation. The expansion is, in fact, key for the move from *The Cost of Discipleship* to *Letters and Papers from Prison*. The theological expression of this is given in Bonhoeffer's formula:

> The more exclusively we acknowledge and confess Christ as our Lord, the more fully the wide range of His dominion will be disclosed to us.[39]

In both cases (*Ethics* and *The Cost of Discipleship*) the ethics of formation strikes a clear tone. But in *The Cost of Discipleship* ethics as formation is predominantly a churchly ethic. In *Ethics* it is the expanded ethic of the Christian in the world. The "wide range of His dominion" has been uncovered. Bethge's summary is again succinct:

> The exclusiveness of the Lordship of Christ—that is the message of *The Cost of Discipleship*. The expansiveness of Christ's totality—that is the new accent of the *Ethics*.[40]

In the section on formation in *Ethics* we first encounter the notion of the mandates. It is not so much which mandates are discussed[41] that is of ranking importance, but rather that they are Bonhoeffer's attempt to treat the christological unity in a concrete, even empirical fashion, as well as a theological one. The mandates are the media of conformation.

In summary, the *Gestalt Christi* as a moral category has taken on theocratic breadth. With that, method has moved away from a wholly atomistic contextual ethic to a contextual ethic that speaks easily of universal rights, duties, and relationships. These may indeed vary through time and be imbedded in the movement of cultures and history. But they share the coherence and continuity of Christ's own form in the world.

The last mention of this motif leaves the reader with whetted appetite and a touch of frustration.

> The question how there can be a "natural piety" is at the same time the question of "unconscious Christianity," with which I am more and more concerned. Lutheran dogmatists distinguished between a *fides directa* and a *fides reflexa*. They related this to the so-called children's faith, at baptism. I wonder whether this does not raise a far-reaching problem. I hope we shall soon come back to it.[42]

> God is in the facts themselves.[43]

ETHICS AS COMMAND

The Path of Ethics as Command

While ethics as command is a genuine methodological motif in Bonhoeffer, we see it chiefly as a borrowing from Karl Barth. To be sure, Bonhoeffer was not an uncritical Barthian. Nonetheless, where Bonhoeffer makes the most of ethics as command he is actually borrowing directly from Barth and appropriating the motif for uses of his own.

Still, ethics as command is related to the *original* Bonhoeffer motif—ethics as formation—as we will indicate further on.

The Barcelona lecture serves again as a convenient starting point. There is little mention of "command" as such, although there are some affinities in terms such as "being addressed," "God's call," and "claim." One passage must be cited at length. It carries premonitions of a theme later found under the rubric of ethics as command.

Ethics is a matter of earth and blood, but also of him who made both; the trouble arises from this duality. There can be ethics only in the framework of history, in the concrete situation, at the moment of the divine call, the moment of being addressed, of the claim made by the concrete need and the situation for decision, of the claim which I have to answer and for which I have to make myself responsible. Thus there cannot be ethics in a vacuum, as a principle; there cannot be good and evil as general ideas, but only as qualities of will making a decision. These can be only good and evil as done in freedom; by contrast, principles are binding under the law. Bound up in the concrete situation, through God and in God the Christian acts in the power of a man who has become free. He is under no judgment but his own and that of God.[44]

The address entitled "A Theological Basis for the World Alliance" was given three years later in July 1932. It contains theme after theme found in later writing; for example, reality and command. That most amazing statement is here: "What the command is for the preaching of the Gospel, the knowledge of firm reality is for the preaching of the command. *Reality is the sacrament of command.*"[45] Bonhoeffer insists:

The word of the church to the world must . . . encounter the world in all its present reality from the deepest knowledge of the world, if it is to be authoritative. The church must be able to say the Word of God, the word of authority, here and now, in the most concrete way possible, from knowledge of the situation. The church may not therefore preach timeless principles, however true, but only commandments which are true today. God is "always" *God* to us "*today*."[46]

The example is timely.

In the event of taking a stand on war the church cannot just say, "there should really be no war, but there are necessary wars" and leave the application of this principle to each individual; it should be able to say quite definitively: "engage in this war" or "do not engage in this war."[47]

The conclusion is this:

But, if the church really has a commandment of God, it must proclaim it in the most definite form possible, from the fullest knowledge of the matter, and it must utter a summons to obedience. A commandment must be definite, otherwise it is not a commandment. God's commandment now requires something quite definite from us. And the church should proclaim this to the community.[48]

"Today God's commandment for us is the order of *international peace*."[49] On a page that parallels discussion of the 1932 seminar on ethics[50] we again find Bonhoeffer addressing Christology and ethics. This time there is explicit reference to the command of God.

The command can come from nowhere else than the origin of promise and fulfillment, from Christ. From Christ alone we must know what we must do. But not from him as the preaching prophet of the Sermon on the Mount, but from him as the one who gives us life and forgiveness, as the one who has fulfilled the commandment of God in our place, as the one who brings and promises the new world. We can only perceive the commandment where the law is fulfilled, where the new world of the new order of God is established. Thus we are completely directed toward Christ. Now with this we also understand the whole order of fallen creation as directed solely towards Christ, towards the new creation.[51]

At least this can be said about ethics as command: the command is a specific, prophetic word to the concrete situation, or it is not God's command; its center is in Christ; and the command itself, if it is truly God's command, corresponds with reality.

Before leaving the 1932 address we should note Bonhoeffer's growing interest in ethics. From this juncture onward, it never left him and it culminated in his consideration of *Ethics* as his major life project.[52] In August 1932 he wrote a friend:

I gave an address in Czechoslovakia on the theological foundation of this work [that of the World Alliance] and attempted in so doing to quiet my theological conscience, but there are still many questions to bring up. At bottom, everything hangs on the problem of ethics, that is, actually in the question of the possibility of the proclamation of the concrete command by the church.[53]

There is no gainsaying that *The Cost of Discipleship* is a wholly "ethical" book punctuated with the concrete commands of Christ to his disciples. Yet while it is a passionate moral tract for the times and a call to battle, it lacks an explicit hermeneutic of ethics as command. Reflection on method is simply missing, despite the important formula that "*only he who believes is obedient, and only he who is obedient believes*."[54] In fact, it is only in the fourth approach of *Ethics* that we find a prolonged reflective effort on the method of ethics as command.

Here is the borrowed Barth. This is striking for several reasons. Barth's name is not mentioned. In fact, it is mentioned nowhere in *Ethics*. Second, Bethge does not mention Barth in the long list of books he records as Bonhoeffer's reading during the time Bonhoeffer wrote material for *Ethics*.[55] Bethge does list *Church Dogmatics 2/2* as Bonhoeffer's reading in Tegel in December 1943–January 1944. Bonhoeffer requested *CD 2/2* in a letter to Bethge at Christmas in 1943.[56] He fails to mention, however, whether he has or has not seen parts or all of it before. But, we now know,[57] Bonhoeffer did use it the winter before, when the portions of *Ethics* on "The Command of God" took form. It is rather curious that Barth himself does not mention the coincidence of this portion of Bonhoeffer's ethics already in his own, even though he commented at length on Bonhoeffer's ethics.[58]

If Bonhoeffer, Bethge, and Barth do not mention the coincidence of ethics as command in *Ethics* and ethics as command in *Church Dogmatics 2/2,* can it in fact be so? The parallels are clear. The sections in question in Bonhoeffer are "The Commandment of God"[59] and "The Commandment of God in the Church."[60] The portion of *Church Dogmatics 2/2* under scrutiny is "The Command of God."[61] Bonhoeffer writes:

> The commandment of God is permission. It differs from all human laws in that it commands freedom.[62]

Barth writes:

> The form by which the command of God is distinguished from all other commands, the special form . . . consists in the fact that it is permission— the granting of a very definite freedom.[63]

The original texts are as follows:

> Das Gebot Gottes ist *Erlaubnis.* Darin unterscheidet es sich von allen menschlichen Gesetzen, dass es die *Freiheit—gebietet.*[64]

> Die Form, durch die das Gebot Gottes sich von allen anderen Geboten unterscheidet, die besondere Form . . . besteht darin, dass es *Erlaubnis* ist: Gewahrung einer ganz bestimmten *Freiheit.*[65]

Barth makes this point again and again.

> The command of God orders us to be free. . . . This is what characterizes the command of God, distinguishes it from all other commands.[66]

> The command of God sets man free. The command of God permits. It is only in this way that it commands.[67]

From Bonhoeffer we hear:

The commandment of God permits man to live as man before God."[68]

On another matter Barth enters this paragraph.

It is this definiteness that the command is unconditional, leaving us no other choice than that between obedience and disobedience. Its unconditional character consists in the fact that, independently of our views, always and in every relationship in which I find myself placed, it has the particular form that God demands from me in all seriousness, this or that concrete thing.[69]

A few pages later Barth, illustrating the definiteness of the command, weaves his way through the Old and New Testaments. He finds multiple examples of God's definite instruction to humankind, including Abraham, Jacob, Moses, Jesus Christ, the disciples, and Paul.[70]

Compare Bonhoeffer's paragraph on the definiteness of the command and the examples that follow.

God's commandment is the speech of God to man. Both in its contents and in its form it is concrete speech to concrete man. God's command leaves man no room for application or interpretation. It leaves room only for obedience or disobedience. God's command cannot be found and known in detachment from time and place; it can only be heard in a local and temporal context. If God's commandment is not clear, definite and concrete to the last detail, then it is not God's commandment. Either God does not speak at all or else He speaks to us as definitely as He spoke to Abraham and Jacob and Moses and as definitely as in Jesus Christ He spoke to the disciples and through His apostles to the Gentiles.[71]

Another time Bonhoeffer says:

God's commandment is always concrete speech *to* somebody. It is never abstract speech *about* something or *about* somebody. It is always an address, a claim, and it is so comprehensive and at the same time so definite that it leaves no freedom for interpretation or application, but only the freedom to obey or disobey.[72]

Another time Barth says:

The command of God is a claim addressed to man in such a way that it is given integrally, so that he cannot control its content or decide its concrete application. . . . It comes to us with a specific content, embracing the whole outer and inner substance of each momentary decision and epitomising the totality of each momentary requirement. It does not need any interpretation, for even to the smallest details it is self-interpreting.[73]

On still another aspect of the command Bonhoeffer writes of its effects:

> The commandment of God becomes the element in which one lives without always being conscious of it, and thus it implies freedom of movement and of action, freedom from the fear of decision, freedom from fear to act; it implies certainty, quietude, confidence, balance, and peace.[74]

No single passage in Barth contains the compactness of the foregoing paragraph. But an entire section, entitled "The Goodness of the Divine Decision,"[75] contains every single one of these elements at one point or another.

In the chapter on the command of God in the church Bonhoeffer discusses, over several pages, the command as proclamation. Then follows a section on Christology. Although hardly surprising in its subject matter, it is surprising in its length and in its relative disconnectedness from the preceding and succeeding portions. These three pages are among the finest and in some ways the most original in Bonhoeffer. There are pathfinding, liberating passages under the headings, "Jesus, the eternal Son with the Father from all eternity," "Jesus Christ, the crucified Redeemer," and "Jesus Christ, the risen and ascended Lord." Yet what is striking are the similarities to the three pages of intense christological reflection in *Church Dogmatics 2/2* in the section "The Presupposition of the Divine Judgment."[76] Both are too lengthy to quote here. Nor are excerpts as telling as the whole, since the distinctive stamp of each author is evident throughout. But the reader is referred to this comparison as further evidence of the influence of *Church Dogmatics 2/2* on Bonhoeffer's approach to a method in ethics.

What is to be made of all this? First, the portions on the command of God apparently received no revision. They were part of the last writings of Bonhoeffer for the present *Ethics*, and were on his desk at the time of his arrest. Certainly they were never intended by him for publication in their present form.[77] Thus, an innocent borrowing occurs here and there. But what may have been only raw material for Bonhoeffer himself later emerged as the end product when the editor patched pieces together for publication. Bethge knows, of course, that these are not the polished pieces Bonhoeffer would have produced for publication.

Second, the content here is genuine Bonhoeffer, though not original. The themes of the concreteness and specificity of the command, the emphasis given obedience, the christocentricity of the command, the embrace of all life by the command and the conferring of freedom—all these have genuine and strong antecedents predating Bonhoeffer's study of *Church Dogmatics 2/2.* There is no doubt whatsoever this last approach to an ethic is authentic Bonhoeffer, albeit Bonhoeffer as the grateful student of Barth.

Third, there are changes in, and additions to, the material used from 2/2. These show the difference between Bonhoeffer and Barth. For example, whereas Barth usually writes that the command of God confers a permission, a freedom, to do this or that, Bonhoeffer drops the article! Bonhoeffer's strongest emphasis is not Barth's—Barth's theme is of constant accountability before God. Bonhoeffer's, rather, is God's permission for us to live "as man, and not merely as a taker of ethical decisions."[78]

> The commandment of God permits man to be man before God. It allows the flood of life to flow freely. It lets man eat, drink, sleep, work, rest, and play. It does not interrupt him. It does not continually ask whether he ought to be sleeping, eating, working or playing, or whether he has some more urgent duties.[79]

This would not be denied by Barth. But it does not carry the emphasis with him it does for Bonhoeffer. Lehmann rightly judges this subtle change in Bonhoeffer from Barth: the attempt to break from any "formal and concrete rigidities" of the conception of command while yet holding onto the command of God. After Lehmann quotes Bonhoeffer's definition of the command as permission to live as "man," he concludes: "To put the matter this way has the two-fold advantage of emphasizing in Christian ethics the personal relations between God and man established by God's action and *will*, rather than the *command* of God."[80]

An important addition to the material from Barth is Bonhoeffer's concretizing the command in the mandates. The mandates are solely dependent upon the one command,[81] but no *single* mandate can claim to embody the one command of God or even claim a position of superiority over any other mandate. They are conjoined so that only by cooperation and coordination do they properly function in fulfillment of the one command.[82] They exist for one another, and one cannot replace another. In fact, mutual limitation is an aspect of their activity as God's mandates.[83]

> The supremacy of the commandment of God is shown precisely by the fact that it juxtaposes and coordinates these authorities in a relation of

mutual opposition and complementarity and that it is only in this multiplicity of concrete correlations and limitations that the commandment of God takes effect as the commandment which is manifest in Jesus Christ.[84]

The mandates are definite historical forms of the command of God.[85] In fulfilling duties within the mandates (as a husband or wife, for example, or father or mother, as friends, as breadwinner, citizen, or church member) we do God's will, whether we are cognizant of it and intend it or not. Here the "flood of life flows freely." Bonhoeffer regards this normal discharge of moral responsibilities as "pre-ethical."[86] For him, the rather self-evident nature of duties in marriage and family, state, church, and work is certainly a matter of morality, but not ethics in a technical sense. The ethical arises only when the moral course itself is brought into question.

> There are, of course, undoubtedly occasions and situations in which the moral course is not self-evident, either because it is not, in fact, followed or because it has become questionable from the point of view of its contents. It is at such time that the ethical becomes a theme.

A few pages earlier, Bonhoeffer had concluded that the ethical is "tied to a definite time and a definite place."[87] It is a matter only when the "shall" and "should" impinge from the periphery of existence because a particular, assumed moral course has been rendered questionable.

Such a conception of the ethical yields two methodological results for Bonhoeffer. First, it makes ethics contextual. Bonhoeffer's ethics are contextual on other grounds as well, but here the conclusion is derived from the fact that the mandates structure life in such a way that the "ethical" only arises at exceptional times. It arises when the duties and obligations required by the mandates are *not* clear. At those times, Bonhoeffer insists that discovering the proper course can only come about through the link with the particular persons, times, and places of this pre-ethical environment and its characteristically "built-in" responsibilities. Ethics must be done contextually.[88]

Bonhoeffer's conception of the ethical also serves, as he expresses it, "to prevent a pathological overburdening of life by the ethical," "to prevent . . . abnormal fanaticization and total moralization of life."[89]

The conclusion is this: the ethical is *part* of the command of God. It is far from the whole. The command comprises the ethical. But the reverse is not true.[90] Indeed, the command first of all "sets free for *unreflected* doing"[91] by forming life in the mandates. Only when this divinely warranted life-process goes astray does its rectification take the form of God's command as the concrete "ethical."

On the subject of the mandates Bonhoeffer's discussions of ethics as formation and ethics as command are arranged precisely alike. For ethics as formation the mandates are historical forms of the *Gestalt Christi* which embody and direct the normal processes of life. The ethical as a theme arises when "who Christ is for us today" is in question as that engages our responses to his changing forms. The ethical arises in these exceptional times and can be answered only with an eye to these times, that is, contextually.

In ethics as command the mandates are historical forms of the command of God. This command first of all sets humanity free, in the mandates, for unreflected doing, for the "free-flowing flood of life." But when the "shalls" and "shoulds" are not clear, "the fixed place and the fixed time of the ethical"[92] arises and the command of God takes the form of the specifically ethical. Decision making is then again done contextually and reflectively.

In both cases, Bonhoeffer's contextual ethic has become increasingly "filled" with moral, but pre-ethical, content. The "ethical" is increasingly marked off as a vital, but "peripheral" event.

> To confine the ethical phenomenon to its proper place and time is not to invalidate it; it is, on the contrary, to render it fully operative. Big guns are not the right weapons for shooting sparrows. In respect of its contents as well as of its character as an experience the ethical phenomenon is a peripheral event.[93]

In both cases the outcome of the "filled" contextual ethic is the same, an increased emphasis upon a kind of natural law. Creation is so formed in Jesus Christ that moral continuities span time and space. We cited this earlier for ethics as formation. Now we note it for ethics as command.

> The commandment of Jesus Christ, the living Lord, sets creation free for the fulfillment of the law which is its own, that is to say, the law which is inherent in it by virtue of its having its origin, its goal and its essence in Jesus Christ.[94]

So we have done more than note Bonhoeffer's addition to the material taken from Barth. We have seen the mandates as forms of the one command and observed the parallel outcome in Bonhoeffer's separate treatments of the mandates.

But the original purpose was to make a judgment on Bonhoeffer's use of Barth for the ultimate reason of clarifying Bonhoeffer's own method. He went beyond borrowing. He altered the material in accord with his own emphases and used it in connection with an original theme, the mandates.

While Bonhoeffer's distinctive emphases and theme cannot be compared with Barth's in detail, considerable contrast between the two should be noted. Bonhoeffer chooses to focus theologically on the human pole of God's command and describe how the living of life proceeds under the command. How we live fully, precisely as humanity, occupies Bonhoeffer's attention. The mandates and, in other sections, the natural and the penultimate, are his categories for explicating this. Yet in the Barth galleys Bonhoeffer read, the human dimensions of the command of God are engaged only to give expression to how the gracious command, as God's, dominates and shapes those dimensions. Bonhoeffer, but not Barth, chooses to focus on "the temporal character of human life, its fulness and its frailty."[95] This is Bonhoeffer's own mark, not that of *Church Dogmatics 2/2*. There are, incidentally, intimations here of the *Letters and Papers from Prison* theme that the Christian life is one of genuine and complete "worldliness" (*Welt-lichkeit*).[96]

The Place of Ethics as Command

The final question is whether this motif, ethics as command, holds the same rank for Bonhoeffer as does ethics as formation. There are clearly elements with a pedigree in Bonhoeffer's writings. The genuineness and importance of ethics as command are thus not to be doubted. But does it carry the load, and the interest, that ethics as formation does? I think not. *Letters and Papers from Prison* gives good indications to that effect, if not conclusive ones.

The theological letters contain little that is explicit about method. But they show direct lines between theology and ethics[97] (if such a distinction is even meaningful in Bonhoeffer's later writings). In *all* instances, the concern is who Christ is for us today. For Bonhoeffer, this is the same as the question how Christ takes form in a world come of age. Only once is the command of God even mentioned. Even then it is only a passing remark about an explanation to the Ten Commandments Bonhoeffer was writing at the time. The remark itself has little to do with method. It is quite significant, then, that for every passage bearing on the Christian life, the starting point is a discussion about the *Gestalt Christi* and/or the world come of age.

That ethics as formation is the motif foremost in Bonhoeffer's latest thought is perhaps best illustrated from the outline of the book he planned and on which he had begun work. (A book usually represents a stronger commitment than do occasional letters.) In this outline the impressive factor is the unity of theology, ecclesiology, and ethics. The movement is from Jesus as "the man for others" to the church as church only when it "exists for others," to a new life in the world as "existence for others," a new life "through the participation in the being of Jesus," interpreted nonreligiously.[98] The *vita Christiana* is not spoken of in a way that even hints of the command of God. The focus is simply "participation in the being of Jesus" (*Sein Jesu*).

The piece that does speak of the command of God is, as mentioned, the Ten Commandments, an assignment done on request. The few comments that might be construed to bear upon method are in line with those in *Ethics*. There are none Bonhoeffer has not expressed earlier, and there are none he felt of sufficient excitement to share with Bethge.[99] The clear excitement in the prison literature is christological discernment and formation in a world come of age.

If we conclude from this that ethics as formation is not only the more original methodological motif in Bonhoeffer but also the one that captures his most intense interest, are there further available reasons for such a conclusion? Here again the answers must be acknowledged as inconclusive. They are offered tentatively.

First, Bonhoeffer claimed a new appreciation of the nineteenth century and of liberalism in theology. He stated his desire to combine the trends of liberalism and neoorthodoxy.[100] This high evaluation of the heritage of liberalism and of the nineteenth century can be interpreted as amiable to the christological content and method of ethics as formation. It is far less friendly to ethics as command, which has such heavy Barthian bases.

> The question is: Christ and the world that has come of age. The weakness of liberal theology was that it conceded to the world the right to determine Christ's place in the world; in the conflict between the Church and the world it accepted the comparatively easy terms of peace that the world dictated. Its strength was that it did not try to put the clock back, and that it genuinely accepted the battle (Troeltsch), even though this ended with its defeat.[101]

Second, Bonhoeffer took obvious delight in his discovery of the world come of age. It stands to the fore in letter after letter. He immediately sought to relate his Christology to this analysis. "Let me just summarize briefly what I am concerned about—how to claim for Jesus Christ a world that has come of age."[102] The result was an even heavier emphasis on Bonhoeffer's already strong theology of the cross.

> He [God] is weak and powerless in the world, and that is precisely the way, the only way, in which he is with us and helps us. Matt. 8:17 makes it quite clear that Christ helps us, not by virtue of omnipotence, but by virtue of his weakness and suffering. . . . The Bible directs man to God's powerlessness and suffering; only the suffering God can help. To that extent we may say that the development towards the world's coming of age outlined above . . . opens up a way of seeing the God of the Bible, who wins power and space in the world by his weakness. This will probably be the starting-point for our "secular interpretation."[103]

Because Bonhoeffer sees the "Mundigkeit" (adulthood) of the world as the occasion for proclaiming the utter "Weltlichkeit" (worldliness) of God, it would appear that ethics as formation is more conducive as a way of proceeding. This is underscored with Bonhoeffer's view of the world's "Mundigkeit" as itself a result of Christ's taking shape among humans and his view that it is God who compels us to recognize that we live in the world *etsi deus non daretur* (as though God did not exist).[104]

This does not of itself exclude the motif of ethics as command. Yet not only is it absent as a subject of discussion; apparently it fits less well than ethics as formation. Certainly the theological and ethical excitement of the letters rotates about the form of Christ in a world come of age.

The last reason is equally remote from truly hard data but it merits consideration.

> It was not in ethics, as is often said, that [Barth] subsequently failed— his ethical observations, as far as they exist, are just as important as his dogmatic ones—; it was that in the non-religious interpretation of the-ological concepts he gave no concrete guidance, either in dogmatics *or in ethics*.[105]

How serious is this deficiency, this lack of nonreligious interpretation with guidance in dogmatics and ethics? For Bonhoeffer, it was as serious as "claiming for Jesus Christ the world come of age"!

> What is bothering me incessantly is the question what Christianity really is, or indeed who Christ really is for us today.[106]

> If our final judgment must be that the western form of Christianity, too, was only a preliminary stage to a complete absence of religion, what kind of situation emerges for us, for the Church? How can Christ become

the lord of the religionless as well? Are there religionless Christians? If religion is only a garment of Christianity—and even this garment has looked very different at different times—then what is a religionless Christianity? Barth, who is the only one to have started along this line of thought, did not carry it to completion, but arrived at a positivism of revelation, which in the last analysis is essentially a restoration. For the religionless working man (or any other man) nothing decisive is gained here.[107]

If Barth does not offer concrete guidance for nonreligious interpretation in ethics, as Bonhoeffer says, is Bonhoeffer finished with Barth's ethics? That would be concluding too much. Still less can it be asserted that Bonhoeffer would be finished with ethics as command, which in any case is authentic Bonhoeffer. What can be concluded, however, is that Bonhoeffer wants an ethic which can be given expression in a nonreligious interpretation of theological concepts. It is also clear he does not find that ethic in Barth's writings. He finds it in "participation" in the being of Jesus, "the man for others." "The man for others" is Bonhoeffer's own nonreligious christological title, and for him it is pregnant with the stuff of ethics. Bonhoeffer is on the trail of what he regards as essential, a Christian ethic that can be expressed nonreligiously. This ethic is closer to ethics as formation than ethics as command. In his last thoughts Bonhoeffer pursues ethics wholly in the mode of ethics as formation.

We conclude from the extant evidence that ethics as formation is not only the more original methodological motif in Bonhoeffer; in the end it is also the reigning one. Had Bonhoeffer's ethics had a future of his own crafting, it would likely have been developed along this line, with less mention of the command of God and more of the discernment of Christ's form in a world come of age, and the shape of the Christian life appropriate to that form.

ONE METHOD OR TWO?

The fragmentary nature of Bonhoeffer's most provocative writing set us upon the course of pursuing dual methodological motifs. Now the question is: are there in fact two methods? If there are, how do they compare if placed side by side?

In both, the overriding thrust is toward concreteness.

In both, the ethic is an ethic of reality and realization. The *Gestalt Christi* and the command of God both have correspondence with reality. They bring to concrete expression in this world the cosmic reality given in Christ.

In both, ethics is done contextually. The ways Christ takes form among human beings vary through time. God's concrete command can only be heard in a local and temporal context.

In both, ethics is relational. The supreme importance of the command of God is that it is the command of Jesus Christ, true humanity. The supreme importance of the gestalt of reality is that it is Christ's form. The Christian moral life is an ongoing, dynamic relationship with its center, God-in-Christ.

In both, the relational, contextual ethic becomes increasingly "filled." Both methods move from an atomistic ethic to an ethic emphasizing the coherence and continuity of the form of Christ, or the command of God. The outcome in both is a large place for the "natural" and for the mandates and their innate laws.

In both, the mandates play an indispensable role. In one, they are the media of conformation; in the other, the media of obedience. In both, they compose the pre-ethical, though moral, environment, and they prevent life from an overburdening by the ethical.

In both, the ethical occupies a peripheral location. It has a fixed time and place. The ethical arises when the structured flow of life in the mandates has been subjected to disruption and severe questioning; when "who Christ is for us today" is in doubt; or what the command of God is concretely is itself problematic.

In both, moral action is the same. Obedience to the command of God is, for moral content, identical with conformation to Christ.[108] (Here is a resolution of the two methods, if there are two.)

For both motifs, all the faculties of the self are employed in ethical discernment: in the one case, in order to discover the present concrete command; in the other, to discern the current, specific form of Christ.[109]

In both, the methodological direction is from the question and answer about the indicative to the question and answer about the imperative. From: "How is Christ taking form among us here and now?" to: "What action on my part conforms to his action?" From: "What is God-in-Christ commanding here and now?" to: "What action on my part is action in keeping with this command?" In both, the weight is clearly on the indicative. It is permissive, authorizing life.

In both, the underlying assumption for Christian ethics is reconciliation, that is, the recovered unity of God and the world in Christ.[110] In both, the point of departure for Christian ethics is the body of

Christ.[111] Christian ethics, on these counts, stands alone in relation to all other ethics.

In both, deputyship or vicarious action has an ontological base and the supreme ethical deed is the deed of free responsibility.[112] This deed is the breakthrough to reality at the particular time and place of the "ethical." In both, however, the final judgment of the deed lies in the hands of God. Both are ethics firmly grounded in justification by grace alone.[113]

What are the differences, if these are two methods? Methodologically considered, there are probably none of great consequence. Müller is correct in pointing to the "Roman Catholic" *tone* in ethics as formation, in contrast to a classically Protestant one in ethics as command.[114] But he is wrong in characterizing the former as a Lutheran brand of *gratia non tollit, sed perficit naturam* (grace perfecting nature, rather than replacing it).[115] This underestimates the methodological importance of the *dialectic* of the natural and the unnatural, the ultimate and the *dialectic* of the natural and the unnatural, the ultimate and the penultimate, and the yes and no to the world within the *Gestalt Christi*—incarnation, crucifixion and resurrection. Ott's comparison of Bonhoeffer with Teilhard de Chardin and Thomas Aquinas suffers the same error.[116]

Is there one method or two? The more cautious answer would be that this remains an open question because Bonhoeffer's theology and ethic remain open-ended. Continuities are very strong, but his method is not complete.

The riskier, but probably more precise, conclusion is that Bonhoeffer's is an ethic of reality and realization which finds methodological expression in two basic motifs, one of which is both more original and more enduring. In the end, ethics as command should be regarded as a genuine motif, but a subordinate one. Both are authentic but ethics as formation is in better tune with Bonhoeffer's christocratic vision of humanity, nature, and history. Its "fit" is better. Still, it would be an unwarranted projection backward from *Letters and Papers from Prison* to name ethics as formation the method of Bonhoeffer's ethics. By his own testimony, his ideas were unfinished. That holds for matters of method, as well as for others. He struggles toward a more competent method of moral discernment, as do we.[117]

7

DIVINE PRESENCE AND
HUMAN POWER

A distinctive mark of our time is the quantum leap in human knowledge and human power. There is a novel range, and there are novel objects and consequences, of enhanced knowledge and power. While the heightened knowledge and power are unevenly distributed, they affect the entire globe, and bring more and more people within striking distance of each other's lives, for better and for worse. Whether the subject is the radical intervening in life processes (the new powers of biotechnologies), the plausible and actual termination of life on a mass scale (nuclear reality and weapons of mass destruction), the heightened and cumulative impact of human effects, especially from industrial society, on the planetary environment (acid rain, ozone layer depletion, deforestation, solid and toxic waste), the gathering and dispersion of vast quantities of information (mass media and electronic technologies), or the integration of systems on a global scale (world-wide economic linkages), the point is everywhere the same: greatly increased powers now rest in the hands of these mysterious and exuberant animals we call human beings.

How shall we think about these new powers? More to the point, how shall we think of them theologically, up against the ancient confession that God is the source of all power and the one to whom we are accountable for the powers we hold? Just what do we understand to be the relationship of divine to human power now, in our time? And how do Christians in North America, and citizens of the United States in particular, approach the subject, living as we do on the busy site of many of the epoch-making developments? The new powers are already so much with us that it is not uncommon to read what should be an utterly startling sentence, and yet react to it with a knowing nod: "The balance [of accountability for the ordering of life]," writes James Gustafson, "has shifted, in a sense, from God to [humanity]" and "is shifting more rapidly in this century than in all the previous centuries of human culture combined."[1]

What is *not* commonplace, however, is careful attention to Gustafson's little prepositional phrase, "in a sense." It is not clear what the relationship of human and divine power in our time is. What does his sentence actually mean, theologically—"the ordering of all life is shifting in a sense from God to humanity"? What does it mean in moral terms? What is the nature of God's presence now? Or, to respect the testimony of many, what is the nature of God's absence now? Is God's presence and/or absence different from ages in which human beings held less power and had less impact on the world of which they were a part? In short, what are we to make of divine and human power in our time, as "God-talk" and as "ethics-talk"?

Rather than foolishly attempting a full inventory of current ruminations about divine and human power, we will compare two thinkers. One is Bonhoeffer, the other is Irving Greenberg, an Orthodox rabbi. There are striking parallels in their separate work. The parallels are especially provocative for any who will venture into the mind-twisting subject of divine presence and human power at the end of one millennium and the beginning of the next.

We have only fragments from these two theologians from different continents. In Bonhoeffer's case, we have fragments because he first came to the subject in the last year of his abbreviated life. We possess the theological letters of a four-month period, from the last day of April to 23 August 1944, together with some attenuated materials and a few premonitions from earlier years. These are found in *Letters and Papers from Prison* and, to a lesser extent, in *Ethics,* both of which are themselves literary fragments published posthumously. In Greenberg's case, the work is fragmentary simply because it is contemporary and still very much in process. Greenberg travels widely and holds to a rather intense schedule as president of the National Jewish Center for Learning and Leadership (CLAL). The chief documents are occasional essays written for various audiences in the 1970s and 1980s. Most of what follows here has appeared in the publication of CLAL entitled *Perspectives.* The exception is an important chapter in the 1975 volume, *Auschwitz: Beginning of a New Era?* The essay is "Cloud of Smoke, Pillar of Fire: Judaism, Christianity, and Modernity after the

Holocaust." It prepares for the extraordinary essay, "The Third Great Cycle of Jewish History" (1981) and the timely "The Ethics of Power" (1988).

Whatever their personal histories, the fragmentary character of Greenberg's and Bonhoeffer's treatment is actually more typical than unusual for our subject. A full treatment of the relationship of divine power to human power in our time has yet to be written which addresses crucial ethical issues while it formulates theological baselines.

The following will be largely expository. The eventual goal, critique and a constructive theological proposal, must await future publication. The necessary first step is simply to present Bonhoeffer and Greenberg on the subject of human power and divine presence in a new era. Their own exploratory and creative thought helps provide what we need most at the moment: not critique, but conceptual clarity and promising paths for this formidable subject.

The exposition pursues two lines, both dictated by the authors' preoccupations. The first line treats their theological conception of divine presence and human power in our era. The second gathers their comments on the moral use of human power, especially political power.

GOD AND HUMAN POWER

An Epochal Shift

For both men, ours is a new era that carries with it an altered relationship to the Ancient of Days. We stand, both men say, awkwardly astride a break in time. Bonhoeffer calls it "the world coming of age," Greenberg describes it in conjunction with "the third great cycle of Jewish history." The break is experienced by both as the cataclysmic event of Nazism and its far-reaching consequences. Together they conclude that the murderous events in Germany in the 1930s and 1940s reveal the deep failure of inherited cultural, religious, and intellectual frameworks—Christian, Jewish, and secular. They also conclude that what remains after the civilizational collapse is the utter, brute fact of heightened human power to affect all of life and to break past limits. For Greenberg, after the ovens of the death camps have been stilled and the reconstruction has gotten well under way, after the State of Israel has become the reality of a millennial dream and a new Europe has risen from the rubble, the fact of growing human power and its use for massive good and equally massive evil remains. For Bonhoeffer, a like conclusion exists. In the outline for the book that he hastened to write in the waning months of his life, he asks, "What protects us against the menace of organization? Man is again thrown back on himself. He has managed to deal with everything, only not with himself. He can insure against everything, only not against man. In the last resort it all turns on man."[2]

In many ways the very purpose of the last thoughts of Bonhoeffer and the present work of Greenberg is to confront with consummate honesty the fact of grave and great power and, for the sake of the future, to render it religiously meaningful and morally accountable. Both men betray a keen sense that vulnerable dimensions of God's own reality and our very humanity lurk in the reality of heightened human power, and are at stake in its use.

If an epochal break is the stimulus for bold thought, what are Greenberg's and Bonhoeffer's perspectives on it?

Greenberg

For Greenberg, all credible talk of God and humanity in this age must orient itself from the polar events of historical destruction and redemption. This means the Holocaust and the State of Israel as counterevents, and genuinely revelatory ones. They are revelatory because they are formative for our time and normative for our understanding of it. What is revealed by them is "the hiddenness of the divine, the holiness in secularity, the sacrilege of powerlessness, . . . and the commitment to a shattered covenant."[3] From a theological point of view, these are the dynamics of a new era. They are palpably a Jewish perspective and for the Jewish people in the first instance. But they bear a truth that is paradigmatic for all of us as members of the same world and collectively shaped by its recent history. It is important to add that the credibility of Christianity and its faith claims is utterly shattered by the the Holocaust. If Jewish believers after Auschwitz dare talk at all about a God who loves and cares and protects, without making a mockery of the millions of innocents who suffered and died, how dare Christianity claim to hold to this God when Christian complicity in the Holocaust was international in scope and centuries deep?[4]

For Greenberg, all reconstructive theological-moral work is governed by a certain kind of dialectical thinking which issues from the polar events of destruction and redemption. Theological-moral work is also oriented to "moment faiths" and a particular relation of concrete human acts to human and divine reality. We must take this items in turn.

Greenberg's dialectic moves between known categories and unknown or faintly emerging ones. It is precisely the characteristic of new epochs that inherited patterns are inadequate for understanding them. It is doubly so when the events themselves shatter inherited beliefs and ways.

The Holocaust is such. It cannot be theologically fathomed in the terms of classical theism. Theism would try to make sense of the Holocaust as punishment for sins, for example, or as an event somehow to be understood in light of the redemptive power of innocent suffering. Both notions are ludicrous. The Holocaust cannot be fathomed on the terms of classical atheism, either. Dogma-free reason, human autonomy, and the liberal confidence in justice—all these tenets of modernity failed to stop, or even explain, this massive evil.[5] The Holocaust is a brutal breaking of past categories of understanding, and a grotesque instance of human evil crashing through past moral limits.

Differently said, the religious and cultural life of the West could not fathom the reality of the Holocaust and did not adequately prepare us either to see it coming or to prevent it. (Greenberg is keenly aware that this is true of Jews as well as of Gentiles.) The modern democratic liberalism of secular Enlightenment rationality and autonomy, and ancient Christian and Jewish traditions—all these were impotent to impede the Holocaust *or to render it meaningful after the fact*. Only as-yet-unknown categories might explain the Holocaust and an era of evil power which has outstripped past power.

At the same time, we have no choice but to use inherited categories as we wrestle with the Angel of the Night for a new identity and the hard-won blessing of understanding. We cannot start simply from "scratch"; there is no "scratch" to start from. That is, there is no place to begin which is not already a part of the communities and traditions from which we have come and which have been seared by the fires. We are condemned to use the past. It is an inevitable part of the dialectic.

Yet in light of epoch-shaking and epoch-making events, past categories must be open to radical revision. Radical revision means that the second term of the dialectic is the yet-unknown and the emergent, the admittedly frail children of human pain, searching criticism, and forced imagination.

Greenberg's dialectic thus moves between inadequate legacies at one pole and uncertain and unformed futures at the other. With a movement like this, no *final* explanations or conclusions can yet be drawn about either God or humanity. His dramatic sentence is: "After the Holocaust, there should be no final solutions, not even theological ones."[6] To one side, he repudiates those who draw conclusions from the logic of long and deeply held, but unrevised, theological notions. The German church's 1948 Darmstadt Confession, which interpreted Holocaust suffering as a divine visitation that might yet lead Jews to repeal their rejection of Christ, is a chilling example. On the other side, he dissents from those who, fully realizing the utter inadequacy of the past deep in the marrow of their bones, draw final conclusions from the shattering experience of the Holocaust. Richard Rubenstein's conviction that "Jewish history has written the *final chapter* in the terrible story of the God of history"; and that "the world will *forever* remain a place of pain . . . and *ultimate defeat*"[7] is rejected by Greenberg as an unwarranted "final [theological] solution." It is not rejected because it *may* not turn out to be true, but because we cannot know *any* epistemological finality in this axial-age moment. Auschwitz and the rebirth of Israel are the orienting events, to be sure, and all authentic and credible theological talk must account for them. Yet even they permit no absolute affirmations or denials in this bewildering, searching period. We must think *from* these events as people who are stretched between the known and unknown, as people who must reflect from within an experience which is simultaneously undeniable and incomprehensible.

With this unsettling dialectic shaping how we think, we can turn to issues of the substance of faith and morality. Faith itself is deeply affected by our age. For Greenberg, faith is "living life in the presence of the Redeemer, even when the world is unredeemed."[8] After Auschwitz there can be only "moment" faiths, however. Only "moments" exist when the Redeemer and a vision of redemption are present. And even they are crossed by times "when the flames and smoke of the burning children blot out faith."[9] Yes, moments do occur when the divine presence and vital living are fused, and redemption is fleetingly experienced. But faith is soon overwhelmed again by the powers of unredemption, by devastating nihilism and nihilistic destruction. And even when fragile faith does reassert itself, "the smoke of Auschwitz obscures the presence of God."[10]

Believers, then, have only momentary experiences of God's saving presence. The difference between the modern skeptic and the modern believer, Greenberg writes, "is frequency of faith, and not certitude of position."[11] Believers are necessarily both believers and unbelievers in our time. Theists are both theists and atheists. Believers also experience the terrible presence of God's absence.

In mandatory Jewish fashion, all this has a most concrete historical reference. It is linked to datable times and real places, tied inextricably to formative historical events. Greenberg writes:

> If the experience of Auschwitz symbolizes that we are cut off from God and hope, and that the covenant may be destroyed, then the experience of Jerusalem symbolizes that God's promises are faithful and His people live on. Burning children speak of the absence of all value—human and divine; the rehabilitation of one half million Holocaust survivors in Israel speaks of the reclamation of tremendous human dignity and value. If Treblinka makes human hope an illusion, then the Western Wall asserts that human dreams are more real than force and facts.[12]

Greenberg's theological movement is thus the intellectually and spiritually precarious enterprise of a search which moves between vital but inadequate legacies and the as-yet-unknown. It is conducted by believers who are permitted by the burden of history to have "moment faiths" only, as they live amidst religiously contradictory events.

We must add a note about the relationship of faith, thought, and action. Theological understanding and even faith itself does not happen simply by giving thought. They arise from re-creating human relationships and even re-creating the image of God itself, full in the face of all the counterevidence of massive evil. The only testimony that can still be heard, against the awful silence of God, is the affirmation of life through the concrete enactment of goodness and mercy. That means: through the building up of dignity by way of acts of caring for one another. "To talk of love and of a God who cares in the presence of burning children is obscene and incredible; to leap in and pull a child out of a pit, to clean its face and heal its body, is to make the most powerful statement—the only statement that counts."[13] Secular acts like these become the critical religious acts, and indeed the only form religious "speech" itself can credibly take now. Such acts, only "a million or billion" of which begin to right the balance of testimony "so drastically shifted by the mass weight of six million dead,"[14] are the only way to "create, save, and heal the image of God."[15] In a very real sense, the redemption of God and humanity are simultaneously at stake in simple, secular acts of moral import. Faith and understanding are bound up in the actions themselves.

In different words, there is an ethical intensification and qualification for all theological discourse and theological reality. One can only live into faith and understanding. Faith is as faith does; all the rest is talk.[16] Ethical revolutions precede dogmatic ones.

Despite these sharp breaks, some strong, crucial continuities exist for Greenberg. He speaks of "the shattered covenant," but covenant remains the core metaphor. Judaism remains an historical faith for him. Events in history bear revelatory meaning. Furthermore, Judaism continues as a religion of redemption. Greenberg clings tenaciously to his belief in the ultimate perfection of creation. He finds creation's center in a God with an elected people whose vocation is to give social embodiment to their faith, a faith lived on behalf of all the peoples of the world. These are classic Jewish tenets. Together they mean that Greenberg's wrestling with the subject of secular human power today will be indelibly theological and moral, as stamped by a profound Jewishness.

Bonhoeffer

The insights that lead Bonhoeffer to reconceive the divine presence and human agency occur while he languishes in Tegel Military Prison. "Languishes" is perhaps ill-chosen, since Bonhoeffer becomes so taken with the new perspectives on Christ and a world coming of age that extraordinary concentration, and even delight, comes over him and he takes even very turbulent times in remarkable stride. "Knowing," he writes just three weeks after the failure of the plot, "is the most thrilling thing in the world, and that's why I'm finding the work so fascinating."[17] "The work" is the new book he has begun, interrupting his intended completion of *Ethics.* The vital impetus is not so much his reading, important though it was. Rather, it is the configuration of experiences which brought him to Tegel Prison in the first place, and his reflection on those.

In the course of a decade Bonhoeffer experienced a double movement: the failure of the Confessing Church and the ecumenical church forcefully and successfully to oppose Nazism, in the one instance; and the location of the most responsible anti-Nazi action among the people of the military/political resistance, in the other. It was Bonhoeffer's family involvement in the resistance and his work on what posthumously became *Ethics* which clarified for him his own deepening participation in the conspiracy against Hitler. But it was his experience with the participants in the resistance itself which became the impulse for the new theology of the new project. He saw in the resisters the incarnation of responsibility and the morally sensitive use of power. They exhibited the consciousness and qualities of what he would, in his theological letters, describe in necessarily exploratory and tentative ways under the rubrics of "world come of age" and "nonreligious interpretation of biblical concepts." He saw in them what he would call "participation in the sufferings of God in the life of the world." Indeed he saw in them salient qualities he also saw in Jesus. And Jesus, for Bonhoeffer, is the disclosure of none other than God.

Yet many of the resisters would never have named their action religious at all nor conceived it theologically. Quite a number of these "participants with God" were utterly innocent of churchly piety. They were secular and humanist. They were morally strong of character, embodying what for Bonhoeffer becomes the key ethical term as he contemplates a new human era, namely, "responsibility toward history." This experience of the resisters, together with Bonhoeffer's disappointment with the church he cherished, generated his need to recast basic theological concepts. As he does so he interacts very little with any of his theological colleagues other than his closest friend, Eberhard Bethge. He offers only a few comments on the work of other theologians as he makes his way forward—a passing remark or two on Bultmann, Tillich, even his revered Barth. Rather, his active conversation partner is his own German past and this recent experience of massive evil. The overall subject is, as he expressed it in an essay for fellow resisters, "responsibility for the course of history,"[18] a task laid on them "by God."[19]

> The ultimate question for a responsible man to ask is not how he is to extricate himself heroically from the affair, but how the coming generation is to live. It is only from this question, with its responsibility towards history, that fruitful solutions can come, even if for the time being they are very humiliating.[20]

The church experience requires further mention. When prisoner Bonhoeffer turns to the great articles of Christian faith, he finds them "remote" and impotent, certainly not the source of immediately "fruitful solutions." The traditional words and acts—"reconciliation and redemption, regeneration and the Holy Spirit, love of our enemies, cross and resurrection, life in Christ and Christian discipleship"[21]—carry no power. They are, he says, words that are "bound to lose their force and cease." "Our being Christian today," he concludes, "will be limited to two things: prayer and righteous action. . . ."[22] "All Christian thinking, speaking, and organizing must be born anew out of this prayer and action."[23]

Bonhoeffer does not contemplate leaving the church, despite its incapacity for making sense of the present and responding to it. He even thinks the church should preserve the great articles of the faith, albeit in a certain silence during a time of renewal. There may well yet be "something quite new and revolutionary"[24] in them, he says, if they can be freed from the "religious" consciousness in which they have been soaked for centuries; and if they can find voice in a new "nonreligious" language.

It is, then, the positive experience with the resisters, in tension with the church experience, that stimulates Bonhoeffer to begin the search for the meaning of a new age of power, its relationship to God, and God's relationship to it. Bonhoeffer senses in that experience the materials of a major "break," one of theological significance.

The break is genuinely epochal for Bonhoeffer. Later uses of his thought, such as Harvey Cox's *Secular City* and William Hamilton's *Life in Stride,* have badly understated this. Bonhoeffer and his colleagues were interpreted as bold partisans of Enlightenment confidence and ardent champions of modernity. This was true only in the most carefully qualified way (see chapter 1 by Renate Bethge). Bonhoeffer was not attracted to the resisters because they were the unperplexed who were sure of their ground and clear-sighted about the future.[25] In the very essay in which he writes of what the conspirators have learned together, he asks whether "ever before in human history" there had been people "with so little ground under their feet—people to whom every available alternative seemed equally intolerable, repugnant, and futile."[26] He reports that "the great masquerade of evil has played havoc with all our ethical concepts"[27] and has undone traditional appeals to reason, principle, conscience, freedom, and virtue! "Who stands fast?" he goes on to ponder, echoing their own perplexity, and answers that only the one "who is ready to sacrifice all this" and take up risky responsibility "in faith and in exclusive allegiance to God" can get his or her bearings in such a time. He finishes with the query, "Where are these responsible people?"[28]

It is true that Bonhoeffer's mood is not really despairing—he had gotten his own bearings. But the mood is one of utter candor about a sharp break, about the stark inadequacy of the past, and about uncertainty in making a way into the future.

His own answer to the question, "Where are these responsible people?" was, in part, "in the resistance." Bonhoeffer was drawn to the resisters because they willingly took on the moral responsibility of using dangerous power at the certain risk of utter humiliation and their own lives, should they ever be found out. They risked themselves amidst a chaos in which, Bonhoeffer says,

> It will be the task . . . not to "seek great things," but to save and preserve our souls out of the chaos, and to realize that it is the only thing we can carry as a "prize" from the burning building. . . . We shall have to keep our lives rather than shape them, to hope rather than plan, to hold out rather than march forward.[29]

In "holding out," yet looking to "how the future generations might live," Bonhoeffer, like Greenberg, uses the past. He strongly affirms some important theological and moral continuities. At the same time, he asks "what we ourselves really believe"[30] of all that we have inherited. And he concludes that "we are once again being driven right back to the beginnings of our understanding."[31] The Christian cause "will be a silent and hidden affair"[32] for the foreseeable future. Being Christian will be limited to "prayer and righteous action,"[33] or "participation in the sufferings of God in the secular life."[34]

Bonhoeffer, too, then, experiences deep discontinuity. And like Greenberg, he sees religious and moral reconstruction in the form of concrete, secular acts of responsibility toward history. If what he said in 1932 was true then, it held with even greater force in 1944: "The first confession before the world is that action that immediately interprets itself."[35]

THE PRESENCE OF GOD AND THE GOD OF THE PRESENCE

We turn now to Bonhoeffer's and Greenberg's thoughts on the relationship of divine and human power.

Bonhoeffer

Bonhoeffer's overriding concern is theological. He is, to be sure, fascinated with reading that yields insight into the evolution of European culture and the character of his time, especially the demise of religious consciousness and the ascent of world-come-of-age consciousness. But his real quest is less to discover the modern world than it is to discern God-in-Christ in that world. It is knowledge of the presence of God, and the form of that presence in the world come of age, that drives Bonhoeffer.

One of the most compact theological discussions appears in the letter of 16 July 1944. Bonhoeffer traces the development of growing human autonomy, concluding that "God as a working hypothesis" has been "surmounted and abolished" in "morals, politics . . . , science . . . , philosophy and religion."[36] "Anxious souls will ask," he goes on, "what room there is left for God now"[37] and will reserve an indispensable place for God even at the cost of intellectual honesty. These religiously anxious ones will abandon "mental integrity"[38] rather than sever themselves from the security of the God-of-the-gaps. In one of the most extraordinary and suggestive passages in twentieth century theology, he continues:

> And we cannot be honest unless we recognize that we have to live in the world *etsi deus non daretur* ["even if there were no God" or "as though God did not exist"]. And this is just what we do recognize— before God! God himself compels us to recognize it. So our coming of age leads us to a true recognition of our situation before God. God would have us know that we must live as men who manage our lives without him. The God who is with us is the God who forsakes us (Mark 15:34). The God who lets us live in the world without the working hypothesis of God is the God before whom we stand continually. Before God and with God we live without God. God lets himself be pushed out of the world on to the cross. He is weak and powerless in the world, and that is precisely the way, the only way, in which he is with us and helps us. Matt. 8:17 ["This was to fulfil what was spoken by the prophet Isaiah, 'He took our infirmities and bore our diseases' "] makes it quite clear that Christ helps us, not by virtue of his omnipotence, but by virtue of his weakness and suffering.
>
> Here is the decisive difference between Christianity and all religions. Man's religiosity makes him look in his distress to the power of God in the world: God is the *deus ex machina*. The Bible directs man to God's powerlessness and suffering; only the suffering God can help. To that extent we may say that the development towards the world's coming of age outlined above, which has done away with a false conception of God, opens up a way of seeing the God of the Bible, who wins power and space in the world by his weakness. This will probably be the starting-point for our "secular interpretation."[39]

An earlier letter spoke of everything getting along without "God" and the "tutelage of 'God.' "[40] Bonhoeffer places "God" in quotation marks, indicating that this God of religion is a false God, albeit one Christians have clung to for centuries, and still do. And who is the real God, in this new era? The "Outline for a Book" asks the question straight-out and answers, in part,

> Our relation to God is not a "religious" relationship to the highest, most powerful, and best Being imaginable—that is not authentic transcendence—but our relation to God is a new life in "existence for others," through participation in the being of Jesus. The transcendental is not infinite and unattainable tasks, but the neighbour who is within reach in any given situation. God in human form.[41]

The form of the presence of God and the relationship with God and neighbor in a new historical moment are the center of attention in these late letters. The letter of 18 July states that "man is summoned to share in God's sufferings at the hands of a godless world,"[42] so "he must therefore really live in the godless world, without attempting to gloss over or explain its ungodliness in some religious way or other. He must live a 'secular' life, and *thereby* share in God's sufferings."[43] By a "secular" life Bonhoeffer means one of intense "this-worldliness." In such a life one meets God, learns faith, and becomes a human being.

In the very next letter Bonhoeffer continues his train of thought. The letter is written the day after the failed attempt to overthrow Hitler. Bonhoeffer knows of the failed putsch and must reckon with the ominous consequences for his own life. (With the letter is enclosed the poem, "Stations on the Road to Freedom," the last stanza of which is entitled "Death.") The letter is retrospective. He muses about what has been learned since the fateful decision to join the resisters, and includes this.

> I'm still discovering right up to this moment, that it is only by living completely in this world that one learns to have faith. . . . By this-worldliness I mean living unreservedly in life's duties, problems, successes and failures, experiences and perplexities. In so doing we throw ourselves completely into the arms of God, taking seriously, not our own sufferings, but those of God in the world—watching with Christ in Gethsemane. That, I think, is faith; that is *metanoia*; and that is how one becomes a man and a Christian (cf. Jer: 45!).[44]

The example of such faith is Jesus, where we learn of God.

> All that we may rightly expect from God, and ask him for, is to be found in Jesus Christ. The God of Jesus Christ has nothing to do with what God, as we imagine him, could do and ought to do. If we are to learn what God promises, and what he fulfils, we must persevere in quiet meditation on the life, sayings, deeds, sufferings, and death of Jesus.[45]

Jesus, for Bonhoeffer, is both the prototype of the person of responsible faith and the one in whom we discern the very being of God. Jesus as example comes increasingly to the fore at the same time that Bonhoeffer complains that the concrete, earthly, human Jesus is "disappearing from sight"[46] in the church. But precisely who is this Jesus?

Jesus drinks the earthly cup to the dregs and even knows utter godforsakenness. He is, in a totally exposed and unprotected way, there for others, to help them find their own strength. He turns away from the privileged, and from available power to control, in order to sit with the outcasts. He is tempted to use his God as the deus ex machina but turns back the temptation. He centers his life in an intense, trusting, and prayerful way in God. He does not require of people that they hold certain beliefs or conform to certain moral standards as a qualification of his companionship with them. He frees those whose life he shares to find their own responsible answers, and does so through participation in their sufferings. He confronts the sins of weakness in people, in order to make them strong ("Christ not only makes people 'good,'" Bonhoeffer writes, "he makes them strong, too").[47] He also confronts the sins that arise from people's strengths, in order to render power accountable to the welfare of others, including future generations. He affirms people's "health, vigour, [and] happiness" and does not "regard them as evil fruit."[48] ("Else why should he heal the sick and restore strength to the weak?" (Bonhoeffer asks.)[49] He "claims for himself and the Kingdom of God the whole of human life in all its manifestations."[50]

All this is an intensely this-worldly life, comprised of very secular, public acts. It is an ethical faith that takes its cues from Jesus' example. It is a faith discovered and lived in the specific acts of taking responsibility for history.

This is so crucial to our discussion that we must say it again, in somewhat different words. The God discerned in Jesus is consummately the suffering God who strains to render people strong and responsible. This God is, in one sense, weak and powerless in the world, yet precisely in order to draw people out so that they might muster and develop their own powers and use them for the humane world for which God yearns. God is therefore not omnipotent in the way religious people often claim and hope, using interventionist power to direct and control. Rather, God wins power and space in the world via the development and responsible exercise of human power. God fosters this through an identification with those in need of power, in order that they might become active participants in their own destiny. God is also present with those who already possess power, in order to bend them to a morally sensitive use of their power by holding them accountable for it.

The place most in need of divine empowerment is amidst human suffering, for suffering renders people powerless. There God meets people in order to tap power from them of which they were unaware, and turn their preoccupation with their own distress toward knowledge and alleviation of the sufferings of others. The suffering God who wins power in this way is the God seen in the Jew named Jesus. It is God utterly hidden in, with, and under the concrete persons, relationships, and events of this world. It is the *deus absconditus* of pathos and empowerment.

Human maturation (coming of age) means, then, the responsible use of enhanced, grave, and great human power, without recourse to an illusory dependence upon a God who will bail us out when our power goes astray. And it means the use of that power to overcome the world's suffering and its attendant powerlessness. The disabling God of religion must go, in Bonhoeffer's judgment. And it is precisely "with" and "before" the God seen in Jesus that we learn to live "without" the God of religion.[51] "The God [of Jesus] who lets us live in the world without the working hypothesis of God [the God of religion] is the God before whom we stand continually."[52]

"The God before whom we stand" is transcendent. But as the hidden and quietly empowering God, this God is "beyond in the midst of our life."[53] The transcendental is a dimension of everyday secular acts. The transcendent is discovered in actions with "the neighbor who is within reach in any given situation."[54]

In summary, the divine presence, through compassion and *mitleiden* [suffering with], works to bring to pass that strength whereby human beings regard themselves irrevocably accountable for their answers to life's questions, together with the answers chosen and acted upon. When there is failure, as there certainly will be, there is no recourse to God as an "out." Furthermore, this strength of person is turned, in the manner of Jesus, to evoking a like strength in others. It does so by "imitating" God, that is, by participating in the suffering of others and being there for them, so as to join them in the way out.

We will return to Bonhoeffer for a discussion of the moral use of power. First we must consider Greenberg's presentation of divine presence and its relationship to human power. As a faithful Jew, Greenberg thinks about the subject from the vantage point of historical experience itself.

Greenberg

"How to use the power [of the re-created Jewish state] is the new halakhah [guidance for judgments in specific circumstances], but denial or endangering the power is considered the unforgivable sin."[55] The one hundred eighty degree turn from powerlessness to power for Jews is the revolutionary turn in the religious situation—and the life situation—marking "the third great cycle" of Judaism. Attaining power distinguishes the third cycle from the preceding phase of exile and landlessness. The period of exile and landlessness exposed the massive immorality of powerlessness. Indeed, as we noted earlier, nothing less than "the sacrilege of powerlessness" was revealed in the unfathomable gruesomeness of the Holocaust. The shift from powerlessness to power is thus an imperative of the Holocaust and a normative condition for Jews in our time. It is exemplified, in the first instance, by the State of Israel. (In the modern era, when great power is concentrated, people who are stateless are defenseless.) The acquisition of power holds for the Diaspora as well; the burden of its absence was evident often enough during the centuries of exile. Powerlessness corrupts and dehumanizes, and jeopardizes survival itself.

The assumption of new and strong power permits the realization of Jewish values. The dream of a Jewish society can be realized. At the same time, the new possibilities carry all the temptations of the imperial abuse of power. Since power does indeed tend to corrupt, and absolute power corrupts absolutely, Greenberg worries mightily that Jewish power will replicate those uses of power which include bloodshed and exploitation. He is aware that many Palestinians themselves are stateless and without adequate defense against Jewish exploitation. He calls for a balancing and checking of Jewish power from without, and, internally, for "strong models and constant evocation of the memory of historic Jewish suffering and powerlessness."[56] "Memory is the key to morality,"[57] he writes, and memory of the Holocaust in particular will help enable Israel "to be a responsible and restrained conqueror."[58] Nothing quite so agitates Greenberg as the pitfalls in this pursuit of the morally responsible use of power, not least because it includes killing power. What he cannot deny, however, is the imperative of its possession. It is a requisite of Jewish survival. For this reason "endangering the power [of the State of Israel] is . . . the unforgivable sin."[59]

The subject more immediately at hand, however, is not the moral use of human power in our time, but human power and the presence of God. Still, the point first had to be made that the historical assumption of power by Jews dramatically alters their reality and experience, and is a distinguishing mark of the third great cycle. The second cycle, that of rabbinic Judaism (from the destruction of the Temple in 70 C.E. through the Holocaust) was noteworthy for Jewish powerlessness. This powerlessness deeply shaped religious life. Greenberg writes,

> The great task of religion [in the long exilic phase] was to give dignity to the powerless, to show that one also serves by standing and waiting. Martyrdom was the highest sanctification of God's name. Since the condition itself could not be changed, the stress on exile as punishment for Israel's sins was a way of asserting control over the Jews' fate, a way of reclaiming moral dignity. If only Jews would repent enough, they would be delivered so that they can perform morally responsible actions. The dignity of suffering, the hope for the world to come, the moral heroism of asceticism, penitential prayer—thousands of religious values and practices were conditioned to heal and uphold powerless Jewry.[60]

If the assumption of power is one distinguishing mark of the third cycle, another is the increased hiddenness of God. The first great cycle, biblical Judaism, knew a dramatically revealed God. The Ancient of Days was intensely present in the Temple and with the temple cult. The sacred Presence was manifest in highly specified sacred space. God was dramatically present in the thunderous words of the prophets' speech as well. "Thus saith the Lord" is the amazingly bold and confident formula of the oracles. In the first cycle God was, in short, magnificently known in cult and prophecy.

In the second cycle, rabbinic Judaism, God was less apparent, at least as the resident of a reserved and awesome space or as the source of distinctive oratory. The manifest presence of the divine was more diffuse. It was, by comparison, rather "secular." Many of the priestly cultic activities moved into family life. (The Temple sacrifice became the table blessing, for example.) And the rabbis became a more secular leadership than either priests or prophets were. They achieved their status through learning rather than ordination, and their sacramental duties were (and are) no different from those of other Jews. The synagogue became a distinctive institutional center, to be sure, but it did not (and does not) carry the aura of the Temple as the dwelling place of the Holy One. The rabbis are by no means consistent secularizers, but—and this is the point—there is "a percentage shift"[61] that heightens the role of human power and action in the covenant of redemption, and diminishes the manifest presence of God in favor of a more hidden one.

Greenberg's discussion includes a fascinating example:

> The Rabbis recognized that God's withdrawal and their own new authority meant that an event such as the Exodus in which God directly intervened would not occur again. This led them to postulate a new central redemptive event for their age. The Rabbis saw Purim as the redemptive paradigm for the post-destruction world. In the Purim story, the Jewish people in exile after the first destruction is threatened with genocide. The nation is saved by the actions of Esther and Mordecai. Operating as fallible and flawed human redeemers, the two manage, by court intrigues and bedroom politics, to save the Jewish people and win permission for the Jews to fight off their enemies. The Rabbis point out that the story of Esther marks the end of redemptive miracles; it is not a miracle, it is a natural event. In justifying the new holiday of Purim, the Rabbis connect Esther's name to the Biblical verse "I (the Lord) will hide (*asteer* in Hebrew, closely resembling the word *Esther*) my face on that day." God's name does not appear in the book of Esther, yet this hidden presence is the redemptive force which the people acknowledge. In an incredibly bold analogy, the Rabbis go one step beyond comparing Purim to Sinai as a moment of covenant acceptance. They say acceptance of the covenant at Sinai was "coerced" by the manifest miracles of God and would not be legally binding today. However, on Purim the Jewish people reaccepted that covenant by recognizing God's presence and salvation in the guise of the secular redemption. This acceptance was binding because it occurred in the context of a world in which God does not split the sea but works in mysterious ways through human redeemers. Thus, the reacceptance of the covenant is legally the equivalent of the Jewish people's maturation and the acknowledgment of their new responsibilities.[62]

The rabbis' achievement in the second great cycle was enormous. They renewed the covenant when land, kingship, and temple were all lost, and when a condition of relative political powerlessness had somehow to be united with the reality of a more hidden or withdrawn God. All this was necessary in order to give coherence to the drastic discontinuity in Jewish experience. Drastic discontinuity on a similar scale marks the third and current period. It is the end of almost two thousand years of exile. It begins with the greatest offense in history, the Holocaust, and moves from that ground zero of Jewish powerlessness to the acquisition of power in the State of Israel. It is marked as well by the increased political activity of Jews elsewhere. The third period thus differs from the second in the shift from powerlessness at the extreme of near extinction to new power in a form Jews have not known since the biblical era.

At the same time, the divine presence is more hidden than ever, moving about under the guise of secular human acts. "Religious activity itself must be profoundly immersed in the secular, where God is hidden. In fact, this has been the primary thrust of Jewish activity since 1945."[63]

Whatever we say, then, about God's power and human agency turns on the increased hiddenness of God in this era and the concrete need to solve the problems of power and daily life.[64] Greenberg pursues this theme under the rubric of "holy secularity."

Holy secularity is a restatement of what we stressed earlier: humanity and the image of God are re-created in the face of overwhelming evil by acts of caring. One by one these acts generate value and harbor redemption. Here we emphasize that they are chiefly secular acts in altogether secular enterprises. They address "the neighbor who is at hand in any given situation" (Bonhoeffer's words).[65] Greenberg is as likely to look to the Jewish voluntary organizations for signs of redemption as he is to the synagogue, or to the Knesset and United Jewish Appeal. The laity obviously carry the heaviest load, since the critical "religious" tasks are immersed in secular tasks. These are the tasks of society building, social justice, human politics, and all that belongs to everyday commerce. In a word, the religious enterprise focuses "on the mundane."[66] This is a "holy secularity" in which the former reality-categories of sacred and secular are simply undone. "*Every* act of life becomes potentially holy, the locus of the hidden Divine Presence."[67]

What of God and holy secularity? God is more hidden, yes; but at the same time, God is in more places. God's presence is throughout the secular order.[68] In what way? Greenberg's reply is to point to a God who suffers and who urges human responsibility for the realization of redemption. He writes,

> The divine is experienced neither as the intervening, commanding One of the Bible, nor the law-giving Partner of the Rabbinic experience but as the everpresent Presence of our era. "I [God] am with him in trouble" (Psalm 91:15) means that where Israel suffers, God is present, suffering with God's people. The answer to the question "Where was God at Auschwitz?" is: God was there starving, beaten, humiliated, gassed and burned alive, sharing the infinite pain as only an infinite capacity for pain can share it.

A presence need not formally command. Indeed, it does not command if a command means an order in words from the outside. The fact that I relate to the presence of God means that I sense more clearly the expectations, I feel more obligation and motivation and I am more deeply moved than any words or formalized commands can express. If God did not stop the murder and the torture, then what was the statement made by the infinitely suffering Divine Presence in Auschwitz? It was a cry for action, a call to humans to stop the Holocaust, a call to the people Israel to rise to a new, unprecedented level of covenantal responsibility. It was as if God said: "Enough, stop it, never again, bring redemption!" The world did not heed that call and stop the Holocaust. European Jews were unable to respond. World Jewry did not respond adequately. But the response finally did come with the creation of the State of Israel. The Jews took on enough power and responsibility to act. And this call was answered as much by so-called secular Jews as by the so-called religious. Even as God was in Treblinka, so God went up with Israel to Jerusalem. Says the Talmud: "Whenever Israel was exiled, the Shechinah was with them . . . in Egypt, in Babylon. Even so, when they will be redeemed in the future, the Divine Presence will be with them, as it is said, 'the Loving God, your Lord shall come back with your captivity.'" It does not say "shall bring back" but rather "shall come back" which teaches that the Holy One, blessed be He, comes back with them from the exile. This is the answer to Richard Rubenstein's argument that God cannot be absolved of the Holocaust yet credited with the rebirth of Israel. God is involved with both events in the same way.[69]

How is God "involved with both events in the same way"? God is a suffering Presence who is dependent upon human power and responsibility for the redemption which this very Presence urges and cries out for. God struggles mightily against evil and for good through that human power which chooses life. God, in Greenberg's striking commentary on the rabbis, comes back with the captives in their return from powerlessness to power, rather than bringing them back. Everything, including the realization of God's yearnings, depends on human power and its employ. Everything, to recall Bonhoeffer, "turns on man."[70]

To assert that everything depends on human power and its employ takes our discussion to the last of the elements listed as the dynamics of Greenberg's thought—the hiddenness of the divine, the sacrilege of powerlessness, holy secularity, and the commitment to a shattered covenant.

The shattering of the covenant in the Holocaust leads Greenberg to rethink this most basic metaphor of Jewish life. The Holocaust and the rise of the State of Israel mean a period of crisis and transformation in the understanding of covenant. The covenant is now a "voluntary covenant." What this means requires some explanation.

The central teaching of Judaism, like Christianity, is redemption.[71] God's covenants have this redemption as their goal—the realization of "the total possibility of being."[72] The covenant with the Jews, like the covenant with the whole planet (God's covenant with Noah), shares this quest for the perfection of all life.

But the roles of the covenant partners have changed. The logic of covenantal partnership has been present from the beginning: human beings join God in the drama of creating a world which reflects the possibilities of redemption. Yet the character of God as the manifest, powerful, initiating, and intervening God of biblical Judaism (the first cycle) is no longer the way of the divine partner. The Holocaust shattered that. Another understanding of partnership must be considered, if partnership still exists at all.

The rabbis, in the second great cycle of Judaism, viewed the covenant as essentially pedagogical. *Shutafut,* partnership, is a motif word in rabbinic literature.[73] It was interpreted to mean that following the destruction of the Temple and the dispersal of the peoples from the land, God was calling Jews to develop the covenant in ways they had not before. There were new roles to play, new responsibilities to take on, new ways to learn.

Greenberg extends the rabbinic legacy, and continues to see covenant as a pedagogy in the service of human redemption. He also presses the unchanged logic of covenant, "that to reach redemption, humans must come to act with full responsibility for their fate."[74] But the Holocaust has reversed the roles of the covenant partners. To be more precise, the Holocaust is the terrible occasion for painfully reconsidering the covenant; and the reconsideration of a covenant in crisis itself leads to the reversed roles. There is no substitute for citing Greenberg directly and at length on this matter.

> If the covenant is not over, then what does the Holocaust reveal about the nature of the covenant? What is the message to us when the Divine Presence was in Auschwitz, suffering, burning, starving yet despite the most desperate pleas, failing to stop the Holocaust?

> The Divine Presence need not speak through prophets or Rabbis. The Presence speaks for itself. If the message of the Destruction of the Temple was that the Jews were called to greater partnership and responsibility in the covenant, then the Holocaust is an even more drastic call for total Jewish responsibility for the covenant. If after the Temple's destruction,

Israel moved from junior participant to true partner in the covenant, then after the Holocaust, the Jewish people is called upon to become the senior partner in action. In effect, God was saying to humans: you stop the Holocaust. You bring the redemption. You act to ensure that it will never again occur. I will be with you totally in whatever you do, wherever you go, whatever happens, but you must do it.[75]

The Holocaust is thus the occasion (not cause) for understanding that in our era human beings must come of age. They must become fully responsible, covenantal agents. Greenberg, continuing the analogy, uses the image of parenting. The ultimate logic of parenting is to raise children to address life's challenges with their own strengths and take responsibility for their own actions.

Greenberg calls this changed covenant "voluntary." But what precisely does "voluntary" mean? The power of the notion is again best conveyed by direct citation.

The fundamental shift in the nature of the covenant can be put yet another way. It can no longer be commanded. Covenantally speaking, one cannot *order* another to step forward to die. One can give an order like this to an enemy, but in a moral relationship, one cannot demand the giving up of the other's life. One can *ask* such a sacrifice, but one cannot order it. To use another image of Elie Wiesel's: when God gave us a mission, that was all right. But God failed to tell us that it was a suicide mission. One cannot *order* another to go on a suicide mission. Out of shared values, one can only ask for volunteers. Similarly, God can no longer enforce or educate for the covenant by punishment. The most horrifying punishments threatened in the Torah for failing to live up to the covenant pale by comparison with what was done in the Holocaust. All Jews now know that by being Jewish they expose not only themselves but their children and even grandchildren to ultimate danger and agony. No divine punishment can enforce the covenant, for there is no risked punishment so terrible that it can match the punishment risked by continuing faithfulness to the covenant. If the Jews keep the covenant after the Holocaust, then it can no longer be for the reason that it is commanded or because it is enforced by reward or punishment.[76]

Many Jews do keep the covenant after the Holocaust. They remain so committed to the dream of redemption that they volunteer to carry on as Jews, despite the fact that to do so is to risk danger and even death. Indeed, this is the renewal of the covenant; but it is now a voluntary covenant in which the human partners take on full responsibility for redemption as commensurate with the powers in their hands. They take on responsibility even for the Messiah!

A messiah who is triumphant and does it all for Israel would be utterly inappropriate in such an age [as ours]. The arrival of such a messiah would be morally outrageous, for the Messiah would have come at the wrong time. As Elie Wiesel has written, if any messiah was going to redeem us by divine strength, then the time to have come was during the Holocaust. Any Messiah who could have come and redeemed us, and did not do so then but chooses to come now is a moral monster. Wiesel is right: it is too late for the Messiah to come. *Therefore we will have to bring the Messiah.* Bringing the Messiah is the crowning response to the divine call for humans to take full responsibility in the covenant.[77]

Greenberg's striking formulations are those of a renewed covenant. Bonhoeffer's formulations, as those of a Christian theologian, are quite different, though equally striking: "God lets himself be pushed out of the world on to the cross."[78] Yet the forceful point is the same: "the divine call for humans to take full responsibility."[79]

This creative theological recasting brings us right up against the hard reality that preoccupies both men and that earlier was edging into our discussion: the moral use of power.

THE MORAL USE OF POWER

The provocation for this chapter is not Bonhoeffer and Greenberg per se, helpful and intriguing as they are, but rather the heightened state of human power in the waning years of the twentieth century and what that portends for the coming millennium. This enhanced power manifests itself in the arenas cited at the outset of this chapter. It is important to recall this because the discussion of Bonhoeffer and Greenberg which now ensues makes no claim to cover the full range of the powers mentioned or speak to all the issues implied. We must keep faith with Bonhoeffer's and Greenberg's discussions and not insist they address matters they never intended to. They do, however, share a strikingly similar judgment about the general relationship of divine presence and the use of human power. That commonality is a good point at which to enter a more specific treatment of one kind of power. The following passage is Greenberg's. With alterations, it might also have been Bonhoeffer's.

Today we live after the Holocaust. This event is a clear signal that the Divine will not intervene to save miraculously. In this event is a divine call to humanity to take up full responsibility for accomplishing the covenant and for stopping the forces of evil. Those who disregard reality considerations in their actions—including calculation of the balance of power and the effects of policies—and those who ignore the pragmatics of moral stands and of "trust in God"—are guilty of irresponsibility and of deafness to divine instruction. Repeating the prophetic dicta that make possession of the land conditional on obedience and a pre-set standard of perfection, constitutes not upholding Divine authority but an attempt to hold God to an earlier stage of relationship. Such views are regressive in that they forgo a responsibility now being offered to humans and pass it back to God. This borders on clinging to infantilization or child-like behavior in the face of being called to adulthood.[80]

The specific power that Greenberg and Bonhoeffer address is state power and the use of force, including deadly force. That is only one instance of power, although it is a common one and an inclusive one. Its use is always perplexing from a moral point of view. Given the judgment of Greenberg and Bonhoeffer that the divine presence is now channeled into the reality of the secular human use of power, such morally dangerous political power is, from a religious point of view, genuinely awesome.

As earlier, we will treat each figure in turn.

Greenberg

The relationship of religious to moral is a direct and intimate one for Rabbi Greenberg, as the previous quotation makes clear. The agonizing issue, a religious one, is the moral exercise of power in a blatantly unredeemed world, as lived in the presence of a Redeemer who now invests human responsibility with the work of redemption itself. A certain critical test is the exercise of power in Israel, since the State of Israel is the locus of a great redemptive act of our time and the opportunity, after millennia, for the realization of Jewish values through the Jewish exercise of newly acquired power.

Greenberg is keenly aware of how the human condition and human experience impinge upon the exercise of power. He avoids any notion of inherent Jewish exceptionalism, and warns Jews that they will repeat historic patterns of oppression unless they remember well their own experience as victims of oppressive power. He is acutely aware that wielding dominant power invariably dulls moral sensitivity and serves selfishly utilitarian ends. It easily falls prey to beguiling ideologies which sanctify the power-wielders' own ways as necessary and just when they may well be neither. Not least—and complicating an already treacherous moral landscape—the exercise of morally responsible power cannot be carried out in a morally pure manner.

The boundaries of the moral use of power in an unredeemed world are succinctly stated in his 1988 essay, "The Ethics of Jewish Power": "Here, then, are the parameters of the new condition. Jewish powerlessness is absolutely incompatible with Jewish existence. But Jewish power is incompatible with absolute Jewish moral purity."[81] In a passage even more reminiscent of Reinhold Niebuhr than Dietrich Bonhoeffer,[82] Greenberg continues,

> Moral maturity consists of grasping both these truths without evasion or illusion. Moral responsibility consists of the continuous struggle to contain both truths without letting them paralyze either the will to power or our moral faculties. To take power is to give up innocence and take up greater responsibility. If we understand that we are pledged to the covenant of life for everyone and that we are accountable to a Divine covenantal partner who dwells "with the oppressed and humble in spirit," then we will be more self-critical and humane in the exercise of strength.[83]

But what is the morally responsible way to exercise strength, given both the impossibility of innocence and the simultaneous accountability to a divine partner? With due recognition that Greenberg's work is still in process, we lift the following from his discussion.

• Jews "must have access to the kind of power and guaranteed haven that only a government and an army can provide."[84] At the same time, power tends to corrupt. Thus the historical challenge to exercise newly acquired power justly "must be taken with eyes open."[85]

Greenberg's discussion includes a tantalizing exegesis of the Jacob and Esau tale, a story that underlines the moral precariousness and turbulence of wielding deadly power. When Jacob, Israel's ancestral father, paused in his flight and turned to defend himself against his brother Esau and Esau's advancing armies, the record states that "Jacob feared and was greatly distressed" (Gen. 32:7). "Jacob feared," the rabbis commented, because he might be killed, and he was "greatly distressed" because he might kill others.[86] Moral necessity is often without any clear winners, and is deeply ambiguous.

• The renunciation of power by Jews (and Christians) has often been glorified and romanticized. Without intending a comparison, Greenberg echos the kind of remark Augustine made about the innocence of a baby: "The moral purity of victims is often a function of the fact they have no power to inflict evil."[87] Faced with the impossibility of wielding power, and experiencing the oppressive uses of power, Jews often subscribed to religious views that renounced power as evil, as Christians with parallel experience have. While this is understandable, it effectively abandons the ancient Jewish vocation of using power to help model a society faithful to God and symbolic of the possibilities for all human communities. Moral purity came to mean the renunciation of power rather than a morally responsible use of it.

• The dilemmas of power are far different from the problems of powerlessness, and the experience of the latter is an inadequate pedagogy for the former. "Religions legitimately play their classic role of comforting the afflicted by focusing on such teachings as the dignity of the powerless, the preciousness of suffering, the moral heroism of renunciation and asceticism."[88] Yet these are often counterproductive for the appropriation and exercise of power. Indeed, their actual impact has frequently meant that the wielding of power has been given over to those with the fewest qualms about its use.

• If "the truly moral do not avoid stain by not exercising power,"[89] are there moral measures for its use? Greenberg subscribes to what in both the Greco-Roman legacy and the Christian traditions are called "just war" criteria. We need not list the criteria,[90] only Greenberg's general position and his example. Morally sensitive persons act,

> But only when necessary [and they seek] to reduce suffering caused by their actions to the minimum. The firm moral principle is that *given the evil that cannot be avoided, there is still an ideal way of exercising power.* A moral army uses no more force than necessary. If it uses less force than necessary, and fails, it betrays those it seeks to protect or its own soldiers who died in vain. If the amount of force necessary is unclear, then willingness to take losses to avoid causing innocent suffering is the ethical test.[91]

Just-war criteria can thus be used to help discern "the ideal way of exercising power" in an unredeemed world. (The term "just war" is unfortunate, not only because it seems to justify war in principle, but because the criteria are to govern any use of potentially deadly force, not only instances of war.)

• "In a perfect world, there will be no gap between reality and principle, which is why Judaism strives to bring the Messiah. In the interim, the good is often advanced by a morally ambiguous process."[92] Sometimes, Greenberg observes, moral acts produce immoral side effects while flawed ones yield good results. The moral test, then, is that of results. Is there less suffering, on balance? Is there a discernible increased good, on balance? At the same time, sheer utility and a thoroughgoing "realism" are not acceptable. They render the inescapable moral ambiguity not only normal but normative, not only common but acceptable. They thereby abandon or disregard the "continual refreshment of judgement through exposure to prophetic norms."[93] For Greenberg the moral course requires both the harsh exposure of the prophets' vision and knowledge that responsible actions invariably entail guilt. "Show me a people whose hands are not dirty and I will show you a people which has not been responsible. Show me a people which has stopped washing its hands and admitting its guilt, and I will show you a people which is arrogant and morally dying."[94]

• Given both the propensities of power to corrupt and the necessity of wielding it for the achievement of any historical good, the most effective ethical structure is the balance of power.[95] "To put it in classic Jewish theological terms: only God's power is absolute (and God has waived that power through commitment to operating through covenant!)."[96] Evil flows from imbalanced power. The balance should be both external (between states) and internal (between centers of power within the state).[97]

• While the balance of power is the desirable ethical structure, it must be yoked to Jewish moral utopianism and the Jewish "pragmatic methodology of perfectionism."[98] This cherished combination, already experienced in the Exodus and the covenant, is the difficult synthesis of moral vision, hard-headed analysis, and the practical steps necessary to move incrementally toward the desired goals.

• The classic Jewish belief in the perfectability of humanity (moral utopianism), and the commitment to a balance of power, should be supplemented with the memory of Jewish suffering. Memory increases empathy "for those who are oppressed or those who will suffer because of Jewish exercise of power."[99] "To encourage Jews to turn Arabs into refugees or into victims is to continue the Holocaust, not oppose it," Greenberg says in a remarkable response to Meir Kahane's rhetorical use of the Holocaust to advocate banishing the enemy by brute force.[100]

• With respect to the State of Israel, power must be exercised in view of two compelling elements in tension with one another. At the one pole, the responsible use of power bends to the realities and requirements of being a normal state in an unredeemed world. At the other pole, power is responsible to a covenant that imposes special expectations upon Jews.

The former—Israel as a normal state—means there must be no double standard. Israel cannot be required to abide by moral standards other nations do not expect of themselves and will not hold to. "Since Israel is functioning in the real world, its morality must be exercised and judged in that arena."[101] Greenberg's moral radar is extremely sensitive here. He senses the anti-Semitism of double standards, even among well-meaning Jews.

> If you insist that Israel's right to exist *depends* on its being perfect then you are making common cause with the anti-Semites. If your self-image as a Jew demands that Israel *never* be morally compromised, in whatever way, then you are making common cause with the anti-Semites. Obviously, there is a difference whether the individual making those absolute judgments is a sworn enemy of the Jewish people or a devoted and spiritual Jew who cannot abide the limits of the flesh. Imposing absolute messianic demands on flesh and blood people in an unredeemed world does not bring the Messiah closer; rather it endangers the fragile first blossoms of Jewish redemption.[102]

Greenberg goes on to say that the moral perfectionists fail to understand the nature of spirituality itself, and the vocational task of Jews. Any embodiment of the ideal, which must be held to on theological grounds, has to be an embodiment that respects human finitude and creatureliness.

> Those who insist on an absolutely spiritually superior Israel and are embarrassed by the moral ambiguities of the actual Jewish body politic, show how little they understand spirituality. There must be a body to embody ideals. Even in its cloddish or earthiest moments, this particular body's existence in defiance of the forces of hatred and history is a testimony to the Hidden God's concern and a tribute to the infinite commitment to life of a people. By existing and overcoming death, the survival of Israel's body points to the legitimacy of covenantal hope and the power of the transcendent.[103]

None of this attack on a double standard denies the existence of a rigorous moral standard rooted in Jewish covenantal values. But now that Israel is a flesh-and-blood state, Israel can only be properly judged by other nations in the context of their shared world, with all its attendant constraints and possibilities. Israel may, in that context and in accord with its own demanding moral heritage, "be five percent better, or ten percent more restrained, perhaps twenty percent more judgmental of its own behavior than the rest of the world."[104] If so, the achievement would make Israel a shining star among the nations, a city set on a hill. But this begins to approach the limits of survivability, Greenberg says.

> Put it this way: If Israel proves to be ten percent better ethically than the rest of the world, it will be "a light unto the nations." If it proves to be twenty-five percent better, it will bring the Messiah. [If it] is fifty percent better, it will be dead.[105]

No group can survive in this world if it acts fifty percent better than the rest![106]

Reinhold Niebuhr, the Christian theologian whose views on morality and power most closely approximate Greenberg's, expresses this sentiment also:

> So nations crucify their moral rebels with their criminals on the same Golgatha, not being able to distinguish between the moral idealism which surpasses, and the anti-social conduct which falls below that moral mediocrity on the level of which every society unifies its life.[107]

This sketch on the moral use of power does great injustice to Greenberg's detailed discussion of current cases and policies—the very stuff of which power decisions are made and the very place power is exercised. It is hardly consolation that we will commit the same injustice for Bonhoeffer! We must simply assume that by now the reader has some familiarity with Bonhoeffer's involvement in the political-military resistance.

Bonhoeffer

Most of the pertinent texts are gathered in the section entitled, "The Structure of Responsible Life," in *Ethics*. Bonhoeffer's writing, often done between assignments for the resistance movement, was necessarily disguised so as not to endanger the goals of the resistance and the lives of its members. Nonetheless, a retrospective reading by anyone who knows the history of these days and Bonhoeffer's part in it will recognize his reflection on the efforts to secure and use power. The implications about the morality of power are readily at hand, just one layer beneath the surface.

Without neglecting Bonhoeffer's immediate context and the decisions of the day, we will concentrate on those aspects of power and morality which pertain to more than Hitler alone. To see Bonhoeffer's posture of the Christian vis-à-vis state power in general is thus the goal. (The specific case of the coup d'état and the moral guidelines for that attempted use of power are discussed in chapter 3.)

Bonhoeffer characteristically rules out two extremes as positions responsible people might take in their use of political power. He gives these extremes different names in different discussions: "servility" and "revolt,"[108] "compromise" (meaning capitulation to evil forces) and "radicalism,"[109] "sanction" and "destruction."[110] All these chart two unacceptable courses: that of uncritical acceptance of the given state of affairs on the one hand, and full-scale revolution and anarchism on the other. In "The Structure of Responsible Life," Bonhoeffer expresses the dichotomy as follows.

The origin of action which accords with reality is not the pseudo-Lutheran Christ who exists solely for the purpose of sanctioning the facts as they are, nor the Christ of radical enthusiasm whose function is to bless every revolution, but it is the incarnate God Jesus who has accepted man and who has loved, condemned and reconciled man and with him the world.[111]

On the face of it, this seems to indicate a sober middle course as the way the responsible person uses power. Bonhoeffer does indeed say that the responsible person does not know "absolute good" or have "ultimate knowledge of good and evil" as does "ideological man."[112] Rather, the responsible person prefers the relatively better to the relatively worse, assesses in light of the present possibilities, and follows through with an eye to the future. Sobriety, realism, and a measure of pragmatism belong to this course.[113] The tone is evident in Bonhoeffer's comment that "one's task is not to turn the world upside down, but to do what is necessary at the given place and with a due consideration of reality."[114]

Yet to imagine this course as some golden mean or cautious pragmatism would miss both Bonhoeffer's own experience and his reflection on it. The responsible Christian citizen rules out extremes as the normal and the normative patterns and procedures for the use of power. But they are not ruled out as exceptional instances of Christian action brought on by hard necessity. In fact, Bonhoeffer insists that the Christian life be open to vitually every possibility and demonstrate what he called "an elasticity of behavior"[115] which faith itself demands. His reason, as always, is a christological one—the "extremes" of the life of Christ set the basic framework for the Christian life. Thus some actions will be in accord with "incarnation" (affirmation and cooperation), some in accord with "crucifixion" (judgment and rejection), and some in accord with "resurrection" (bold creativity and newness). Only by "living unreservedly in life's duties, problems, successes and failures, experiences and perplexities," [116] can one know which use of power is the appropriate one, including extreme expressions. Thus Bonhoeffer does not exclude exceptional, extremist actions as occasional necessities. He does, however, refuse to make them the binding moral norms and the normal way of using power. They may be crucial actions, but that does not make them normative. The exception is real, but it is not the rule.

The political-military conspiracy was an instance of the necessary extremist exception. Bonhoeffer's was not a normal time, and the circumstances he knew were not normal circumstances. So he writes of "the deed of free responsibility" as a courageous venture of power which simultaneously violates the law of the civil order and conforms to "the form of Christ in the world" (or, to "reality," to use his parallel phrasing). This is Bonhoeffer's rationale for conspiracy. It is not co-incidental that it appears in the limited remarks on "statecraft" and, within this, among comments on the breaking of civil law. His remarks are few, but there is no mistaking their meaning.

> In the course of historical life there comes a point where the exact observance of a formal law of a state . . . suddenly finds itself in violent conflict with the ineluctable necessities of the lives of men; at this point responsible and pertinent action leaves behind it the domain of principle and convention, the domain of the normal and regular, and is confronted by the extraordinary situation of ultimate necessities, a situation which no law can control.[117]

Obeying law is a strong moral boundary for Bonhoeffer, but not an ultimate or final one. And when the deed of free responsibility is called for, it is to be carried out with full resolution, even though illegal.

That the unlawful deed is a moral boundary is clear when Bonhoeffer moves into a discussion of the acceptance of guilt and freedom. "From what has just been said it emerges that the structure of responsible action includes both readiness to accept guilt and freedom."[118]

The reason for Christian citizens' taking on guilt is a christological one. Jesus did not seek first of all to be good or to preserve his own moral innocence. Rather, he freely took upon himself the guilt of others. Responsible persons should do the same.[119]

Bonhoeffer is deeply aware of a difference, however. The responsible Germans who now take on the guilty use of deadly power are not, unlike Jesus, innocent. So Bonhoeffer writes of the guilt of his church, his nation, and his class. In fact, to be historically complicit in this collective guilt and then not to plot Hitler's overthrow but instead attempt to save some measure of moral innocence amidst such guilt by not supporting tyrannicide only compounds the guilt. Not to attempt the overthrow would, in these circumstances, be morally per-verse. Furthermore it would actually be the abandonment of one's own humanity: "If any man tries to escape guilt in responsibility he detaches himself from the ultimate reality of human existence."[120]

In the surreal world of Nazism, this reasoning and action leads to bizarre and repulsive results, and Bonhoeffer knew it. Attaining the necessary power meant mimicking Nazi behavior in order to disguise the resistance, which was lodged in high places in the Nazi institutions themselves. It meant lying and other forms of deception. It meant uses of power in ways that ran full grain against the moral dispositions of the resisters themselves.[121] This and more stands behind seemingly abstract lines like these:

> Whether an action arises from responsibility or from cynicism is shown only by whether or not the objective guilt of the violation of the law is recognized and acknowledged, and by whether or not, precisely in this violation, the law is hallowed. It is in this way that the will of God is hallowed in the deed which arises from freedom.[122]

In a certain sense, then, the use of power at the extremes falls almost entirely upon the character of responsible people who are willing to act in an awesome freedom. There are few moral guides. The required actions violate or conflict with most of the guides that do exist. Most everything depends upon the kinds of persons these exercisers of power are.

The moral guides that are available are instances of "just war" criteria. They are important and have a degree of "objectivity." (See the chapter 3, "Resistance," for the detailed list.) Yet so very much is governed by personal character instead.

Bonhoeffer knew responsible persons of character in the resistance and in his family. Some were Christians, some were not. They acted for others, for themselves, and for the nation even when discovery of their actions would mean certain death. They bore the weight of guilt which accumulated because of the crimes committed in Germany's name, above all, the mass murder of the Jews. They took this guilt upon themselves, knowing it was also theirs. They undertook the necessary but horrendous task of plotting the overthrow of their government, even though conspiracy was contrary to all they considered the normal bearing of peace-loving citizens.

Bonhoeffer does not romanticize the conspirators. In fact, the conspiracy for him is an act of repentance, as it was for some of them.[123] But he does see in them the moral use of dangerous power and the kind of consciousness we have called world-come-of-age consciousness.[124] They longed for the day when their exercise of power could be intrinsic to the normal functioning of a reasonably just social order. Many of them would probably have understood neither their present extraordinary action nor their hoped-for future action theologically, as Bonhoeffer did. But for him they were part of the epochal drama of our time, when none less than God would have us learn the moral use of unprecedented human power. They may not have formulated it so, but they helped show that "before God and with God we live without God." Or, in Greenberg's citing of the rabbis, the presence of the divine is such that the Holy One does not bring them back from exile but comes back with them.

The Holy One, coming back with them—this is the relationship of divine presence and human power today. "Responsibility toward history" (Bonhoeffer) is the way God is present in new human powers. It becomes the primary ethical category for North Americans now.

8

AN ETHIC OF THE CROSS

CONCLUSIONS

It may seem curious to begin with conclusions. But these assertions also serve to orient the reader for all that follows. It seems best to unfold the map and issue fair warning about the journey.

- For historical reasons the ethics of the theology of the cross (*theologia crucis*) have been badly underdeveloped. Dietrich Bonhoeffer is an improvement upon Martin Luther, but further changes are needed.
- The theology of the cross radically alters some common notions of "ethics." Ethics does not address the movement from vice to virtue but from vice and virtue combined to the "realization of reality" (Bonhoeffer).
- This means that the point of departure for Christian ethics is not an analysis of the human condition, or patterns of character and conduct in the world, or our knowledge of good and evil, whether innate or acquired. The point of departure is the new creation in Jesus Christ as Lord.
- Christian faith means living in and with the "old aeon" on the terms of the "new." This is the source of the unrelenting tension in the relationship of Christ and culture. For us neither the formulation of that relationship by Ernst Troeltsch nor its elaboration by H. Richard Niebuhr is the most helpful.
- The "imitation of Christ" is the most promising and most underdeveloped dimension of the theology of the cross. It has been frustrated by continued Constantinian assumptions on the part of those who have held a theology of the cross. Bonhoeffer's own struggle here is significant for us.

144

• A Christology that is not simultaneously a social ethic is not a biblical Christology.

• An ecclesiology that is not simultaneously a social ethic is not a biblical ecclesiology.

• Against the North American theology of glory (*theologia gloriae*) of bourgeois optimism and its religion of legitimation and human "coping," the theology of the cross (*theologia crucis*) understands Christ existing as community as the church's societal vocation; and the way of the cross, especially messianic suffering, is the strong musical line (*cantus firmus*) in a celebration of the full range of human experience.

INTRODUCTION

While on a sojourn in East Africa I read Douglas John Hall's *Lighten Our Darkness*.[1] Hall's Canadian perspective is a devastating critique of North American culture and North American enculturated Christianity. The critique was only reinforced by my days in Tanzania, Kenya, and then South Africa. But since I already stood in basic agreement with Hall's assessment, my attention turned with anticipation to his constructive proposal: "Toward an Indigenous Theology of the Cross" (the volume's subtitle).

Hall essentially asks two questions: (1) Can the theology of the cross be sustained, that is, does it invariably resolve itself into a theology of glory? (2) Is the theology of the cross adequate ground for a viable social ethic? Does it not invariably lead to ethical quietism and passivity?

Hall's questions are the right ones, and Bonhoeffer, little used by Hall, assists constructively in responding to them. In the process Bonhoeffer provides cues for North Americans and an ethic of the cross appropriate to our setting.

THE SETTING

Junk mail can sometimes be revelatory, yielding insight into North American society and refracting the culture's working theology. One of the items in the day's pile was from DATALERT, "a newsletter interpreting events, trends, and views for religious leaders." It included the following:

REAGAN AND OPTIMISM

If your organization is troubled, you may want to take a leaf from President Reagan's book and give special attention to building optimism among your people. The "key-note" of the inaugural address combined with comments by persons in the new administration suggests that early actions will be almost as much addressed to the goal of building American confidence as to goals of specific improvements in various programs. That goal has classically been a concern of Presidents, and it is probably essential at present—even if it does later complicate judgments on how well any specific economic program worked (it will always be possible that the sheer increase in confidence created a positive change, not the economic program). In any event, there is a manifest desire in the American public to have its confidence restored.

Certainly our religious tradition testifies to the importance of symbol and attitude in affecting real change. Further, it always seems that when confronted with serious problems, those organizations handle them best that start with the conviction that they are able to solve their difficulties. Optimism about eventual outcome seems to be a human requirement for heavy investment of effort and self.[2]

This is an authentic expression of a dominant tone in a strong segment of North American culture. With a little bravado, it would be an adequate expression of triumphalistic bourgeois optimism, buttressed by "our religious tradition" and the irrepressible requirements of human nature. Yet there is a certain measured tone in the text. It knows of "troubled" waters and "serious problems" and, indeed, is written as counsel for flagging organizations with a sagging esprit de corps.

The text can be interpreted on the basis of Hall's work. The point of the interpretation is that the working theology of much of both North American culture and Christianity is a "theology of glory."

Our lives happen somewhere between our actual experience and our expectations. We exist in a space somewhere between our lived history and our fervent hopes. The cultural ethos and ideology of socioeconomically privileged North America has built a secondary world of expectations in this space. It has been named "progress," or gathered other labels of upward historical mobility. This creation is reflective of the master image of humanity regnant since the Enlightenment, the image of mastery itself. Humanity as master in history is the short form for the awesome point where widespread silent assumptions about life all converge. The opening up of new worlds everywhere, the exhilarating explorations of new territories, of outer space as well as psychic space, would have generated credence enough.

But the heady and unbounded confidence that came with the transforming power of scientific knowledge and technological application clinched the lived conviction that we could have a world of our own making, on our own terms. "Organization" replaced "nature" as our immediate environment, to recall Bonhoeffer's description, and "technical" rather than "spiritual" means became the mode of human conquest.[3] The Industrial Revolution, the Enlightenment, the planet, and even the human self as frontier converged for an extraordinary chapter in the human story.

Despite the consciousness of sin in the Calvinist beginnings of North Americans from northern Europe, a sense of innocence triumphed. No doubt the reason was their strong sense of breaking ties with the Old World and establishing a holy commonwealth in the New World. H. Richard Niebuhr's theological caricature holds true for far more of American life than the Protestant liberalism he was describing.

> A God without wrath brought men without sin into a kingdom without judgment through the ministrations of a Christ without a cross.[4]

There is evil, of course. We all recognize racism, sexism, classism, imperialism, and other "isms" in the moral catalog of social woe. But the triumph of innocence meant that we learned to "dissociate this evil from our own essence, to believe it would be eliminated, and to see ourselves in the role of its eliminators."[5] Not only can we have a world of our own making, it can be good; we shall make it so.

There is no damnation of the human condition here. There is no admission that the human condition is one of truly profound "darkness, sorrow and . . . need."[6] There is no recognition that "the whacks of life"[7] render the shape of life itself cruciform. There is no understanding that humanity is on the cross. Differently said, there are religion and ethics in North American culture but no *theologia crucis*.

Readers well acquainted with Bonhoeffer's writings will recall that it is this very lack of the *theologia crucis* that Bonhoeffer sensed almost everywhere in the United States, not just in the theological "rubbish" of Riverside Church on Sunday morning.[8] The 1939 essay, "Protestantism without Reformation," includes the observation that despite "Reformation" thinkers such as the Niebuhrs, Pauck, and others of the younger set, Christianity in America is still essentially "religion and ethics," without a Christology of radical judgment and grace. It is Christ without a cross, it is Protestantism without Luther's *simul iustis et peccator*, it is Christian liberalism without *The Epistle to the Romans*, hurled in hardbound from Safenwil. (The reference is to Barth's explosive commentary.)

Triumphalist and innocent bourgeois optimism thus constructed a certain world of expectations, and Christianity in North America adapted to it. The doctrine of providence was transmuted into the doctrine of progress (with that change the notion of the presence of pervasive, persistent evil at the heart of things disappeared). The doctrine of creation was purged of elements offensive to rationalism (with that change humanity's immersion in nature and a deep, keen sense of the limits of finitude faded). The biblical anthropology of sinful humanity was truncated in certain consistent ways (with those changes we no longer asked whether or not becoming masters of history was actually the distortion of our humanity). And the understanding of the cross was reduced either to the symbol of "home" ("This is, after all, a Christian nation") or the symbol of personal piety and borne suffering ("We all have our crosses to bear").

Whatever the innocence, we now know we have experienced failure as a culture. There is a sober side to even the most unqualified resolve "to get this country moving again." Yet we cannot bring ourselves to contemplate that failure straight on. We do not possess the kind of hope that "does not have to look away from death in order to find the courage to live."[9] Thus we construct a religious world to "answer" the genuine experience of negation that shimmers in our bones. This religion duly functions in accord with the culture's theology of glory. It is essentially "a bundle of defense mechanisms against disappointment."[10] It is protection from the abyss we sense but cannot face. What Karl Marx posited as the proletariat's inauthentic coping with its real-world suffering and its skewed perception of reality—namely, religion as a narcotic—is now manifestly the case with much of the middle class in North America. Repressed and denied cultural failure gives rise to a fantastic flowering of religion as a coping or counseling mechanism for "getting through the night" and ersatz fulfillment. But it does so without changing that which in the real world feeds the religious flowering itself. It bolsters the "can do" culture, albeit by what in the end is illusion. Christianity remains "the official religion of an officially optimistic society" (Hall) that cannot face its own acute sense that its gods have feet of clay "all the way up to their necks" (Martin Marty). Or, when some residents of the culture do face the failure without illusion, they are without the culture's hope and without its God. North American religious streams offer few resources that are themselves not wholly acculturated. Hope has been hopelessly confused with optimism.

The point to be made, as forcefully as possible, is this: North American culture and Christianity have, as their working theology, a theology of glory which moves between a human and essentially god-less confidence about "handling" the world, on the one hand, and "religion" as a means of coping when they do not handle the world well, on the other. It is, in Bonhoeffer's words, albeit stripped of their context, a theology of glory which is "the religious rounding off of an [essentially] profane conception of the universe."[11] Our way of addressing the experience of negation is first to reassert with considerable vigor the basic tenets of the cultural faith itself (see "Reagan and Optimism," cited above) and then to call upon religion for legitimating and revitalizing the cultural world in which we live and move and have our being. The electronic church is only a crasser form of something that has a thousand religious and secular expressions, from "my shrink says," to store aisles full of self-help books, to inflated promises about supply-side economics. Reagan himself stayed close to the script here. It is the reason he was popular even when his policies failed.

CRUX SOLA EST
NOSTRA THEOLOGIA

It would be a sin against those who have brought us this far not to acknowledge their part in the contouring of our lives. We turn to the enormously influential Luther and a critique of his theology of the cross.

Luther's treatment of the socioeconomically poor is a convenient case that has special pertinence for us, for two reasons. First, hardly a more thoroughgoing challenge is posed to North American Christianity than that of various liberation theologies, and indeed by the vast majority in the ecumenical church. This challenge is centered most sharply on the response to the poor of the world. Christianity itself is rapidly moving from its status as the religion of the rich to the faith of the poor.[12] Second, part of Bonhoeffer's own theology of the cross is his discovery of the illuminating perspective that comes via "the view from below," that is, from the perspective of those who suffer.

The Peasants' Rebellion took place in Germany in 1524–1525. For reasons that extended even beyond the natural search for allies, the peasants turned to Luther. After all, in the Ninety-five Theses, he had expressed his solidarity with the socioeconomically poor. The theses had been massively distributed and the peasants had them in hand. Others of Luther's writings were also interpreted by the peasants as documents for battle—the ringing essay on "The Freedom of the Christian" was published in 1520 and Luther had often appealed to Scripture as an authority for faith and life, direct and without intermediaries. In short, much from Luther supported their cause.

The peasants' direct appeal to Luther and others was framed in the Twelve Articles. The plea there was for the remedy of grievances against the feudal lords. The articles hurl challenges in the manner of Luther himself—peasant demands are grounded in Scripture and can only be legitimately refuted on scriptural grounds.

The pivotal text in Luther's own passionate reply to the Twelve Articles is as follows:

> Not one of the articles teaches anything of the Gospel. Rather everything is aimed at obtaining freedom for your person and for your property. To sum it up, everything is concerned with worldly and temporal matters. You want power and wealth so that you will not suffer injustice. The Gospel, however, does not become involved in the affairs of this world, but speaks of our life in the world in terms of suffering, injustice, the cross, patience, and contempt for this life and temporal wealth. How, then, does the Gospel agree with you?[13]

Had you and I been peasants, we would have been deeply angered, utterly mystified, and suspicious that the Reformer was on the take, or at least hopelessly compromised by city hall or the local lords and princes. It was precisely Luther's gospel that agreed with us!

Before this episode, in the period 1516-1519, Luther had spoken of poverty as a socioeconomic reality and had argued that both church and state had responsibility for remedying the causes of that poverty. He did not hesitate to label poverty the outcome of oppression and injustice. In the lectures on Romans, where so many Reformation insights first sprang to life, he "tirelessly repeated" that "members of other social classes hate the poor."[14] He traced the matter to its theological core: the rich, showing the pan-human trait of the heart turned inward, idolize themselves and their way of life and undertake both oppression and charity for the same self-serving, self-interested reasons.

What the peasants did not know was that a sharp break in Luther's meaning of "poverty" occurred in late 1518 or early 1519, at the very time Luther gave formulation to the theology of the cross. The peasants heard only the outcome:

> The Gospel . . . does not become involved in the affairs of this world, but speaks of our life in the world in terms of suffering, injustice, the cross, patience, and contempt for this life and temporal wealth.[15]

Bloody swords accompanied the outcome.

While there are many reasons for Luther's change in the meaning of poverty and the poor, what concerns us is what Lee Brummel cites as the "decisive factor," namely, the "emergence of the theology of the cross."[16] The general lines of the *theologia crucis* are these:

- God does not want to be known by that which is invisible, but only by what God has disclosed.

- The knowledge of God, veiled in revelation, is a matter of faith. What is known is God's humanity and weakness revealed through the cross.

- As revealed, God is, at the same time, hidden. The revealed God is hidden under suffering and the cross.

- This means that the revelation of God is apprehended in suffering and the cross, understood as Christ's passion and at the same time as the Christian's suffering and cross. The suffering of Christ and of the Christian belong together.

- This way of knowing God shows the necessity of suffering and excludes all works-righteousness. Suffering is most precious while works-righteousness is useless and deceptive; God accepts only those who are lowly and despised.[17]

This theology, first mentioned in the Heidelburg Disputations of 1518, was, as Brummel notes, developed as an instrument for reforming the church. Luther used it to do theological combat with Rome in the decisive period of the formulation of Reformation policy and practice, the half decade from 1520 to 1525. In this combat, and in order to buttress his case theologically, he took up the biblical language of poverty. Yet, for Luther, the Bible no longer means by "poor" the socioeconomically needy, as it did for him in the period 1516–1519. Rather, Luther returned to a meaning held even earlier. In the earliest pieces, from 1513 to 1516, the poor are the spiritually humble, or "true Christians," as Luther called them. He now retrieves the meaning of "true Christians" as part of the new theology.

Poverty becomes a crucial notion in the *theologia crucis*. It is a way of speaking about several closely related matters. First, "we are all beggars," as Luther is fond of saying. It means that we come with absolutely nothing as a contribution to our salvation. Second, only in this poverty of spirit is there hope of salvation. Until we are poor in spirit we will not find the gracious God. Third, our experience at the cross, as the mortification of the "old Adam," is rightly described as a journey of poverty. We experience *Anfechtung*—anguish, despair, the descent into hell, death, godforsakenness. This is Jesus' experience but it is also truly our own. In short, poverty becomes the way Luther speaks of the suffering of the true Christian under the cross. This is the passage from anguish to grace, in which we are all beggars, and where, at the cross, God meets us in saving mercy. "God's eyes are ever upon the afflicted and the poor. The more abject the man, the nearer and more present God is to him. But the proud he knows from afar."[18]

There came a time, after 1530, when Luther returned to the socioeconomic poor as the subject of biblical texts. Indeed, only the preaching of the gospel held higher rank than responding to the plight of the poor. But this is not a moral admonition grounded specifically in the theology of the cross for Luther at this time.

We must return to the development of the *theologia crucis* shortly before the Peasants' War. The crucial turn for ethics happens here.

There is no doubt that Luther's emphasis in the *theologia crucis* is upon passive suffering and utter trust in the God who hears the cries of the poor and afflicted. There is no doubt, either, that this emphasis was fashioned in response to his passion for reform in the midst of the early battles with the Babylonian captors in Rome. Cross was linked to ecclesiology in the first instance. At this time Luther pointed to "the true church" as a small band of willing sufferers who would endure "through tearful prayers."[19] Framing ecclesiology from the *theologia crucis* also meant that the community of God's people, who became that people in their own crucifixion under the cross, is a community "hidden" in the world, upheld by a God who comes to us *sub contrario*, that is, a God whose own power is cast as weakness, whose glory is wrapped in rags, whose divinity is masked in finitude. All this ran full grain against the triumphalism and cheap grace of the established Roman church of the age.

Two developments took place which greatly affected the ethics of the *theologia crucis*. By 1519 Luther had come to distinguish "private" from "public" persons. Public persons held positions of civil responsibility in which they wielded the sword for the sake of the common good. Private citizens were to endure injustice rather than inflict it if and when their civic appeals went unanswered. Luther categorically rules out insurrection, insisting that any inclinations toward vengeance should be left with God.

We need to note an extension in this stance of passive suffering. It moves from one located in the church and in the context of ecclesiastical reform, to one applicable to a division of ruler and ruled in society. This becomes elaborated upon in the second development, the teaching on the two kingdoms (*Reiche*) and the two governances (*Regimente*). Here was Luther's "social theory" for ethics. What thus began as the proper stance of "true Christians" before God, and was seen as the mark of the true church, namely, expectant but passive suffering, was transposed by Luther into a social ethic for different sectors of society.

This ominous transfer is seen in all its confusion in two remarks of Luther to the peasants' appeal. Both remarks advocate the same course: the peasants must abandon their bellicosity and suffer whatever injustice might come their way, if they really intend to be "true Christians." "We have all we need in our Lord, who will not leave us, as he has promised [Heb. 13:5]. Suffering! Suffering! Cross! Cross! This and nothing else is the Christian law."[20] Luther also says that what the peasants have in mind is not a "Christian" matter at all! It is an affair of one and only one of the two governances and kingdoms, a matter between those set in place by God to effect order and those contemplating rebellion against the ordained authorities. So he snorts, "Now, dear sirs, there is nothing Christian on either side and nothing Christian at issue between you."[21]

This brief stop in Wittenberg is in the interest of the next subject, Bonhoeffer's revisions of the theology of the cross in ways that form a quite different ethic. At least two revisions leap off the page, given this glimpse of Luther.

1. The cross for Luther, humanly experienced, is primarily the God-wrestle of the sensitive soul with self and sin. By comparison, Bonhoeffer wants to connect the cross and coming-of-age in a way that does not assume the journey through *Anfechtung* and does not find us nearer to God in our despairing weakness than in our strength. Moreover, it is not the mortification of self that the cross symbolizes, but the suffering that comes when one is caught up in the way of Jesus in the world. It is more "social" than "psychological" in character, though the distinction itself is not a happy one.

2. There are dualisms in Luther that Bonhoeffer fully rejects (in the name of Luther, of course!) The gospel, Luther told the peasants, has to do with "suffering, injustice, the cross, patience, and contempt for this life and temporal wealth." It has nothing to do with "worldly and temporal matters."[22] In contrast, few Lutheran theologians are more consistently antidualistic than Bonhoeffer. He is as antidualistic in his understanding of the gospel as Luther was antilegalistic. Bonhoeffer will distinguish, but never separate, the "ultimate" (God's justifying action) from the "penultimate" (the concrete conditions of our lives, including the material conditions of "worldly and temporal matters").

A BETTER START

John Godsey writes: "Like Luther, Bonhoeffer is inclined toward a theology of the cross."[23] This could not be more understated! What Bonhoeffer is "inclined toward" runs down the middle of his theology and ethics, and most strongly of all in the *Letters and Papers from Prison*, from which we will draw most heavily.

The first excerpt is from an earlier letter, from 1939, one Godsey himself cites. Bonhoeffer wrote to Theodore Litt:

> Solely because God became a poor, suffering, unknown, successless man, and because from now on God allows himself to be found only in this poverty, in the cross, we cannot disengage ourselves from man and from the world. For this reason we love the brethren. Because in the Christian faith it is understood that, indeed, out of the sovereign freedom of grace, the "unconditioned" has enclosed itself in the "conditioned," the "otherworldly" has entered into the "this worldly," the believer is not torn asunder but finds God and man united at this one place in the world, and from now on love of God and love of the brother are indissolubly united with one another.[24]

At least three matters must be noted: (1) God is found "only in this poverty, in the cross"; (2) this *kenosis* keeps us pegged to the world; (3) a fundamental unity of God and world is won by God's enclosing the "unconditioned" in the humanity of a particular poor Jew.

Of the extant letters to Bethge, the one we cited in an earlier chapter, from 21 August 1944, includes the following paragraph:

> Dear Eberhard,
>
> It's your birthday in a week's time. Once again I've taken up the readings and meditated on them. The key to everything is the "in him." All that we may rightly expect from God, and ask him for, is to be found in Jesus

Christ. The God of Jesus Christ has nothing to do with what God, as we imagine him, could do and ought to do. If we are to learn what God promises, and what he fulfils, we must persevere in quiet meditation on the life, sayings, deeds, sufferings, and death of Jesus. It is certain that we may always live close to God and in the light of his presence, and that such living is an entirely new life for us; that nothing is then impossible for us, because all things are possible with God; that no earthly power can touch us without his will, and that danger and distress can only drive us closer to him. It is certain that we can claim nothing for ourselves, and may yet pray for everything; it is certain that our joy is hidden in suffering, and our life in death; it is certain that in all this we are in a community that sustains us. In Jesus God has said Yes and Amen to it all, and that Yes and Amen is the firm ground on which we stand.[25]

The meaning of this letter is lost if it is heard only as the piety and longing of a prisoner who misses a great and good friend. He certainly does miss him, and must "talk" with him via letter. But what is written is less piety than credo. The credo is a precise and succinct statement of the *theologia crucis*.

The theology of the cross, then, is this: that God happens for us in the humanity of Jesus of Nazareth; that everything we know of God and God's purposes, or of ours and the world's nature and destiny, is buried in the details and drama of that life, death, and resurrection; and that Christian faith is a participation in the *Sein Jesu*, in messianic suffering, where cosmic joy and victory are both hidden and passed along.

But where does this take us for ethics? Bonhoeffer shares with Luther the starting and ending point of ethics in the understanding of justification by faith. He also shares with Luther the consequences for the very notion of ethics itself.

Gerhard Forde cites a lovely text from Luther's *Romans* commentary:

The exodus of the people Israel has for a long time been interpreted to signify the transition from vice to virtue. But one should, rather, interpret it as the way from virtue to the grace of Christ, because virtues are often the greater and worse faults the less they are regarded as such and the more powerful they subject to themselves all human affections beyond all other goods. So also the right side of Jordan was more fearful than the left one.[26]

Christian ethics has invariably become synonymous with a movement *from vice to virtue*. The process of sanctification is regarded as moral growth or, to employ the modern liberal version in Kantian dress, as those stages of moral development toward individual autonomy. For Luther such thinking in terms of movement or progress is considered *ad modum Aristotelis* (after the manner of Aristotle) "where everything depends on what the person does" and where righteousness is "real only to the degree that sin is expelled."[27]

For both Luther and Bonhoeffer, to think *ad modum scripturae* (after the manner of Scripture) is to think in a radically different way about ethics. If there is movement, it is not from vice to virtue, but from both vice and virtue to grace. Cross the Jordan if you wish, but life on both banks is really much the same and equally in need of a fundamental transformation that does not come with better boats or a friendlier welcoming party.

Moving from vice and virtue to the grace of Christ is in fact a shattering of all our schemes of moral development and aspired-for salvation. All the movements on our part to attain "salvation," however we name it—as security or wholeness or "meaning" or "goodness" or just a "good time"—are simply brought up short and put out of business by the righteousness of God through the cross of Jesus of Nazareth. As Forde says, God's putting things right (the meaning of justification) is "neither at the beginning or end of [any] movement [on our part]."[28] Rather, it creates—it establishes—a wholly different situation. It is the new age breaking in upon the old. It is the reign of God come in our midst. It is the world of "recovered unity" (Bonhoeffer's phrase). It is eschatological reality present among us.

The new reality exposes the old for what it is. We did not regard ourselves as "sick unto death" before. Only now is it revealed that we are. (We thought we were just good folks trying to do a decent job down at the ammunition factory.) What the new reality does is expose our darkness. We thought our darkness was light and our evil good.

The new reality in Christ shatters our schemes at the same time that it creates the "new humanity." This is the precise meaning of Luther's *simul iustis et peccator* (sinful and justified at the same time). We are both, and simultaneously, *totus iustis* (completely justified) and *totus peccator* (still a sinner throughout). Luther's *simul iustis et peccator* is not a way of saying that some nasty residue of vice remains even though we have been grabbed by virtue. It is a way of saying the new aeon has illumined the old to expose it for what it is, that the two aeons are opposed to one another, and that the battle over allegiance goes on within us and without.

While the battle is existentially our own, the establishment of the new reality and our grasping it by faith have nothing to do with the particular psychic condition that is ours. Whether we suffer Luther's "guilty conscience" or possess Paul's "robust conscience," whether we are mired in despair or "having a nice day," does not alter what for Luther and Paul is first of all a cosmic event, the sounding of the "last word" by God in Jesus Christ. The connection of cosmology to anthropology is not one in which one first becomes a "sinner" via the introspective conscience or some other route. One becomes that sinner and the new person in Christ simultaneously as faith grasps the reality of God's making righteous. Indeed, our consciousness is, in the end, no measure at all. Thus Luther on *Romans*: "by faith alone we must believe that we are sinners, for this is not obvious to us; indeed, quite often we are not even conscious of it."[29]

One's experience may be that of *Anfechtung*. But it has about the same meaning for the reality of justification as circumcision has as a "condition of justification" and "religion" as a "condition for salvation"![30]

Forde provides further elucidation:

> This [blasting of both our vices and virtues by God's righteousness] requires a radical reorientation in theological thinking and in the way we look on the Christian life. The old argument whether we are only "declared" righteous or actually "made" so is largely beside the point. It presupposes that our schemes remain intact. Justification is, however, a creative act of God which ends all previous schemes and begins something absolutely new. Usually what has happened in Protestant thought is that the radical point has been missed and the attempt made to combine justification by faith with previously existing schemes—to put new wine in old skins. We are perhaps willing to admit we should get rid of our vices but not our virtues. We fear what would happen then. What results is a theology afflicted with a profound inner contradiction: the attempt to mix justification with thinking *ad modum Aristotelis*. Justification will then always come off second best. It will be a dangerous doctrine which threatens all our plans and ideas about how to get on in this world and will have to be domesticated in some fashion or other. So one will indulge in endless debates about "all this and sanctification too," "good works," and so on. The *simul iustis et peccator* will turn to poison—merely the word that no matter how hard we try in our struggle from vice to virtue we have to settle for the fact that we will never *completely* make it. We are, after all, *simul iustis et peccator* (pronounced with a sigh of resignation). So justification and the *simul* serve simply as a counsel of last resort: rescue in the case of the failure of the old rather than the beginning of something radically new.[31]

Let me say it differently. Justification by faith, the "last word," rather than being the beginning and ending point of Christian ethics as Luther intended, becomes instead the very element that generates anxiety "over against ethics, moral progress, and virtue."[32] Perversely, "justification" is even set in opposition to ethical vigor.

There is no question that justification correctly grasped, and the *theologia crucis* of which it is here a part, radically alter our way of thinking about ethics. Bonhoeffer is thoroughly aware of this, and writes of it in *Ethics.*

> Whoever wishes to take up the problem of a Christian ethic must be confronted at once with a demand which is quite without parallel. He must from the outset discard as irrelevant the two questions which alone impel him to concern himself with the problem of ethics. "How can I be good?" and "How can I do good?" What is of ultimate importance is now no longer that I should become good, or that the condition of the world should be made better by my action, but that the reality of God should show itself everywhere to be the ultimate reality. . . . The point of departure of Christian ethics is the realization among God's creatures of the revelational reality of God in Christ, just as the problem of dogmatics is the truth of the revelational reality of God in Christ. The place which in all other ethics is occupied by the antithesis of "should be" and "is," idea and accomplishment, motive and performance, is occupied in Christian ethics by the relation of reality and realization. . . . The question of good becomes the question of participation in the divine reality which is revealed in Christ.[33]

It is in the meeting between Jesus and the Pharisee that we see most clearly the radical departure of Christian ethics. The Pharisee "is that extremely admirable man who subordinates his entire life to his knowledge of good and evil and is as severe a judge of himself as of his neighbor to the honor of God, whom he humbly thanks for this knowledge."[34] All his choices are choices of vice and virtue and he is constantly caught in conflict as he aspires to square them with the will of God. By contrast, the ethics of the follower of Christ begins at a point "beyond the knowledge of good and evil," that is, in the unity of God and world in Jesus Christ effected by God's creating righteousness.

> Now anyone who reads the New Testament even superficially cannot but notice the complete absence of this world of disunion, conflict and ethical problems. Nor man's falling apart from God, from men, from things and from himself, but rather the rediscovered unity, reconciliation, is now the basis of the discussion and "the point of decision of the specifically ethical experience." The life and activity of men is not at all problematic or tormented or dark; it is self-evident, joyful, sure and clear.[35]

But how does one arrive at this beginning point for ethics and the Christian life? Surely there is some method of moral hitchhiking that takes us from point A or B (the penultimate) to home (the ultimate). Bonhoeffer addresses the issue. One of the passages in *Ethics* discusses a way "of attaining to this final word,"[36] only to refute the notion that we have a step-by-step procedure. There is no Lutheran method, Bonhoeffer writes, nor a Pauline one. Indeed, both the "way of Paul" and the "way of Luther" were "condemned" in the judgment of God's righteousness, and only the "sinner Paul" and the "sinner Luther" were justified.

> Strictly speaking, we may no more retread the path which Luther followed than we may go the way of the adulteress, of the thief on the cross, of Peter who denied Christ, and of Paul who was filled with zeal against Christ. The qualitatively final word excludes every kind of method once and for all. . . . It is senseless and wrong . . . if one preaches . . . that each and every man must first become like Mary Magdalene, like the beggar Lazarus, like the thief on the cross, like all these dim "peripheral figures," before he can become capable of hearing the final word of God. . . . The purpose of the Christian message is not that one should become like one or other of those biblical characters, but that one shall be like Christ Himself. No method leads to this end, but only faith.[37]

It is with this understanding of justification as the radical cancellation of all our movements, and the living from faith alone, that we should read the later Bonhoeffer as well. The letter of 21 July 1944 is especially poignant, coming as it does on the day following the failure of the putsch and while Bonhoeffer is reflecting on the course of his own life, now in great jeopardy.

> I remember a conversation that I had in America thirteen years ago with a young French pastor. We were asking ourselves quite simply what we wanted to do with our lives. He said he would like to become a saint (and I think it's quite likely that he did become one). At the same time I was very impressed, but I disagreed with him, and said, in effect, that I should like to learn to have faith. For a long time I didn't realize the depth of the contrast. I thought I could acquire faith by trying to live a holy life, or something like it. I suppose I wrote *The Cost of Discipleship* as the end of that path. Today I can see the dangers of that book, though I still stand by what I wrote. I discovered later, and I'm still discovering right up to this moment, that is it [sic] only by living completely in this world that one learns to have faith. One must completely abandon any attempt to make something of oneself, whether it be a saint, or a converted sinner, or a churchman, . . . a righteous man, or an unrighteous one, a sick man or a healthy one. By this-worldliness I mean living unreservedly

in life's duties, problems, successes and failures, experiences and perplexities. In so doing we throw ourselves completely into the arms of God, taking seriously, not our own sufferings, but those of God in the world—watching with Christ in Gethsemane. That, I think, is faith; that is *metanoia*; and that is how one becomes a man and a Christian.[38]

Earlier in the letter Bonhoeffer explains "this-worldliness." This-worldliness is not "the shallow and banal this-worldliness of the enlightened, the busy, the comfortable, or the lascivious." That we can leave to triumphalist bourgeois optimism! It is "characterized by discipline and the constant knowledge of death and resurrection." "I think Luther lived a this-worldly life in this sense."[39]

Differently said, Bonhoeffer sees the path of a *homo religiosus* as a subtle *theologia gloriae* in action. It has a method for "making something of oneself" so as to move from vice to virtue and garner salvation, or fulfillment. To be a human being and Christian, however, is to live "unreservedly" and "throw ourselves into the arms of God" who slays our ways and in the same moment gives us new life. Profound this-worldliness lives from "death and resurrection." This dynamic generates Christian ethics.

Church, Christ, and Culture

If knowing death and resurrection in "profound this-worldliness" is the inaugural point for Christian ethics, its concrete community context is the church. By Bonhoeffer's definition, the church is "nothing but a section of humanity in which Christ has really taken form."[40] "The form of Christ" in "the form of the Church" is where "reality" is being "realized," to use his terms. Or, "what matters . . . is not religion but the form of Christ, and its taking form amidst a band of men."[41]

We turn now to the relationship of church, Christ, and culture. The contention is that the ethics of the *theologia crucis* have been frustrated in their development because of the ongoing presence of Constantinian assumptions. While this holds true for Bonhoeffer as well, he has nonetheless begun a new and promising direction. It is that of a revived "imitation of Christ" ethic, seen as the church's societal vocation.

> If we are to learn what God promises, and what he fulfills, we must persevere in quiet meditation on the life, sayings, deeds, sufferings, and death of Jesus.[42]

This is part of the hidden discipline, the pole of "prayer" in the indispensable dialectic with "doing justice" from which "all Christian thinking, speaking, and organizing must be born anew"[43] in the coming epoch. But it is also a concrete expression of the theology of the cross with clear import for ethics. It is a way of speaking of the "form of Christ" to which we, as church, are to be conformed. Everything known of God and what God seeks to effect among us is "hidden" in the humanity of Jesus. To discern "who Christ is for us today" means to persevere in that "quiet meditation."

Is it weaving too much from too slender a thread, or is there not in Bonhoeffer increased attention to the concrete humanity of Jesus (and of other biblical figures)? Is there not now more attention to example, more talk of the way of Jesus and the being of Jesus, and somewhat less talk of "Christ the center of man, nature, and history?" The reach of the christological claims is not diminished, but Bonhoeffer in prison moves even deeper into the radical claim of the *theologia crucis* for both epistemology and ethics. The details and drama of the humanity of a certain poor Jew, at the heart of the theology of the cross, takes on greater importance for ethics specifically.

We need not catalogue all the supporting references. But attention should be given to a line from the next paragraph in the same letter of 21 August 1944 that so clearly articulates Bonhoeffer's theology of the cross: "if such *a man* as Jesus lived, then, and only then, has life a meaning for us. If Jesus had not lived, then our life would be meaningless, in spite of all the *other* people whom we know and honour and love."[44] (Emphasis added).

This is not the slightest of retreats from the claims of Christ's lordship. But it does suggest that there is a specificity about the Way of Jesus which had not been tapped for the *theologia crucis* and which is different in *Letters and Papers* from *The Cost of Discipleship*. The difference is the place of human example and the particulars of the way of the cross: "quiet meditation on the life, sayings, deeds, suffering and death of Jesus." The same "Outline for a Book" which discusses the being of Jesus as concrete "being-for-others," discusses the church. The nature of the church is a strict corollary: "the church is the church only when it exists for others."[45] Then comes an interesting note. It follows immediately upon a short section of moral discourse in which Bonhoeffer names vices the church must counter (such as *hubris*, power-worship, envy, and illusion) and virtues it must exalt (including moderation, purity, trust, constancy, patience, discipline, and humility).

[The church] must not underestimate the importance of human example (which has its origin in the humanity of Jesus and is so important in

Paul's teaching); it is not abstract argument, but example, that gives its word emphasis and power. (I hope to take up later this subject of "example" and its place in the New Testament; it is something that we have almost entirely forgotten.)[46]

Bonhoeffer himself uses examples extensively when he wants to show the shape of the ethics of the cross, of what it means to share in the sufferings of God in the life of the world, as Jesus did.

This being caught up into the messianic sufferings of God in Jesus Christ takes a variety of forms in the New Testament. It appears in the call of discipleship, in Jesus' table-fellowship with sinners, in "conversions" in the narrower sense of the word (e.g., Zacchaeus), in the act of the woman who was a sinner (Luke 7)—an act that she performed without any confession of sin, in the healing of the sick (Matt. 8:17; see above), in Jesus' acceptance of children. The shepherds, like the wise men from the east, stand at the crib, not as "converted sinners," but simply because they are drawn to the crib by the star just as they are. The centurion of Capernaum (who makes no confession of sin) is held up as a model of faith (cf. Jairus). Jesus "loved" the rich young man. The eunuch (Acts 8) and Cornelius (Acts 10) are not standing at the edge of an abyss. Nathaniel is "an Israelite indeed, in whom there is no guile" (John 1:47). Finally, Joseph of Arimathea and the women at the tomb. The only thing that is common to all these is their sharing in the suffering of God in Christ. That is their "faith." There is nothing of religious method here. The "religious act" is always something partial; "faith" is something whole, involving the whole of one's life. Jesus calls men, not to a new religion, but to life.[47]

We should not be distracted from Bonhoeffer's larger subject. The matter at hand is "faith" contrasted with "religion." Yet it must not be overlooked that the "faith" discussed includes its ethic, and that human example, especially the premier example of Jesus, shows forth just such faith.

One more citation is appropriate.

The Christian . . . has no last line of escape available from earthly tasks and difficulties into the eternal, but, *like Christ himself* ("My God, why hast thou forsaken me"), he must drink the earthly cup to the dregs, *and only in his doing so is the crucified and risen Lord with him, and he crucified and risen with Christ.*[48]

"Like Christ himself" is the language of the moral tradition of the "imitation of Christ." Bonhoeffer does not often use the term per se. His preference is "conformation to Christ." The point here is simply that in *Letters and Papers from Prison* the "imitation" ethic is present and is presented as a sharing or participating in the being of Jesus, seen in the human example of Jesus and his way.

But where does this put Bonhoeffer vis-à-vis Luther and the Lutheran legacy in ethics? What are the revisions that would follow for the understanding of church, Christ, and culture?

"What can and must be said is not what is good once and for all, but the way in which Christ takes form among us here and now."[49] The revival of the tradition of the *imitatio Christi* imbedded in Bonhoeffer's theology and ethics of the cross does not alter the starting point and basic dynamics of Christian ethics. Ethics emerges on the other side of God's recovering of "unity" in the world and beyond any movement from vice to virtue. It is Christian ethics, "beyond" the knowledge of good and evil in its starting place, and calling simply for "participation in the sufferings of God in the life of the world" so that ultimate and true reality might be concretely, historically "realized."

If Bonhoeffer shares this basic starting point with Luther, why did Luther, unlike Bonhoeffer, flinch in drawing out the "imitation of Christ" for the social ethics of the cross? The reason is largely historical. What Luther knew of the *imitatio Christi* tradition was its active life in medieval piety. And there it was part of the *theologia gloriae* that incensed Luther. It was a trek from vice to virtue in order to achieve salvation. It was works-righteousness. Since Luther rejected moral and spiritual growth as a way to salvation, he emphatically rejected the *imitatio Christi* ethic as its means.

The Lutheran rejection of an *imitatio* ethic for the social ethics of the cross continues, albeit on different grounds. The concluding chapter in *Two Kingdoms and One World: A Sourcebook in Christian Social Ethics* is an important document of the Lutheran World Federation's Commission on Theology. The title is: "Bases for a Christian Ethic." The following is stated in conjunction with the first topic, "The Scope of Christ's Lordship":

> No sphere of our life can be excluded from Christ's Lordship. . . . Christ is the church's Lord and the world's. All our actions, whether public or private, whether in the church or in society, must be based on Christ's lordship.[50]

The topic of the next paragraph is: "But No Ethical Code." The explanation runs as follows:

> The thesis that Christ's Lordship is the basis of ethics needs qualification. To be based on the lordship of Christ does not mean that ethics is to be derived from it. To imagine that the entire content of ethics could be

deduced from the concept of the lordship of Christ would mean illegitimately stretching this concept beyond proportion.[51]

The next paragraph continues:

> To define the *content* of ethics we have to turn to the reality of the world around us.[52]

Then follows the Lutheran move away from Jesus as norm, to creation as the place of discerning God's "demand" (as the document puts it).

In three short paragraphs, the theologians have simply walked away from Jesus and his lordship as the source of content for Christian ethics. Further reading clarifies the fears of the Commission:

> One major concern in thus bracketing together ethical demand and the reality of the world is to ensure that we understand the evangelical ethic as an ethic of freedom. If we were simply to deduce from, or construct the entire content of ethics on, the concept of the lordship of Christ, we should be in danger of transforming Christian freedom into obligatory obedience to instructions. Christ our Redeemer would then appear as the legislator for the world, and the gospel would be turned into a demand for obedience or into an ideal of human conduct and social order which it would be our task today to copy. But Christian discipleship is under the sign of the gospel, not under that of law.[53]

It is difficult to know where to begin the discussion of a Lutheran social ethic of *imitatio*, or conformation to Christ, when the discussion is already so confused. The *imitatio* ethic we have in view, drawing upon Bonhoeffer, is Christian discipleship as under the gospel, not the law. It is an ethic of response to grace, not in order to garner virtue or attain salvation, but simply to participate faithfully in the way in which God has chosen to be among us, the way of Jesus. *Imitatio* ethics—participation in the sufferings of God in Christ—means having our character and conduct formed in keeping with God's; and this is seen with the most compelling clarity where God has chosen to reveal it, in the humanity of Jesus. An *imitatio* ethic of the theology of the cross has nothing whatsoever to do with "law," or with making "Christ our Redeemer" the "legislator for the world." It is the response to justification which trusts that in the moral life God's way shows itself most vividly when our faithfulness is like unto the faithfulness of Jesus. This is not ethics as "deduced" from a "concept," even that of the lordship of Christ. It is ethics as participation in the way of Jesus, who is Lord.

Kierkegaard's language for all this is the language of obligation. That is an unfortunate choice: the Lutheran association of obligation with law places obligation in opposition to Christian freedom. But Kierkegaard is worth citing at length, nonetheless.

> In the case of Christianity the situation is this: the gift and the obligation correspond to one another in exact proportion. In the same degree that Christianity is a gift it is also an obligation. The knavish trick of "Christendom" is to take the gift and say good day to the obligation, to want to be heir to the gift, but without assuming the obligation, to want to make it appear that mankind is indeed the heir, whereas the truth is that only by performing the obligation is mankind, or rather . . . I would say every single individual . . . the heir. . . . However, hypocritical as everything is with "Christendom," they have made it appear as if Christendom too did maintain that Christianity is an obligation—one has to be baptized. Ah! That is making confoundedly short work of obligation! A drop of water on the head of an infant, in the name of the Trinity—that is obligation! No, the obligation is: *the imitation of Jesus Christ*.[54]

In Bonhoeffer's language, cheap grace is justification and forgiveness (the "gift") without moral consequence. Costly grace is "nachfolge" (the German for "discipleship" means "following after"), participation in the sufferings of God in the life of the world in the manner of Jesus. The imitation of Christ is the form of Christian freedom. It is the shape of a voluntary response made with one's whole being. It is taking up the cross as one's own.

We turn to further reasons Luther and Lutherans have failed to develop a social ethic of the cross, at the same time investigating what Bonhoeffer offers. Bonhoeffer rejects the notion that one can believe in Christ without actually having to follow Jesus.

Many of the Anabaptists had an imitation-of-Christ ethic which was a social ethic grounded in a *theologia crucis* very different from that of medieval piety. There are multiple reasons Luther rejected the Radical Reformation and pressed forward with the Imperial Reformation instead. Only part of that complex, the "Christendom" or "Constantinian" assumptions held by Luther, will be treated here.

Discussion of those assumptions, which are still with us in subtle ways, requires other prefacing remarks, namely, comment on the tradition in social ethics which has shaped many North American Protestant views.

Largely missing in North American Protestant church life and culture are a distinct ecclesiology and a clear ethic as part of the understanding of "church." The social significance of the church as a piece of the world with an integrity peculiar to itself, and the meaning of that for the moral life, has been given too little consideration.

Stanley Hauerwas's polemics force the issue.

> It is not the task of the church to try to develop social theories or strategies to make America work; rather the task of the church in this country is to become a polity that has the character necessary to survive as a truthful society.[55]

> The first task of Christian social ethics . . . is not to make the "world" better or more just, but to help Christian people form their community consistent with their conviction that the story of Christ is a truthful account of our existence.[56]

To many ears this will ring too sectarian. Nonetheless, it has striking familiarity with Bonhoeffer's words:

> What is of importance is now no longer that I should become good, or that the condition of the world should be made better by my action, but that the reality of God should show itself everywhere to be the ultimate reality.[57]

For Bonhoeffer, as for Hauerwas, this happens for the world by letting the church be the church; that is, a piece of world where Christ is taking community form. And so the social formation of the Christian community itself becomes a prime focal point for Christian ethics. The focal point is not initially, and not only, the social formation of the wider world.

Of course, church and world are indissoluble, since the church is a piece of world. But the attention of Christian social ethics, which is often focused primarily and sometimes only on the world beyond the church, has neglected, and sometimes distorted, the relationship of ecclesiology and ethics.

It is almost startling to read Ernst Troeltsch in this connection. In *The Social Teaching of the Christian Churches* he writes:

> It is a great mistake to treat the ideas which underlie the preaching of Jesus as though they were primarily connected with the "Social" problem. The message of Jesus is obviously purely religious; it issues directly from a very definite idea of God, and of the Divine Will in relation to man. To Jesus the whole meaning of life is religious; His life and His teaching are wholly determined by His thought of God.[58]

No Jew (like Jesus) would understand this. To have one's "life and . . . teaching . . . wholly determined by [one's] thought of God" but not connect that intimately to social reality and every aspect of life was unthinkable to the observant Jew.

Of the early community Troeltsch writes:

It is worthy of special note that Early Christian apologetic contains no arguments dealing either with hopes of improving the existing social situation, or with any attempt to heal social ills. Jesus began His public ministry, it is true, by proclaiming the Kingdom of God as the great hope of Redemption; this "Kingdom," however, . . . was primarily the vision of an ideal ethical and religious situation, of a world entirely controlled by God, in which all the values of pure spirituality would be recognized and appreciated at their true worth.[59]

When the "Kingdom" is "the vision of an ideal ethical and religious situation," the social ethic of Jesus and the early community is of little help, except as a judging, transhistorical norm. It functions as a statement of an ideal or ideals that provide a critique and standard. In Reinhold Niebuhr's work, for example, there is indeed a central place for the cross. It is the revelation of the ultimate ethical norm, namely, *agapē* (sacrificial love), and it is the revelation of the divine mercy in the form of the forgiveness of sins. The latter serves as the core of a powerful spirituality for political engagement which succumbs neither to illusion nor to cynicism. This is certainly helpful in its own deeply Lutheran way, but it is not yet a social ethic of the cross.

Reinhold Niebuhr, the most influential North American social ethicist, here reflects the Troeltschian formulation of liberal Christianity. What is crucial for our attention is the assumption that social ethics, in order to be valid, has to be relevant to society as a whole and to its governance. Its attention is not to the formation of the church community as such. (That would be the introversion of sectarianism.) As Hauerwas correctly points out, Troeltsch specifically exempts from social ethics and lists as "purely religious" such matters as the "right kind of congregational organization, the application of Christian ideals to daily life, self-discipline in the interest of personal holiness, and appropriation of spiritual inheritance."[60] These items do not intersect the problem Christians have when they participate in running society, and *thus* are not matters of social ethics. Differently said, when the Jesus story does not help in the managing of "empire" (Hauerwas's term), it is not an adequate story for a Christian social ethic. Why? Because after Constantine and the legacy of Christendom, it is precisely the partnership of throne and altar, of a nation or a people and the church, that sets the very terms of "social ethics." Thinking from inside a post-Constantinian paradigm shifts ethics away from the New Testament focus on the shape of the believing community as a community of the new aeon and as a "public" in its own right. It simultaneously shortcuts the possibilities that await an ethic of the cross as a community ethic of the *imitatio Christi*. Until the so-called sectarian vocation is permitted, there will be no communitarian social ethic of the cross, except on the terms of a Niebuhr or a Troeltsch.

Social ethics must include the concrete organization of the imitation of Christ in the world as Christian community. That is the contention here, and it is also Bonhoeffer's. Polity is politics, sharing and table-fellowship are economics, fellowship and joining with others in their suffering and joy are healing, and lifting up the Jesus story is worship. Social ethics is *Gemeinsames Leben*, to cite the title of Bonhoeffer's book on Christian community (*Life Together*). "Christ existing as community," the theme of his earlier work, *Sanctorum Communio*, is what the church is both to be and to do in the world.

To talk about the ecclesial vocation in ethics in these terms requires further discussion of the church's relationship to culture, especially in North America. For here we live with both a strong sense that our "calling" is to conquest and control and with a religious history in which many of the strains of Christianity have seen the social ethical task as that of making the North American world "better."

Both liberal Protestant Christianity and American evangelicalism have suffered from the neglect of a clear, distinctive sense of the church as a collective moral agent. The "church" in much of American Protestantism, with the notable exception of the African American churches, has been largely the individual and the nation, with denominations supplying ecclesiastical structure. Both the stance of the Moral Majority in the 1980s and the opposition of liberal Protestants to it betray an acculturated Christianity markedly lacking a sense of a community (the church) whose normative shape is positioned over against its own wider world.

In this setting we should emphasize Christian social ethics as ecclesial in character, and the church as the *ecclesia crucis* (the community of the cross). The direction taken will, as hinted, lean as much toward the Radical Reformation as toward Luther. The shift to the left wing of the Reformation is best seen in the meaning given the cross itself. We can do no better than include a passage from Mennonite theologian John Yoder:

> The believer's cross is no longer any and every kind of suffering, sickness, or tension, the bearing of which is demanded. The believer's cross must be, like his Lord's, the price of his social nonconformity. It is not, like

sickness or catastrophe, an inexplicable suffering; it is the end of a path freely chosen after counting the cost. It is not, like Luther's or Thomas Muntzer's or Zinzendorf's or Kierkegaard's cross of *Anfechtung*, an inward wrestling of the sensitive soul with self and sin; *it is the social reality of representing in an unwilling world the Order to come.*[61]

There is a strikingly similar passage in *The Cost of Discipleship*:

To endure the cross is not a tragedy; it is the suffering which is the fruit of an exclusive allegiance to Jesus Christ. When it comes, it is not an accident, but a necessity. It is not the sort of suffering which is inseparable from this mortal life, but the suffering which is an essential part of the specifically Christian life. It is not suffering *per se* but suffering-and-rejection, and not rejection for any cause or conviction of our own, but rejection for the sake of Christ.[62]

To represent, in an unwilling world, the order to come is to "realize [true] reality," to call to mind Bonhoeffer's language. It happens when the church participates in the being of Jesus by traversing the often costly way of Jesus. "The cross means sharing the suffering of Christ to the last and to the fullest."[63]

The development of the church's social ethic has been truncated by certain assumptions and arrangements described here as Constantinian. I list a few, drawing heavily from John Yoder.

1. When H. Richard Niebuhr defines "culture" in his classic volume, *Christ and Culture*, he does so in a way that assumes "culture" is something whole. We must be "of" it or "against" it, or "above" it, "transforming" it, or holding it "in paradox." We are inconsistent, maybe we even cheat, if we as Christians do not take responsibility for the whole. Culture is a package deal and there is only one fare. Thus Niebuhr criticized Tertullian for using and applauding the Latin language as a great and good gift of the Roman Empire, and then turning around and categorically rejecting Roman imperial violence.[64] Culture is a seamless web, a single garment.

2. "The civil order [meaning government] is the quintessence of the cultural mandate."[65] It takes little reflection to note there are many dimensions of culture—family, education, the arts, the economy, religious life, and so on. Yet mainline social ethics has it that the one critical for all the rest is civil governance. Without sovereignty of government all would be lost. Such sovereignty is ordained by God or imbedded in the very order of nature, according to most of Western social ethics.

3. "The sword is the quintessence of the civil order."[66] While coercion, including lethal coercion, may be the means of last resort

(ultima ratio) for governing, it is so central to the state that the civil order cannot be understood apart from it. It is necessary if society and culture are not to dissolve in anarchy. The sword is God's instrument for order. It belongs to the very essence of the state that the state wields it.

As Yoder notes, this identification between the sword and the civil order is, theologically, a fusing of creation and the Fall. That there must be order is not in doubt, nor that order is a created mandate. Genesis 1 and 2 are about such patterning of creation. But that the sword belongs to creation is not part of that ordering. Such arguments—more frequently, simply assumptions—have overlaid life under the Fall onto creation and its ordering. It has made sin not only normal, but normative.

4. God's will is univocal. We have nurtured a notion that God's will is the same for all peoples, perhaps because all share a common created nature, or a common destiny in God, or hold common potential. So we strive for a common ethic. Indeed, in ethics, "universalizability" is a test of the moral integrity of any contemplated behavior.

There is probably very little that supports this biblically. Again, Yoder:

> There is no self-evident reason that the will of God has the same meaning for a Jew as for a Gentile in the age of Moses, when tabernacle worship and circumcision are not expected of the nations. There is no self-evident reason to assume that the obligations of Christians and non-Christians are the same in the New Testament when one decides and acts within the reestablished covenant of grace and the other does not. There is no reason to have to assume that the moral performance of which God expects of the regenerate [God] equally expects of the unregenerate. Of course, on some much more elevated level of abstraction, our minds demand that we project a unique and univocal ultimate or ideal will of God. But it is precisely the nature of [God's] patience with fallen humanity that God condescends to deal with us on other levels.[67]

What must be emphasized is that the above Constantinian assumptions betray the perspective of those who formulate their ethic, its nature and purpose, "from above." These are the assumptions of people more accustomed to making history than "taking" it. Ethics here are for "running society," forging and enforcing public policy for both the clean and the great unwashed. "The view from above" (Bonhoeffer's phrase) sees culture as a totality, or demands that it be such and aspires to make it so. "From above," that is, from the point of view of the privileged, the nod is given the governing function as the one where final sovereignty must rest. "From above" the heart of governance is holding and wielding of power in the form of coercion and its threat. "From above" the constant inclination is to fuse the realities of the fallen world with requirements supposedly rooted in creation itself. "From above" universalism is a test of the validity of an ethic which corresponds to God's singular will.

Of course, such assumptions can be argued on grounds other than the interests of the privileged and the requirements of rule. Order is a social necessity, and coercion as well. But it would be naive and foolish not to suspect the pervasive play of social interests here and the remnants of a Christendom marriage of the church to power.

In any case, if we do speak of some universal reach for an ethic of the cross, it should not be that of the "Christendom" ethic, either in its more theocratic forms or in its more liberal dress (the acculturated Christianity of democratic societies). The liberal version, says Yoder:

> affirms the adequacy of the religious expression of almost everyone or at least of people in almost every condition, sometimes in other religions or perhaps even in no religion, because of some inherent human qualities for which one considers the label "Christ" to be a symbol.[68]

In Bonhoeffer this way of proceeding comes clearest when, on christological grounds, he wonders whether the ethic of agnostic world-come-of-age people might not be something like "unconscious Christianity." One way or another, with faith or without, the world will be shaped "in keeping with Christian principles!" This is the Constantinian hangover in Bonhoeffer's own thought.

The universalism of the cross, which is even stronger in Bonhoeffer, is markedly different. It is in accord with Yoder's own description, where the way of the cross is

> that of the confessing minority whose commitment to her Lord, despite its being against the stream, is so convinced of the majesty of his Lordship that she risks trusting that his power and goodness can reach beyond the number of those who know him by his right name.[69]

Yoder adds: "The former universalism [Constantinian] is a high view of the human; the latter a high view of Jesus."[70]

We must draw our conclusions. The ethics of the community of the cross need not share *any* of the above Constantinian assumptions in order to be a theologically and morally valid, and "reasonable," social ethic. Indeed, to carry these Constantinian assumptions subverts the ethic of the cross and the character of its community. By such prevailing assumptions about the relationship of church, Christ, and culture, the theology of the cross is forced to be something it is not, namely, a perspective for society at large. The *theologia crucis* is certainly about faithful engagement in and for the world. But it is not about controlling culture and exercising dominance. The social ethic of the cross is a communitarian ethic of "life together" in Christian community, an ethic that may or may not be appropriated by the wider world. But that it is not so appropriated is not an invalidation of the ethic. The rigors of the ethic ought not be compromised just so that it will be accepted in all quarters.

Differently said, the moral vocation of the church is to "be for others." But it does so as a community of the cross. Its social ethics are thereby formulated from the nature of the new order under the lordship of Jesus, and not from the requirements of culture and its maintenance by whomever happens to possess access to power in the moment. The confidence that the good and right will triumph does not arise from the church's ability to line up might behind right so that the levers of power favor the good guys over the bad. Its confidence arises from the strange power of Jesus and his way, the power of cross and resurrection. This is life by a very different logic from that of the enhanced strength of the good guys, or the gradual institutionalization of virtue over vice under our wise tutelage.

For people accustomed to being in charge, this way of thinking is literally almost inconceivable. It does not "make sense," given their assumptions. Thus it is labeled hopelessly sectarian, irrelevant, self-righteous, and perhaps even world-hating. Without denying that these are risks for any close community with a distinctive identity, we must also say that for the community of the cross to be such a community in an unwilling world is not to be "against culture" per se (H. Richard Niebuhr's phrase). It is to be against those continual propensities in culture which invariably shift Christian ethics from living in and with the old aeon on the terms of the new, to living in and with the new aeon on the terms of the old! It is to be against the propensity always present to fuse even new creation with the Fall! This has been rampant in our acculturated Christianity. Its most frequent form has been the marriage of throne and altar, nation and church, sword and cross, ethnic community and religion. Or, if not marriages, then, as in the case of the United States, long-term arrangements of "living together."

A CONCLUDING NOTE

Reformation ethics in North America has generally emphasized that Luther's task was to put the church back under the gospel. The phrase important to ethics in this context has been "faith active in love."[71] This names the Christian's moral impulse, rooted as it is in the confidence of justification and the assurance of forgiveness. The unfinished portion of the Reformation, the teaching goes on, is the second task, namely, societal reform. "Love in pursuit of justice" is the motto here.[72]

The conceptualization in this essay is subtly different, though it is opposed neither to the church under the gospel nor to social reform! The contention here is that Luther never got the church he sometimes strove for, and that the link of *ecclesiology* and social ethics has rarely been rightly made in the Lutheran tradition. It is this link that haunted Bonhoeffer in the most existential ways in the church struggle and plagued the Confessing Church itself from within. It remains an unfinished part of the Reformation. It is the link Bonhoeffer labored mightily to forge anew and which occupied him to the end (see the "Outline for a Book"). Luther's initial impulse remains the suggestive one, namely, the theology of the cross. Bonhoeffer's contribution is to envision and embody a community of the cross with an ethic of imitation, or participation, as the church's societal vocation and presence.

But the plea for an ecclesial ethic of the cross expressive of the *theologia crucis* springs not so much from attachment to Luther and Bonhoeffer, despite their stature and contributions. It springs from an assessment of North American culture and Christianity as saturated with a dangerous theology of glory. Every form of religious and cultural triumphalism, innocent and otherwise, must be combatted. That can hardly be undertaken by the means most indigenous to the culture itself: power and wealth coupled with aspirations to control. If it is, the theology of glory will but prevail in another form. Some disarming alternative must show itself. Douglas John Hall's subtitle names our aspiration: "Toward an Indigenous Theology of the Cross." This is the communal task for North American Christians now.[73]

AFTERWORD

Larry Rasmussen discloses a lively sense for the fact that theological concepts, as well as creeds, possess changing degrees of truth. His sense is sharpened since he, an American, is also a Lutheran, and yet, as the representative of a particular Lutheranism in the United States, is still quite American. With this sensitivity he understands Bonhoeffer's message: the message of this German, Lutheran resister and conspirator of the Nazi period; the message of this gifted formulator of, and experimenter with, an adequate Christian answer for a poorly armed German church at a critical time of testing when the church itself tried to amalgamate a nazified patriotism with the Reformation proclamation of *sola gratia.* Thus Larry Rasmussen verifies Bonhoeffer's famous sentence about knowing a truth that can only be appropriated as we ponder the specific situation in which it is formed. Its persuasive power depends upon its contextualization in its actual location, circumstances, and time. And America's place, time, and self-understanding (the plural could be used here) requires such genuine scrutiny in order to see how, after the passing of a half century, Bonhoeffer's intimate attachment to Christ expresses itself in North America through the Christ who identifies with victims.

So one reads with mounting curiousity how Bonhoeffer's witness compares to that of three great Americans—Berrigan, Niebuhr, and Greenberg—and how this witness is interpreted and works itself out for responsible Christians poised, as they are, between self-confidence and fears in this most powerful of all lands. Bonhoeffer's credo leaps to life in the process. Although critical objections occur in the inter-action with the American environment, at the same time it achieves renewed critical functions itself. These are brought to bear on the growing American union of a supposed Christian faith and ethic and a revived patriotism, if not nationalism itself.

What delighted me most is the comparison between the Jew Green-berg and the Christian of *Letters and Papers from Prison*. In the conversation Rasmussen establishes, a dream of mine is fulfilled, name-ly, that both these thinkers, interpreters, and men of action might enter a dialogue. Historically, it could never have taken place, yet it is a dialogue for which their writings cry out for, and one that Rasmussen sets in motion here. It is high time it happen, and has already been successfully launched. The parallels of these two and their demands will command our attention for a long while.

EBERHARD BETHGE

NOTES

CHAPTER 1: BONHOEFFER'S FAMILY AND
              ITS SIGNIFICANCE FOR HIS THEOLOGY

1. *LPP,* 8 (translation slightly emended).
2. *E,* 227.
3. *FFP,* 76.
4. *DB,* 123 (translation slightly emended).
5. J. Zutt, E. Straus, and H. Scheller, eds., *Karl Bonhoeffer* (Berlin and Heidelberg: Springer Verlag, 1969).
6. *E,* 109.
7. *DB,* 836.
8. *LPP,* 6.
9. *GS* 5:85.
10. *E,* 97–98.
11. *LPP,* 9.
12. *DB,* 5.
13. *LT,* 35.
14. Ibid.
15. *LPP,* 271.
16. Ibid., 272.
17. Ibid., 271.
18. *E,* 233.
19. Ibid., 227.
20. Ibid.
21. Ibid., 230.
22. Ibid., 232.
23. Ibid., 234.
24. Ibid., 363.
25. Ibid., 364–65.
26. Ibid., 368.
27. Ibid., 363.
28. Ibid., 245 (translation emended).
29. Ibid., 97–98.
30. Ibid., 60 (translation emended).
31. *GS* 3:25.
32. *CD,* 45, 46.
33. *LPP,* 280.

34. Ibid., 281.
35. Ibid., 280.
36. Ibid., 281.
37. Ibid., 361.
38. Ibid., 383 (translation slightly enended).
39. Letter to Helmut Rössler, 1931, *GS* 1:61.
40. *DB,* 155 (translation slightly emended).
41. *LPP,* 282.
42. Ibid., 295.

CHAPTER 2: PATRIOTISM

1. Charles Krauthammer, "Reagan's Painless Patriotism," *The Washington Post,* 31 May 1985.
2. G. Clarke Chapman Jr., "Approaching Nuclearism as a Heresy: Four Paradigms," *Union Seminary Quarterly Review* 39 (1984): 264.
3. Bonhoeffer, "Der Tod der Mose," *GS* 4:620 (my translation).
4. *Ibid.*
5. Reinhold Niebuhr, *Christianity and Crisis,* June 25, 1945, 6.
6. Letter of 22 December 1943, *LPP,* 174–75.
7. Cited from Keith Clements, *A Patriotism for Today* (Bristol, England: Bristol Baptist College, 1984), frontispiece. I an grateful to Clements for his treatment of Bonhoeffer's patriotism, and I draw heavily from it.
8. *DB,* 86.
9. Paul Lehmann, "Paradox of Discipleship," in *I Knew Dietrich Bonhoeffer,* ed. Wolf-Dieter Zimmermann and Ronald Gregor Smith (New York: Harper & Row, 1964), 41.
10. "After Ten Years," *LPP,* 17.
11. The relative "popularity" of these three church groupings is reflected in the recorded allegiance of the clergy. Claudia Koonz, in *Mothers in the Fatherland: Women, the Family and Nazi Politics* (New York: St. Martin's Press, 1986) reports that, in round numbers, 250 Protestant pastors joined the Deutsche Christen, 2,000 joined the Confessing Church, and 14,000 remained publicly neutral. Cited from The Religion & Society Report, 5, no. 8 (August 1988), 7.
12. *CD,* 57.
13. Letter "An M. Diestel zum 70. Geburtstag," *GS* 6:578 (my translation).
14. *GS* 1:447–48.
15. Ibid., 448.
16. Ibid.
17. Ibid., 412.
18. *B:EM,* 82.
19. "An den Landeskirchenausschuss," *GS* 6:417 (my translation).
20. *GS* 1:205 (my translation).
21. Ibid., 281.
22. *B:EM,* 91.
23. *DB,* 585.

24. "Night Voices from Tegel," *LPP,* 353. I prefer the translation used here, however, as provided by J. B. Leishman in the *Union Seminary Quarterly Review 1,* no. 3 (1946): 7.

25. *GS* 1:40 (my translation).

26. "Christians and Pagans," *LPP,* 349.

27. Letter of 30 April 1944, *LPP,* 279.

CHAPTER 3: RESISTANCE

1. See especially his review of Bonhoeffer's biography in "The Passion of Dietrich Bonhoeffer," *Saturday Review* 53 (May 30, 1970), 17–22.

2. Daniel Berrigan, *To Dwell in Peace: An Autobiography* (New York: Harper & Row, 1986), 243.

3. Robert Coles and Daniel Berrigan, *The Geography of Faith* (Boston: Beacon Press, 1971), 28–30.

4. For example, the Confessing Church's response to the Jews and the jailed was for Bonhoeffer a test of whether the Confessing Church was truly the church. For Berrigan, the response to the victims of war and to the poor is a parallel test.

5. Compare Bonhoeffer's portrayal in *The Cost of Discipleship* with Berrigan's foreword to David Kirk's *Quotations from Chairman Jesus.*

6. Letter of 22 December 1943, LPP, 174.

7. In Berrigan and Coles, *The Geography of Faith,* 82.

8. For Bonhoeffer this is all the more striking because pacifism was a heresy for church as well as state. Conscientious objection was punishable by death.

9. David O'Brien, *The Holy Cross Quarterly* 4 (1971): 55.

10. Chomsky, ibid., 22.

11. O'Brien, 52.

12. The reader will find that the language itself is not Bonhoeffer's. For the evidence that he used what are, in fact, just war criteria applied domestically (thus, "just rebellion" or "just coup d'état" criteria), see Larry L. Rasmussen, *Dietrich Bonhoeffer: Reality and Resistance* (Nashville: Abingdon Press, 1972).

13. *E,* 350–51.

14. Ibid., 239.

15. Berrigan and Coles, *The Geography of Faith,* 63–64.

16. Daniel Berrigan, *The Dark Night of Resistance* (Garden City, N.Y.: Doubleday), 77.

17. Ibid., 78.

18. Berrigan, "The Passion of Dietrich Bonhoeffer," 17.

19. Cf. Berrigan, *The Dark Night of Resistance,* 76. "To take up weapons is to lose one's choice of weapons. Men who take up the sword, die by the sword."

20. Philip Berrigan, *Prison Journals of a Priest Revolutionary* (New York: Holt, Rinehart & Winston, 1970), 89.

21. See the quotation, 47.

22. There is a telling conversation between Bonhoeffer and a resistance figure who could approach Hitler armed and whose conscience was so driven by its knowledge of war crimes that he wanted to bring off the assassination. Bonhoeffer told him not to do so, because the issue was not between the individual conscience and Hitler's deeds, nor was it a matter of some dramatic gesture. The issue was between Nazism and the future, and the latter meant any such act had to be done in light of reasonably assured success that it would contribute to the end of the Nazi operation as a whole. See Rasmussen, *Reality and Resistance,* 141–42; and Wolf-Dieter Zimmermann and Ronald Gregor Smith, eds., *I Knew Dietrich Bonhoeffer* (New York: Harper & Row, 1966), 190ff.

23. To avoid misunderstanding, let me add that the above does not assume Berrigan is consciously proceeding with similar criteria. Even when his public and written utterances do indicate that the concerns of these criteria are important to him, I am not assuming that his order and emphases are Bonhoeffer's. I have simply used some of Bonhoeffer's criteria as a handy way of discussing what are, in fact, critical issues for both of them and upon which they have agreements and disagreements.

24. Berrigan, "The Passion of Dietrich Bonhoeffer," 19.

25. *LPP,* 6.

26. Berrigan, *The Dark Night of Resistance,* 3, 7.

27. Ibid., 70.

28. Berrigan and Coles, *The Geography of Faith,* 25.

29. Ibid., 36.

30. Francine du Plessix Gray *Divine Disobedience* [New York: Alfred A. Knopf, 1970, 57 is here paraphrasing Daniel Berrigan in answer to a question as to why he joined the Catonsville Nine and whether it had been a practical gesture.

31. Ibid., 140.

32. Berrigan, *Prison Journals of a Priest Revolutionary,* 212.

33. *Christianity and Crisis,* December 28, 1970, 30, no. 21, 288.

34. John Raines, *The Holy Cross Quarterly* 4 (1971): 66–67.

35. Berrigan, *The Dark Night of Resistance,* 6.

36. Ibid.

37. Ibid., 17.

38. Berrigan and Coles, *The Geography of Faith,* 44.

39. For further discussion of this, see Bruce C. Birch and Larry L. Rasmussen, *The Predicament of the Prosperous* (Philadelphia: Westminster Press, 1978), especially the chapter, "Which Way Now?"

40. See Berrigan and Coles, *The Geography of Faith,* 80–82.

41. Ibid., 3.

42. Ibid., 84.

43. For a brief sketch, see Berrigan, *The Dark Night of Resistance,* 97.

44. I will not list similarities here—cf. the first section of this chapter, nor have I attempted to enumerate all the dissimilarities. An additional difference, which has the same outcome for the contrasting ethics, is Berrigan's mysticism. Bonhoeffer would never have found St. John of the Cross the guide through "the dark night of resistance."

45. Berrigan, *To Dwell in Peace,* 334ff.
46. Ibid., 348.
47. Ibid.
48. Ibid.
49. Ibid., 349.

CHAPTER 4: WORSHIP IN A WORLD COME OF AGE

1. Letter of 30 April 1944, *LPP,* 279.
2. Ibid., 280.
3. Ibid., 281.
4. Only the outline survives because Bonhoeffer took the remainder of the manuscript along to the Gestapo prison. The fact that his very few possessions there included the manuscript indicates its importance to him ("Outline for a Book," *LPP,* 382).
5. Letter of 30 April 1944, *LPP,* 281.
6. Ibid., 280.
7. Letter of 8 June 1944, *LPP,* 327.
8. "Outline for a Book," *LPP,* 380.
9. "Thoughts on the Day of the Baptism of Dietrich Wilhelm Rüdiger Bethge," *LPP,* 299–300 (trans. emended).
10. Roger A. Johnson, Ernest Wallwork, Clifford Green, H. Paul Santmire, and Harold Y. Vanderpool, eds., *Critical Issues in Modern Religion* (Englewood Cliffs, N.J.: Prentice-Hall, 1973), 287.
11. Letter of 30 April 1944, *LPP,* 279.
12. Ibid., 280.
13. More precisely, Christianity in the West has been clothed in a variety of forms of consciousness, all or virtually all of which have shared certain common "religious" strains.
14. See especially Ernst Feil, *The Theology of Dietrich Bonhoeffer,* trans. Martin Rumscheidt (Philadelphia: Fortress Press, 1984), as well as Bethge, *DB.*
15. "Outline for a Book," *LPP,* 381.
16. Letter of 8 June 1944, *LPP,* 326.
17. Ibid., 327.
18. Letter of 30 April 1944, *LPP,* 281.
19. "Thoughts on the Day of the Baptism of Dietrich Wilhelm Rüdiger Bethge," *LPP,* 300. (trans. emended).
20. Bonhoeffer writes, "The Pauline question whether . . . [circumcision] is a condition of justification seems to me in present-day terms to be whether religion is a condition of salvation," letter of 30 April 1944, *LPP,* 281.
21. See note 19.

CHAPTER 5: THE CHURCH'S PUBLIC VOCATION

1. See the introductory essay by Larry Rasmussen in *Reinhold Niebuhr: Theologian of Public Life,* a volume in the series, The Making of Modern Theology, ed. John de Gruchy (London: Collins Religious Publishing, 1989).

2. The reader may wish to refer to chapter 2, "Patriotism."

3. These dynamics are elaborated in chapter 4, "Worship in a World Come of Age."

4. Gerhard Forde, "The Exodus from Virtue to Grace: Justification by Faith Today," *Interpretation* 34 (1980):38.

5. *E,* 189–90.

6. *E,* 188–89.

7. Peter Berger and Thomas Luckmann, *The Social Construction of Reality* (Garden City, N.Y.: Doubleday, 1966), 93.

8. Gerhard Lohfink, *Jesus and Community* (Philadelphia: Fortress Press, 1984), 123.

9. Paulo Friere, *Pedagogy of the Oppressed* (New York: Herder & Herder, 1970), 34.

10. Thomas W. Ogletree, *The Use of the Bible in Christian Ethics* (Philadelphia: Fortress Press, 1983), 185.

11. Rudolf Bultmann, "New Testament and Mythology," in *Kergyma and Myth* (London: S.P.C.K., 1953), 5.

12. Dominic Crossan, *In Parables: The Challenge of the Historical Jesus* (New York: Harper & Row, 1973), 26.

13. Letter of 21 August 1944, *LPP,* 391.

14. See his volume by this title: *Beyond Tragedy* (New York: Harper & Row, 1937).

15. The reference is to the poem Bonhoeffer wrote, one of his last (see *LPP*).

16. See Hall's chapter in *Reinhold Niebuhr and the Issues of Our Time,* ed. Richard Harries (Grand Rapids: W. B. Eerdmans, 1986), 183–204.

17. Letter of 21 July 1944, *LPP,* 370.

18. See the discussion in chapter 4 above, "Worship in a World Come of Age."

19. Eric W. Gritsch and Robert W. Jenson, *Lutheranism: The Theological Movement and Its Confessional Writings* (Philadelphia: Fortress Press, 1976), 93.

20. A common phrase from Pinchas Lapide, *The Sermon on the Mount: Utopia or Program for Action?* (Maryknoll, N.Y.: Orbis, 1986).

21. *LPP,* 17. From "After Ten Years."

22. The phrases are Bonhoeffer's from the letter cited earlier.

23. For this chapter I am indebted to William R. Herzog, "The Quest for the Historical Jesus and the Discovery of the Apocalyptic Jesus," *Pacific Theological Review* 19 (Fall 1985): 25–39. More extensive discussion of the church's public roles is available in my essay, "The Public Vocation of an Eschatological Community," *The Union Seminary Quarterly Review 42.4 (1988): 25-35.*

CHAPTER 6: METHOD

1. See Clifford Green, "The Text of Bonhoeffer's Ethics," in *New Studies in Bonhoeffer's Ethics,* ed. William J. Peck (Lewiston and Queenstown: Edwin

Mellen, 1987), 3–66. The discussion of exact arrangement of the materials for *Ethics* continues. The most up-to-date conclusions will be reflected in the publication of the *Dietrich Bonhoeffer Werke* by Christian Kaiser Verlag, Munich.

2. E.g., "Vorwort," 14–17.

3. Hanfried Muller, Von der Kirche zur Welt (Hamburg: Herbert Reich Evang. Verlag, 1961), 288–89.

4. *Eg*, 13.

5. Eberhard Bethge, lecture at Union Theological Seminary, 7 February 1967.

6. Letter of 18 November 1943, *LPP*, 129.

7. *CC*, 62.

8. Ibid.

9. *CC*, 28 (emphasis in the original).

10. Ibid. (emphasis in the original).

11. *E*, 70.

12. *E*, 194.

13. *Eg*, 85.

14. *Eg*, 241.

15. *E*, 229.

16. Heinrich Ott, *Wirklichkeit und Glaube* (Zurich: Vandenhoeck & Ruprecht, 1966), 241–42. Translation and emphasis mine. The emphasis is warranted by the preceding sentence. There Ott calls conformation to Christ the "oberstes materielles Prinzip dieser Ethik," 241.

17. Letter of 30 April 1944, *LPP*, 279.

18. One attraction of this method is its applicability for both the Christian and the non-Christian. In the above set, the first is for the Christian, the second for the non-Christian. Yet both are the same because of Bonhoeffer's identification of the world-in-Christ with reality. The problematic arises at the point of epistemology. Can one know the real apart from knowing Christ?

19. *E*, 195.

20. *GS* 3:48. The lecture was given in February 1929.

21. *E*, 85.

22. *E*, 85.

23. Edward L. Long Jr., *A Survey of Christian Ethics* (New York: Oxford University Press, 1967), 117. This is Long's description of relational ethics.

24. *E*, 228.

25. *E*, 228, note.

26. *E*, 80.

27. *NRS*, 45–47 (trans. emended). See *GS* 3:55–56.

28. *E*, 149.

29. See Bonhoeffer's discussion of "The Natural," in *E*, 143–51, and "The Four Mandates," in *E*, 207–13 and 186–87.

30. *E*, 145.

31. Author's translation; see *CS*, 136. The translation of *Gemeinde* is a notorious problem; Bethge sometimes translates it as "Christ existing as church." See Eberhard Bethge, "The Challenge of Dietrich Bonhoeffer's Life

and Theology," *The Chicago Theological Seminary Review* 51, no. 2 (February 1961): 9.

32. Bethge, "The Challenge," 8 (emphasis in the original).

33. *AB*, 90–91. *Act and Being* was written in 1931.

34. *DBg*, 1075. The material "Gibt es eine christliche Ethik?" is an appendix.

35. *DBg*, 1075.

36. *CC*, passim, and *NRS*, 157–73.

37. *CD*, 341. Initial publication was in 1937.

38. *E*, 64–119.

39. *E*, 58. It is intriguing, but not coincidental, that this change occurred in tandem with Bonhoeffer's move from churchly to political resistance.

40. *DBg*, 806 (my translation).

41. Bonhoeffer was experimenting here, in any case. One time he names four (*E*, 207); another time he substitutes one for another (*E*, 286); still another time he wonders where "friendship" belongs and whether culture and education should not be added to marriage and family, work, state, and church (letter of 23 January 1944, *LPP*, 193).

42. Letter of 27 July 1944, *LPP*, 373. In Lutheran dogmatics *fides directa* means unconscious response to God-in-Christ in contrast to *fides reflexa*, meaning reflective, conscious response.

43. Letter of 23 January 1944, *LPP*, 191.

44. *NRS*, 46–47 (translation emended; see *GS* 3:56–57).

45. *GS* 1:147 (translation mine); the emphasis is Bonhoeffer's. The translation in *NRS*, 164, incorrectly reads "for the preaching of the sacrament" instead of "for the preaching of the command" *(Gebot)*.

46. *NRS*, 161–62 (emphasis in the original).

47. *GS* 1:146 (my translation); see *NRS*, 162–63.

48. *NRS*, 163.

49. *NRS*, 167 (emphasis in the original).

50. See notes 36 and 37, citing the essay "Gibt es eine christliche Ethik?"

51. *GS* 1:150 (my translation); see *NRS*, 166. The last line anticipates the mandates, the natural, and the penultimate as discussed in *Ethics*. It is worth mentioning, however, that this line and those which speak of "reality" should not lead us to conclude that *Ethics* is here in nuce. Whatever the anticipation, "reality" in this address is not yet the full-blown christocratic understanding of it that Bonhoeffer presents in *Ethics*. There is much in this address that points to, but is not yet Bonhoeffer's grand Christo-universal vision of this world.

52. Letter of 15 December 1943, *LPP*, 163.

53. *GS* 1:33 (my translation).

54. *CD*, 69.

55. *DBg*, 803–4. Bethge does say, however, that the list is incomplete. Furthermore, later evidence, explained elsewhere, will make for revisions in Bethge's biography of Bonhoeffer, cited here.

56. Advent IV, *LPP*, 171.

57. This chapter was written prior to the June 1981 discovery of letters from Bonhoeffer to Barth. The letter of 13 May 1942 includes the following: "I have been in Zurich for a few days, since yesterday with the Pestalozzis.

Now, armed with the galley proofs of your new volume of the *Dogmatics* which Mr. Frey has procured for me, I want to spend about eight days on the way to Geneva in complete peace and quiet in a boarding house on the lake of Geneva recommended to me by the Pestalozzis. There I want to try to work through at least the second half of your volume." Bonhoeffer's reference is to 2/2 of the *Kirchliche Dogmatik;* the second half is "The Command of God." I am using a translation of the letters provided by John Godsey.

    58. See Karl Barth, *Church Dogmatics* 2/4, trans. A. T. Mackay et al. (Edinburgh: T. & T. Clark, 1961), 258–67. This is fascinating. Barth criticizes Bonhoeffer extensively on one point only—the concrete command in the mandates. This is the one place in all the sections in *Ethics* on the command of God where Bonhoeffer deviates from Barth.

    59. *E,* 277–85.

    60. *E,* 292–302. Between these comes "The Concrete Commandment and the Divine Mandates."

    61. Karl Barth, *Church Dogmatics* 2/2, trans. G. W. Bromiley et al. (Edinburgh: T. & T. Clark, 1957), 509–782. The space used to treat this same subject is typical of each!

    62. *E,* 281.

    63. *Church Dogmatics* 2/2, 285.

    64. *Eg,* 298 (emphasis in the original).

    65. Karl Barth, *Kirchliche Dogmatik* 2/2 (Zurich: Evangelischer Verlag A. G. Zollikon, 1946), 650 (emphasis in the original). This is the second edition. The portions of Bonhoeffer being compared were probably written during the winter of 1942–43.

    66. *Church Dogmatics* 2/2, 588.

    67. *Church Dogmatics* 2/2, 586.

    68. *E,* 282.

    69. *Church Dogmatics* 2/2, 669.

    70. Ibid., 673–74.

    71. *E,* 278.

    72. Ibid., 279–80.

    73. *Church Dogmatics* 2/2, 665.

    74. *E,* 280.

    75. *Church Dogmatics* 2/2, 708–32.

    76. Ibid., 738–41.

    77. See the letters of 18 November 1943 and 15 December 1943, *LPP,* 129, 163.

    78. *E,* 282.

    79. Ibid., 283.

    80. Paul Lehmann, "The Foundation and Pattern of Christian Behavior," *Christian Faith and Social Action* (New York: Charles Scribners Sons, 1953), 101 (emphasis in the original). There is an increasingly open-ended understanding of freedom as one moves from Barth's ethics to Bonhoeffer's to Lehmann's. The place held by obedience to God and service to neighbor in Barth becomes responsibility to God and neighbor in Bonhoeffer and freedom before God and neighbor in Lehmann. This parallels the weight of emphasis

on the indicative over the imperative as one moves from Barth to Bonhoeffer to Lehmann. The subtle changes in the material Bonhoeffer takes from Barth illustrate these shifts of emphasis away from Barth's strong tones.

81. *E,* 288.
82. Ibid., 291.
83. Ibid.
84. Ibid., 279.
85. Ibid., 278.
86. Ibid., 283.
87. Ibid., 267, 264.
88. Ibid., 272–73.
89. Ibid., 265.
90. Ibid., 285.
91. Ibid., 280. Emphasis mine.
92. Ibid., 270.
93. Ibid., 265–66. The German for "peripheral event" is "Grenzereignis." This does not connote "unimportance" as "peripheral" sometimes does in English. It means a particular location, as we have described above. Occupying "a fixed time and a fixed place" does not thereby make the ethical a matter of less importance for Bonhoeffer. On the contrary, it is a matter of "big guns."
94. *E,* 298. Perhaps this is the place to refer the reader to the methodological move to near casuistry as Bonhoeffer wrests moral directives from the innate laws that result from the forming of the command (or the forming of Christ). The sections on "natural rights," albeit unfinished, especially show this. Bonhoeffer discusses euthanasia, abortion, and suicide in this manner. See *Ethics,* 149–72. It is more than methodological coincidence that the same pattern occurs in Barth's ethics. For some illustrations, see *Church Dogmatics* 3/4, on "Respect for Life," 324–97, and "Protection of Life," 397–470.
95. *E,* 282.
96. See, for instance, 18 July 1944, *LPP,* 361.
97. This holds for the following: Advent IV, *LPP,* 169–73; 18 April 1944, *LPP,* 273–82; 5 May 1944, *LPP,* 285; 20 May 1944, *LPP,* 302–3; 2 June 1944, *LPP,* 315–16; 21 June 1944, *LPP,* 332–33; 27 June 1944, *LPP,* 335–37; 16 July 1944, *LPP,* 357–61; 18 July 1944, *LPP,* 361–63; 21 July 1944, *LPP,* 369–70; 27 July 1944, *LPP,* 373.
98. "Outline for a Book," *LPP,* 380–83.
99. Dietrich Bonhoeffer, "The First Table of the Ten Commandments," in John D. Godsey, *Preface to Bonhoeffer* (Philadelphia: Fortress Press, 1965), 50–67.
100. Letter of 3 August 1944, *LPP,* 378.
101. Letter of 8 June 1944, *LPP,* 327.
102. Letter of 30 June 1944, *LPP,* 342.
103. Letter of 16 July 1944, *LPP,* 360–61.
104. Ibid.
105. Letter of 8 June 1944, *LPP,* 328 (emphasis added).
106. Letter of 30 April 1944, *LPP,* 279.
107. Ibid., 280.

108. *E,* 299.
109. Ibid., 37–43.
110. Ibid., 70, 298.
111. Ibid., 85, 299.
112. Ibid., 222, 224, 284–85, 291
113. Ibid., 120–21.
114. Müller, *Von der Kirche zur Welt,* 289–92.
115. Ibid., 290.
116. See Heinrich Ott, *Wirklichkeit und I: Zum theologischen Erbe Dietrich Bonhoeffers* (Zurich: Vandenhoeck & Ruprecht, 1966).
117. A discussion of method which benefits from literature that came after Bonhoeffer's efforts is found in Bruce C. Birch and Larry L. Rasmussen, *Bible and Ethics in the Christian Life,* revised and expanded edition (Minneapolis: Augsburg, 1989). See the chapter entitled "Decision Making" (the earlier edition does not include this chapter).

CHAPTER 7: DIVINE PRESENCE AND HUMAN POWER

1. James M. Gustafson, *Ethics from a Theocentric Perspective,* vol. 2 (Chicago: University of Chicago Press, 1984), 281.
2. "Outline for a Book," *LPP,* 380.
3. From the introduction by Nina Beth Cardin to Rabbi Greenberg's "The Third Great Cycle of Jewish History," in *Perspectives* (The National Jewish Center for Learning and Leadership, n.d.), iv.
4. Irving Greenberg, "Cloud of Smoke, Pillar of Fire: Judaism, Christianity, and Modernity after the Holocaust," in Eva Fleishner, *Auschwitz: Beginning of a New Era?* (New York: KTAV, 1974), 11.
5. A comparison with Bonhoeffer would cite his reflections written as part of *Ethics,* together with parallel remarks in his essay on what the resisters had learned from the Nazi experience. See *E,* chap. 3, "Ethics as Formation," the subsection "The Theoretical Ethicist and Reality"; and *LPP,* "After Ten Years," the subsection "Who Stands Fast?". Note also the sentence in *LPP,* in "Thoughts on the Day of the Baptism of Dietrich Wilhelm Rüdiger Bethge": "We thought we could make our way in life vith reason and justice, and when both failed, we felt that we were at the end of our tether" (298).
6. Greenberg, "Cloud of Smoke, Pillar of Fire," 26.
7. Ibid., Rubenstein quoted by Greenberg, with Greenberg supplying the emphasis.
8. Ibid., 27.
9. Ibid.
10. Ibid.
11. Ibid.
12. Ibid., 32.
13. Ibid., 42.
14. Ibid.
15. Ibid.

16. This is a line from Greenberg, "Cloud of Smoke, Pillar of Fire," 10, but I have substituted the word "faith" for "religion," in keeping with the discussion in this paragraph.

17. Letter of 11 August 1944, *LPP,* 384.

18. "After Ten Years," *LPP,* 7.

19. Ibid.

20. Ibid.

21. "Thoughts on the Day of the Baptism of Dietrich Wilhelm Rüdiger Bethge," *LPP,* 299.

22. Ibid.

23. Ibid.

24. Ibid., 300.

25. Some of the turmoil is reflected in Bonhoeffer's essay "After Ten Years," and vividly in "Night Voices in Tegel." Both are published in *Letters and Papers from Prison.*

26. "After Ten Years," *LPP,* 3.

27. Ibid., 4.

28. Ibid., 5.

29. "Thoughts on the Day of the Baptism of Dietrich Wilhelm Rüdiger Bethge," *LPP,* 297.

30. "Outline for a Book," *LPP,* 382.

31. "Thoughts on the Day of the Baptism of Dietrich Wilhelm Rüdiger Bethge," *LPP,* 299.

32. Ibid., 300.

33. Ibid.

34. Letter of 18 July 1944, *LPP,* 361.

35. From a 1932 lecture that appears as Appendix B in the German edition of Eberhard Bethge's biography of Bonhoeffer, *DBg,* 1065 (my translation).

36. Letter of 16 July 1944, *LPP,* 360.

37. Ibid.

38. Ibid.

39. Ibid., 360–61.

40. Letter of 8 June 1944, *LPP,* 326.

41. "Outline for a Book," *LPP,* 381.

42. Letter of 18 July 1944, *LPP,* 361.

43. Ibid. (emphasis mine).

44. Letter of 21 July 1944, *LPP,* 369–70. In this context, the reference to Jeremiah 45 must refer to Yahweh's words to Baruch. Baruch complains of his own condition: "I am worn out with groaning, and find no relief!" Yahweh says that destruction is being visited upon humankind and Baruch is asking for special treatment. The point for Bonhoeffer is that it is the sufferings of the world and not his own which command attention. More precisely it is joining God in the sufferings of the world.

45. Ibid.

46. "Outline for a Book," *LPP,* 381.

47. Letter of 21 August 1944, *LPP,* 392.

48. Letter of 27 June 1944, *LPP,* 341.

49. Ibid., 341–42.

50. Ibid., 342.

51. Letter of 16 July 1944, *LPP*, 360.

52. Ibid.

53. Letter of 30 April 1944, *LPP*, 282.

54. "Outline for a Book," *LPP*, 381.

55. Greenberg, "The Third Great Cycle," 14.

56. Ibid., 15.

57. Ibid.

58. Ibid.

59. Ibid., 14.

60. Ibid., 15.

61. Ibid., 7.

62. Ibid., 6.

63. Ibid., 9.

64. Ibid., 16.

65. Cited above from "Outline for a Book," *LPP*, 381.

66. Greenberg, "The Third Great Cycle," 10.

67. Irving Greenberg, "Voluntary Covenant," *Perspectives,* 41 (emphasis added).

68. Ibid., 11.

69. Ibid. Given sufficient time and space it would be fascinating to read Bonhoeffer in *LPP* in light of this and other passages from Greenberg. For example, the Jesus of *LPP* is surely an intense presence for Bonhoeffer, precisely in the midst of secular, chiefly political, acts of reconstruction. This Jesus is strikingly no longer the commanding one of *The Cost of Discipleship*. He is far more the empowering companion than the overpowering "Lord."

70. "Outline for a Book," *LPP*, 380. We should not relegate Greenberg's investigations of theological models for the presence of God in our time to this endnote. Alas, for the sake of maintaining the flow of the main text and keeping the overall length in check, that is necessary. Greenberg wrestles with the kind of divine presence that would make sense in the light of the incomprehensibility of the Holocaust and the redemptive event of the State of Israel. What are the analogies from past struggles which might illumine our own? In "Cloud of Smoke, Pillar of Fire," Greenberg reviews three:

1. *Job.* Job is the righteous one from whom everything is taken. His friends suggest he is being punished for his sins. He rejects this explanation. His wife suggests that he "curse God and die," which he also rejects. His suffering is not justified by God, nor is Job consoled by the thunderous speech of the majesty and grandeur of God. All that is meaningful is that in the whirlwind the contact with God is restored, and this sense of the Presence is sufficient to go on living amidst the contradictions (34–35).

2. *Suffering servant.* Greenberg begins by noting J. Coert Rylaarsdam's comment that if being a Christian meant taking up the cross and being crucified for God, then the only practicing Christians were the Jews. Greenberg goes on to say that the description of the suffering one in Isaiah 53 reads like eyewitness accounts of concentration camp inmates, which it certainly does.

But the heart of Greenberg's commentary is the plausible meaning of the key theme that the iniquity of us all lands upon the servant. The treatment of the suffering servant "is a kind of early warning system of the sins intrinsic in the culture but often not seen until later" (37). Greenberg then discusses various modern absolutist claims—Christian claims to absolute spiritual salvation, Stalinist and Nazi claims to absolute social and political salvation, capitalist and superpatriot claims to ultimate national loyalty—and renders the Holocaust the counterpart of the torture of the Suffering Servant. That is, the Holocaust reveals in the treatment of the Jews (and others in the Holocaust) the demonic that is present in modernity's claims. "The Holocaust was an advance warning of the demonic potential in modern culture" (37). "Unfortunately the strain of evil," Greenberg goes on, "is deeply embedded in the best potentials of modernity. The pollution is in the liberating technology; the uniformity in the powerful communication and cultural explosion; the mass murder in the efficient bureaucracy. This suggests a desperate need to delegitimatize the excessive authority claims of our culture" (37). The treatment of the suffering servant then is revelatory of evil, and, in contrast to Christianity's glorification of the servant's submission, the prose poem shows the overwhelming power of evil, a power of such strength that the servant may be driven to yield to it. The servant has indeed borne the iniquities of all— all humankind's sins have been inflicted upon the servant—but the lesson learned is not that innocent suffering is itself redemptive. The lesson is that suffering must be fought, cut down, eliminated before it overwhelms the innocent and they have no recourse but to do anything at all except yield to it. The suffering servant reveals what must be done so that the reality does not repeat itself over and over again.

3. *Lamentations and the controversy with God.* The third chapter of Lamentations contains the image of God "as a bear who stalks, and attacks me like a lion." "God ate up my flesh and skin." The narrator does not, as in another portion of Lamentations, say that the torture is God's response to sin. There is no hint of sinfulness in the account here, only suffering and the agony inflicted by God. From the narrator's side there is anger and pain and spiritual desolation: "And I said: my eternity and my hope from God has been lost." The narrator is not guilty, but the narrator suffers and is cut off from God. Greenberg, who notes the closeness of this to Wiesel's writings, quotes Wiesel on Rosh Hashanah: "This day I had ceased to plead. . . . On the contrary, I felt very strong. I was the accuser, God the accused. . . . I had ceased to be anything but ashes, yet I felt myself to be stronger than the Almighty . . ." (39). Wiesel's lesson, learned in the agony itself, is that a new relationship with God only begins with the anger and controversy, given the experience of massive evil and suffering. The justification is of suffering human beings, not God. Greenberg goes on to say that what may then come forth is a "total and thoroughgoing self-criticism that would purge the emotional dependency and self-abasement of traditional religion and its false crutch of certainty and security. It involves a willingness to confess and clear up the violations of the image of God (of women, Jews, blacks, others) in our values, and a willingness to overcome the institutionalism that sacrifices God to self-interest" (40). For Christians it

would mean repudiating the anti-Semitism in the Gospels themselves and declaring that the God who has sanctioned that in Christianity is no longer the God Christians will worship, lest Christianity again be complicit in a future Holocaust. So what begins in anger at the God one knows moves into a deep critique of one's image of God and relationship to God, with all that that means, and ends up with a moral qualification for any proposed word from God. It may well mean a rejection of the God we have in fact worshiped.

Greenberg finishes his theological grappling with the acknowledgment that none of these models can "fully articulate the tensions of the relationship to God after the Holocaust" (41). Ours is, to recall the discussion above, a time for dialectical thinking stretched between the inadequate past under-standings and the as-yet-unknown future ones. This suggests, Greenberg goes on, that "we are entering a period of silence in theology—a silence about God that corresponds to His silence" (41). He closes the section with a sentence that echoes Bonhoeffer: "In this silence, God may be presence and hope, but no longer the simple *deus ex machina*" (41).

71. Greenberg, "Voluntary Covenant," 27.

72. Ibid., 35.

73. Ibid., 30.

74. From a letter to the author.

75. Greenberg, "Voluntary Covenant," 36.

76. Ibid., 34–35.

77. Ibid., 40.

78. Letter of 16 July 1944, *LPP,* 360.

79. Greenberg, from the quotation just cited.

80. "The Ethics of Power," 35–36 of the typed manuscript. For the sake of brevity, I have cited this draft rather than the longer passage from the published version. Everything included here is part of the lengthier passage.

81. "The Ethics of Jewish Power," *Perspectives,* 27.

82. Niebuhr would not have hesitated to transpose Greenberg's sentences, just cited, as follows: "Christian powerlessness is absolutely incompatible with Christian existence. But Christian power is incompatible with absolute Chris-tian moral purity."

83. Ibid. In another essay, Greenberg writes: "If Jews fail to amass or exercise effectively sufficient military and economic power, and so are overwhelmed by their enemies, then Jewish existence is endangered. If Jews let power brutalize their culture or create an unjust discriminatory system, then the basic values of that culture are betrayed, and the community's ability to main-tain group loyalty may be seriously undermined" ("The Third Era of Jewish History: Power and Politics," *Perspectives,* 46–47). Later in the same essay, he says: "In the Third Era, this ability to exercise power while restraining its excesses will be the major test of whether Jews and Judaism can flourish in the post-modern world" (Ibid., 53).

84. Ibid., 1.

85. Ibid.

86. Ibid.

87. Ibid.

88. Ibid., 5.

89. Ibid.

90. Readers can refer to the discussion of Bonhoeffer and Berrigan and Bonhoeffer's use of modified "just war" criteria. See chap. 3, "Resistance."

91. "The Ethics of Jewish Power," 5.

92. Ibid., 6.

93. Ibid.

94. Ibid.

95. Ibid., 7.

96. Ibid.

97. Unfortunately, space constraints limit our presentation of Greenberg's discussion of concrete cases and policies. This is where power decisions must be made and power exercised. This is also where the complexity of both must be faced. Thus, cases are crucial. Here I only append to our discussion in the main text Greenberg's keen awareness of certain requisite conditions for the balance of power. He firmly believes in it and is committed to it as the ethical structure. At the same time, the varied power contenders must also accept it if it is to work. Thus he says that "Israel should seek maximum Arab autonomy in Judea and Samaria by encouraging the emergence of indigenous leadership willing to live in peace with the Jewish state. Let the word go out unequivocally from Israel that Palestinian Arabs can earn autonomy and even a state by seeking peace and taking risks for it. In theory, the PLO also can earn the status of a negotiating partner with Israel. The PLO would have to disavow its call for the destruction of Israel and purge its 'rejection front' elements—preferably by military confrontation—to make clear that it really intends to live in peace with Israel. Of course, this will not happen until the Arab nations and the world stop romanticizing and encouraging the murderous elements in PLO leadership" (7–8). Short of a commitment to the legitimacy of one another to exist, a balance of power is actually unacceptable: "A situation of approximate equality of force tempts the aggressors to try for one strategy, one breakthrough, that can tilt the balance in their favor" (7). But with a guarantee of intended coexistence, the balance should move in the direction of greater political and military parity, in Greenberg's judgment. He rejects any romanticizing of power, including Jewish power.

98. Ibid., 8.

99. Ibid.

100. Ibid. In a similar vein, and showing the excruciating difficulty of combining balance of power social theory, the lessons of oppression, and the presence of real threats to survival, Greenberg writes: "The same standard of ethical memory suggests that Israel must seek ways of finding room for the Palestinians' dignity and national identity. Whether this takes the form of local autonomy or an Israeli-Jordanian condominium or an independent Palestinian state is a secondary question. The form should grow directly out of historical process, direct negotiations, and the ability of the Palestinians to win the confidence of the Israeli public and world Jews. The Holocaust standard suggests that the Palestinians must earn this trust by getting rid of their murderous leadership and making crystal clear beyond doubt, by actions and words, that they intend to live in peace with Israel" (26).

101. Ibid., 23.

102. Ibid.

103. Ibid., 24.

104. Ibid.

105. Ibid., 24–25.

106. Ibid., 25.

107. Reinhold Niebuhr, *Moral Man and Immoral Society* (New York: Charles Scribners Sons, 1932), 88–89.

108. E, 228.

109. Ibid., 127.

110. Ibid., 133.

111. Ibid., 229.

112. Ibid., 234. Bonhoeffer's acquaintance with power-mad ideologies is, of course, firsthand. Nazism is included when he writes: "Ideologies vent their fury on man then leave him as a bad dream leaves the waking dreamer. The memory of them is bitter. They have not made the man stronger or more mature; they have only made him poorer and more mistrustful. In the hour of this unhappy awakening, if God reveals himself to men as the Creator before whom man can live only as the creature, that is grace and the blessing of poverty" (216).

113. *E,* 233.

114. Ibid.

115. The phrase is from the letter from prison on "resistance and submission," a phrase that itself gave rise to the German title for the letters and papers from prison—*Widerstand und Ergebung.* This portion of the letter reads as follows: "It is therefore impossible to define the boundary between resistance and submission on abstract principles; but both of then must exist, and both must be practised. Faith demands this elasticity of behaviour. Only so can we stand our ground in each situation as it arises and turn it to gain" (letter of 21 February 1944, *LPP,* 217–18).

116. Letter of 21 July 1944, *LPP,* 370.

117. *E,* 238.

118. Ibid., 91.

119. Ibid., 241.

120. Ibid.

121. A proper treatment of Bonhoeffer here would engage his poetry from prison at great length. The pertinent poems are "Night Voices in Tegel," "Jonah," "Der Tod des Mose," and "Stations on the Way to Freedom." All show the emotional turbulence that belongs to the moral turbulence of conspiracy as carried out by fundamentally conscientious agents.

122. *E,* 262.

123. This discussion has drawn heavily and sometimes directly from my earlier work, *Dietrich Bonhoeffer: Reality and Resistance* (Nashville: Abingdon, 1972). The documentation of conspiracy as an act of repentance is found on 56ff.

124. See the discussion in chap. 4, "Worship in a World Come of Age."

CHAPTER 8: AN ETHIC OF THE CROSS

1. Douglas John Hall, *Lighten Our Darkness: Toward an Indigenous Theology of the Cross* (Philadelphia: Westminster Press, 1976).

2. DATALERT: A Newsletter Interpreting Events, Trends, and Views for Religious Leaders, "Reagan and Optimism," vol. 9, no. 5, February 1, 1981: 1.

3. Dietrich Bonhoeffer, "Outline for a Book," *LPP*, 380.

4. H. Richard Niebuhr, *The Kingdom of God in America* (New York: Harper & Row, 1937), 193.

5. Hall, *Lighten Our Darkness*, 60 (emphasis added).

6. Ibid., 101.

7. Joseph A. Sittler, *Grace Notes and Other Fragments* (Philadelphia: Fortress Press, 1981), 118.

8. See the entry of 18 June 1939 in the American diary, *GS* 1. The entry reads in part:

Gottesdienst in Riverside Church . . . Die ganze Sache eine dezent, uppige, selbstzufriedene Religionsfeier. Mit solcher Reiigionsvergotzung iebt das Fleisch auf, das gewohnt ist, mit den Worten Gottes in Zucht gehalten zu werden. Solche Predigt macht libertinistisch, egoistisch, gleichgultig. Wissen denn die Leute wirklich nicht, dass man gut und besser ohne "Religion" auskommt—wenn nur Gott selbst und sein Wort nicht ware? Viellicht sind die Angelsachen wirklich religioser als wir, christlicher sind sie wohl nicht, wenn sie sich noch solche Predigten gefallen lassen. Es ist mir unzweifelhaft, dass in diesen religiösen hand-out der Sturm einmal kräftig hineinblasen wird, wenn Gott selbst überhaupt noch auf dem Plan ist. Menschlich ist die Sache nicht einmal unsympatisch, aber da ist mir die bauerischste Predigt von Br. Schutz lieber. Die Aufgaben fur einen echten Theologen hier druben sind unermesslich. Aber diesen Schutt kann nur ein Amerikaner selbst wegraumen. Bis jetzt scheint keiner da zu sein (300).

9. Hall, *Lighten Our Darkness*, 60. See the remark on culture and death by Bonhoeffer, letter of 23 January 1944, LPP, 193–94, in reply to Bethge's remark on the subject.

10. See the discussion in Dorothee Soelle's *Suffering* (Philadelphia: Fortress, 1975).

11. *E*, 189.

12. I have tried to sketch recent movement in theology and church in "New Dynamics in Theology," *Christianity and Crisis* 48, no. 8 (16 May 1988): 178–83.

13. Lee Brummel, citing from *Luther's Works*, 46:35–36, in his article, "Luther and the Biblical Language of Poverty," *The Ecumenical Review* 32, no. 1 (1980): 40–58.

14. Brummel, "Luther," 45.

15. From the Luther citation above.

16. Brummel, "Luther," 49.

17. These five sentences are but slightly altered quotations from Brummel, ibid.

18. Ibid., 50–51, citing Luther, *Weimar Ausgabe*, 5, 660, 7.

19. Brummel, "Luther," 51.

20. Ibid., 55, citing Luther, *Luther's Works* 46:29.

21. Brummel, "Luther," citing Luther, *Luther's Works* 46:40.

22. See the earlier citation, p. 150 above.

23. John Godsey, "The Legacy of Dietrich Bonhoeffer," in A. J. Klassen, ed., *A Bonhoeffer Legacy: Essays in Understanding* (Grand Rapids: Wm. B. Eerdmans, 1981), 162.

24. Cited by Godsey (162), from *GS* 3:32 (translation Godsey's).

25. Letter of 21 August 1944, *LPP*, 391.

26. Cited by Forde from Martin Luther, *Lectures on Romans*, trans. and ed. Wilhelm Pauck, published as vol. 15 of the Library of Christian Classics (Philadelphia: Westminster Press, 1961), 4.

27. Gerhard O. Forde, "The Exodus from Virtue to Grace: Justification by Faith Today," *Interpretation* 34 (1980): 37.

28. Ibid., 36.

29. Forde, 38, citing Luther's *Lectures on Romans*, 81.

30. *DB;* letter of 30 April 1944, *LPP*, 281.

31. Forde, "The Exodus from Virtue to Grace," 38.

32. Ibid., 33.

33. Excerpts from *E*, 188–90.

34. Ibid., 27.

35. Ibid., 26.

36. Ibid.; 123.

37. Ibid., 123–24.

38. Letter of 21 July 1944, *LPP*, 369–70.

39. Ibid., 369.

40. *E*, 83.

41. Ibid., 84.

42. Letter of 21 August 1944, *LPP*, 391.

43. "Thoughts on the Day of the Baptism of Dietrich Wilhelm Rüdiger Bethge," *LPP*, 300.

44. Letter of 21 August 1944, *LPP*, 391.

45. "Outline for a Book," *LPP*, 382.

46. Ibid.

47. Letter of 18 July 1944, *LPP*, 362.

48. Letter of 27 June 1944, *LPP*, 337 (emphasis added).

49. *E*, 85.

50. "Bases for a Christian Ethic," in *Two Kingdoms and One World*, ed. Karl Hertz (Minneapolis: Augsburg, 1976), 363.

51. Ibid., 363–64.

52. Ibid., 364.

53. Ibid., 365.

54. Søren Kierkegaard, *Attack upon Christendom*, trans. Walter Lowrie (Boston: Beacon Press, 1944), 280. Cited by Hall, *Lighten Our Darkness*, 132 (emphasis added).

55. Stanley Hauerwas, *A Community of Character: Toward a Constructive Christian Social Ethic* (Notre Dame, Ind.: University of Notre Dame Press, 1981), 3.

56. Ibid., 10.

57. *E*, 188.

58. From Troeltsch's *The Social Teaching of the Christian Churches*, 50 of the Macmillan edition cited by Hauerwas, *A Community of Character*, 38.

59. Ibid., 39–40, from Hauerwas, *A Community of Character*, 38.

60. Cited by Hauerwas, *A Community of Character*, 38.

61. John Howard Yoder, *The Politics of Jesus* (Grand Rapids: Wm. B. Eerdmans, 1972), 97 (emphasis added).

62. *CD*, 98.

63. Ibid.

64. John Howard Yoder, "The Apriori Difficulty of 'Reformed-Anabaptist Conversation,' " (unpublished January 27, 1977), 7. The discussion of the four assumptions relies on Yoder's paper, though done here in highly simplified fashion.

65. Ibid.

66. Ibid.

67. Ibid., 11–12.

68. John Howard Yoder, "The Basis of Barth's Social Ethics," (unpublished paper presented to the Midwestern Section of the Karl Barth Society, Elmhurst, Illinois, 29-30 September 1978), 11.

69. Yoder, "Barth's Social Ethics," 11.

70. Ibid.

71. This is the title of George W. Forell's study of Luther's ethics, *Faith Active in Love* (Minneapolis: Augsburg, 1954).

72. As influential representatives of this point of view, see the chapter by William Lazareth, "Luther's 'Two Kingdoms' Ethic Reconsidered," in John C. Bennett, ed., *Christian Social Ethics in A Changing World* (New York: Association Press, 1966), and George Forell, *Faith Active in Love*.

73. Unfortunately I did not secure Hall's newest work, *Thinking the Faith* (Minneapolis: Augsburg, 1989), until after this book was completed. In it he draws much more from Bonhoeffer's *theologia crucis* than he did in his earlier works. I affirm his particular emphasis and would use it to revise this chapter. That emphasis is this: the *theologia crucis* throws us into the concrete realities of this world as the place we meet God, especially in suffering. The quotation from Bonhoeffer cited earlier in the chapter captures Hall's emphasis: "Solely because God became a poor, suffering, unknown, successless man, and because from now on God allows himself to be found only in this poverty, in the cross, we cannot disengage ourselves from man and from the world." (Letter to Theodor Litt, *GS* 3:32.) In other words, the *theologia crucis* is "indigenous" by its very character.

Index

America, v, 13, 31–33, 41
See also United States.
Arcane discipline, 44, 58, 68–70
Assassination, 11, 21, 47–48

Barmen Declaration, 8, 33
Barth, Karl, 96, 99–105, 108, 184 nn.
  58, 61, 65, 80; 185 n. 94; 195
  n.68
Berrigan, Daniel, vi, 43–56, 178 nn.
  2, 3, 4, 5, 16; 179 n.30
Bethge, Eberhard, vi, ix, x, 39, 82, 119,
  183 n.55
Bethge, Renate Schleicher, v, vi, vii,
  30, 39, 120
See also Family
Bultmann, Rudolf, 81, 119

Christ, 16, 19, 21, 22, 24–27, 36, 37,
  41, 52, 56, 57, 59, 60, 66, 68, 72,
  75, 81, 85, 87, 91–96, 98, 100–
  1, 104–10, 116, 118, 120, 122,
  124, 140–41, 144, 145, 147, 151,
  155, 156–57, 159–66, 168–69,
  171, 182 nn.16, 18, 31; 185 n.94
See also Jesus
Church, 8, 15, 16, 18, 24–29, 36–39,
  42, 44, 55, 57–60, 66, 72, 75, 76,
  81, 82, 85–88, 94, 96, 97–99,
  103, 106, 116, 118–20, 124, 141,
  144, 145, 147, 149–50, 152, 153,
  160–61, 163, 165–69, 171, 172–
  73, 178 n.4; 181 n.23; 182 n.31

church renewal, vi, 67–71
church's public vocation, vi,
  72–73, 75, 82, 86–88, 181 n.23
ecumenical movement, 36–42
See also Confessing Church;
  Ecclesiology
Church Struggle, 68, 94, 173
Command, 89, 91, 96–106, 108, 109,
  183 n.45, 184 n.58, 185 n.94
Confessing Church, 7–9, 15, 17, 21,
  33, 36, 38, 118, 130, 132, 177
  n.11; 178 n.4
Conformation, 89, 91, 92, 93, 95, 109
Consciousness, 51, 53–55, 78, 61–66,
  71, 119, 120, 121, 147, 157
See also Religion; World Come of
  Age
Conspiracy, 49, 53, 56, 119, 140–42
Covenant, 76, 114, 117–18, 128,
  130–33, 135, 170
Cross, vi, 44, 56, 73, 75, 76, 81, 83,
  84–86, 120, 122, 133, 144–45,
  147, 149–55, 167–69, 171–73
See also Theology of the Cross
Crucifixion, 82, 110, 140, 152
Culture, v, 35, 36, 42, 74, 75, 78, 80,
  84, 85, 110, 112, 122, 144–47,
  148, 164–70

Deus ex machina, 63, 64, 190 n.70
See also Religion
Discipleship, 50, 52–53, 56, 59, 95,
  96, 98, 120, 178 n.5

196

Ecclesiology, 27, 106, 145, 152, 168, 173
Eschatology, 55, 75–83, 86–88, 181 n.23

Faith, 31, 34, 36, 47, 55, 58, 59, 71, 75, 77, 78, 82, 84–85, 87–88, 96, 114, 116–20, 123–24, 140, 144, 149, 151, 155, 157, 158–59, 178 n.7; 181 n.4
See also Justification
Family, v, 1–14, 15, 17, 18, 19, 20, 25, 27, 28, 29, 30, 31, 34, 72, 79, 81, 119, 127, 176 n.5; 183 n.41
Finkenwalde, 28, 33, 35, 68, 69

Gandhi, 35, 45, 49, 51, 68
Germany, 2, 3, 10, 14, 33–39, 41, 42, 45, 72, 75, 77, 94, 113
Gestalt Christi, 104, 105, 108
See also Conformation; Imitatio
God, 15, 16, 21, 22, 24, 26, 28, 29, 33, 41, 42, 44, 51, 60, 62–68, 76–78, 79–82, 84–85, 87–88, 89, 91–94, 97–110, 111, 112, 114, 116, 117–25, 127–35, 137, 138, 140, 147, 148, 151–57, 167, 169–71, 189 n.70; 192 n.12
Grace, 16, 25, 26, 54, 69, 76, 77, 81, 110, 147, 152, 156, 170, 181 n.3
See also Justification
Greenberg, Irving, vi, 43, 111–43, 186 n.4; 188 n.70; 191 nn.97, 100

Hitler, 1–5, 7–12, 33, 34, 39–40, 48, 49, 52, 119, 123, 139, 141, 179 n.22
See also Assassination; Conspiracy; Germany; Resistance
Holocaust, 33, 189 n.70

Imitatio, 144, 163–4
See also Conformation; Gestalt Christi
Incarnation, 94, 95, 110, 140
Israel, 76, 77, 80, 114, 116, 126, 127, 128, 130, 132, 134, 135, 137, 138

Jesus, 16, 21, 24, 26, 37, 41, 44, 59, 60, 76–78, 80–81, 83, 85–88, 91–93, 100, 101, 103, 104, 106–8, 119, 123–25, 140–41, 144, 152, 154–58, 167, 169, 171, 172, 179 n.7; 181 nn.8, 12, 23
See also Christ; Gestalt Christi
Jews, Judaism, 2, 8, 9–12, 40, 84, 112–13, 118, 126, 127, 131, 134, 136–38
Just war, 53, 136, 142, 178 n.4; 186 n.3; 190 n.83
Justification, 22, 46, 51, 52, 76, 77, 78, 110, 157–59, 173
See also Grace

Law, 9, 20, 24, 47–48, 93–94, 95, 104, 109, 130, 141, 153
Lehmann, Paul, 35, 39, 102, 177 n.9; 184 n.80
Liberation theology, 35–36

Moses, 33, 100

Nationalism, 38, 41
Nazism (Nazis), 1–15, 17, 20, 21, 24, 25, 27, 28, 30, 34, 38, 40, 41, 118, 141, 179 n.22; 186 n.5; 189 n.70; 192 n.112
New (Old) Age, 76–78, 80, 81, 120, 159
Niebuhr, Reinhold, vi, 33–34, 43, 72–88, 135, 139, 177 n.5; 180 n.1; 181 n.16
Nonviolence, 35, 47
See also Pacifism; Resistance
North America, v, 41, 43, 73, 76, 83, 111, 147, 168, 172–73
Pacifism, 21, 45, 178 n.8
See also Nonviolence
Patriotism, vi, 31–33, 35–39, 41–42, 44, 73, 177 nn.7, 9; 181 n.2
See also Nationalism; Resistance
Paul (Pauline), 77, 78, 100, 159, 180 n.20
Peace, 45, 76, 101, 106
Power, vi, 44, 51, 64, 71, 76, 77–81, 82, 84, 86–88, 97, 107, 111–14, 118–19, 121, 124–31, 134–37, 139–43, 147, 150, 152, 190 n.83; 192 n.115
Prayer, 27, 44, 57–59, 66, 68, 70, 120–21, 127

See also Arcane discipline
Prison, 1, 3, 4, 13, 19, 26, 29, 34, 40, 50, 57, 192 n.115
See also Resistance; Tegel

Reagan, Ronald, 31, 32, 83–84, 85, 177 n.1
Reality, 15, 19, 20, 21–22, 54, 61, 77–79, 80–81, 84, 110, 114, 118, 127, 128, 130, 132–33, 140–41, 144, 148, 150, 169, 178 n.12; 181 nn.7, 23; 182 n.18; 183 n.51; 186 n.5
Redemption, 59, 115, 118–19, 128, 129–32, 134, 138, 169
Reformation, 147, 150, 168, 173
Religion, 26, 58, 60–67, 71, 75, 79, 108, 118, 122, 123, 125, 127, 136, 145, 147–49, 171
See also Consciousness; *Deus ex machina*
Religionless Christianity, 25, 26, 44, 58, 67, 70
See also World Come of Age
Resistance, vi, 4–7, 14, 25, 35, 40, 43–51, 53–55, 69, 72, 90, 118–19, 121, 139, 142, 178 n.12; 179 n.22; 183 n.39
See also Hitler; Church Struggle; Conspiracy; Berrigan
Responsibility, 21–23, 44, 47, 52, 63, 72, 110, 119, 120–21, 124, 135, 139, 142–43, 150, 152, 184 n.80
Resurrection, 59, 81, 110, 120, 140, 155

Secularity, 15, 26, 115, 123, 127, 129–30

Society, vi, 51, 61, 70, 79–81, 84, 85, 86–87, 111, 135, 145, 148, 153
Solidarity, 48, 68–70
Suffering, 68–70, 76, 80, 82, 84, 85, 87, 107, 123, 125, 127, 130–32, 135, 136, 144, 148, 150–54
See also Theology of the Cross

Tegel, 29, 40, 118, 178 n.24; 187 n.25
See also Prison
Theology, v, vi, 1, 6, 15–27, 28–30, 41;
of glory 83, 84, 87, 145, 148, 173;
of the cross (*theologia crusis*) 44, 73, 76, 82, 83, 85, 86–87, 107, 144, 145, 147, 151–52, 155, 161, 165, 173
Third Reich, 2–4, 38, 40, 48
See also Germany; Hitler; Patriotism; Resistance

United States, vi, 31, 33, 38, 39, 45, 111, 147, 172, 174
See also America

Vice/virtue, 107, 144, 155, 158, 181 n.4

World Come of Age, vi, 57–61, 63–66, 68–71, 75, 105–7, 119, 124, 142, 181 n.18
See also Consciousness
Worldliness, 105, 123, 160
Worship, vi, 26, 57–62, 66–69, 86–87, 168, 170, 181 n.3
See also Arcane discipline; Prayer